Claiming Power from Below

Claiming Power from Below
Dalits and the Subaltern Question in India

Edited by
Manu Bhagavan
and
Anne Feldhaus

OXFORD
UNIVERSITY PRESS

OXFORD
UNIVERSITY PRESS

YMCA Library Building, Jai Singh Road, New Delhi 110001

Oxford University Press is a department of the University of Oxford.
It furthers the University's objective of excellence in research, scholarship,
and education by publishing worldwide in

Oxford   New York
Auckland   Cape Town   Dar es Salaam   Hong Kong   Karachi
Kuala Lumpur   Madrid   Melbourne   Mexico City   Nairobi
New Delhi   Shanghai   Taipei   Toronto

With offices in
Argentina   Austria   Brazil   Chile   Czech Republic   France   Greece
Guatemala   Hungary   Italy   Japan   Poland   Portugal   Singapore
South Korea   Switzerland   Thailand   Turkey   Ukraine   Vietnam

Oxford is a registered trade mark of Oxford University Press
in the UK and in certain other countries

Published in India
by Oxford University Press, New Delhi
© Oxford University Press 2008
The moral rights of the author have been asserted
Database right Oxford University Press (maker)

First published 2008
Oxford India Paperbacks 2009
Second impression 2011

ISBN-13: 978-019-806348-3
ISBN-10: 019-806348-2

Typeset in Minion 10.5/12.5
by Eleven Arts, Keshav Puram, Delhi 110 035
Published by Oxford University Press
YMCA Library Building, Jai Singh Road, New Delhi 110 001

for Eleanor Zelliot

Sketch by S.Y. Waghmare

CONTENTS

PREFACE

We are proud and happy to present this second of two volumes in honour of Eleanor Zelliot. We two editors are among the many contributors to these volumes whose lives and careers she has profoundly affected. As Manu Bhagavan's undergraduate professor at Carleton College, Zelliot opened up for him the world of committed, analytical historical inquiry, and after he graduated from college she continued to discuss his work with him and to follow his career actively. Anne Feldhaus was not Zelliot's student, but met her as a graduate student in India. Generous as always, Zelliot introduced Feldhaus to numerous friends and colleagues, both in India and in the United States. Most importantly, Zelliot took the young Feldhaus and her work seriously. Not only did Zelliot recommend her for numerous research fellowships, teaching positions, and posts on professional organizations, she also read the manuscript of Feldhaus's first major postdissertation project and made her own written contribution to it ('The World of Gundam Raul', in *The Deeds of God in Ṛddhipur*, translated by Anne Feldhaus. New York: Oxford University Press, 1984).

The two of us are not alone in our debt to Eleanor Zelliot. We are joined in gratitude by the many contributors to this volume and its companion ('*Speaking Truth to Power*': *Religion, Caste, and the Subaltern Question in India*. New Delhi: Oxford University Press, 2008), and also by many other students, protégés, and colleagues of Professor Zelliot's who were eager to felicitate her but whose scholarly work does not fit the themes of the two volumes. To quote one of them, Irina Glushkova of the Institute of Orientology, Moscow:

Though not sharing Bai's [Zelliot's] focused attention to Dalits, I believe that the nature of that attention is far beyond the professional frames, that giving a hand whenever possible is another way of involvement, that going deep into Ambedkar movement studies, contributing to Cokha Mela's legacy, and writing an introduction to Vasant Moon's *Growing Up Untouchable in India*: *A Dalit Autobiography* was a historian's as well as a humanist's commitment. There are grades of 'oppression' which are sometimes recognized by scholarly analysis, and sometimes by a shrill pain in one's own heart, and Bai is an expert in both. 'Oh well, don't despair, Eleanor' is a lovely melody I have learned from her email letters—the implicit teaching and encouragement she addresses to herself has had a profound impact on each of us. Bai, you are a great optimist, moreover, you are a trained optimist, with energy and vigour both imagined and unimagined, constructed and intrinsic, and invariably brought into life and put to creation ....

I remember once asking Anne Feldhaus, 'What will happen to us when we are older?' The answer was, 'Don't worry, we'll be like Eleanor.' Will we manage?

Irina Glushkova's words come from a message that she sent to be presented to Zelliot with the very first draft of these two volumes. In October 2004 we presented our first draft to Professor Zelliot at a surprise party held in conjunction with the annual Conference on South Asia at the University of Wisconsin, Madison. The book has gone through many changes and much editing since then. We are grateful to our editors at Oxford University Press for their interest in the work, and most especially to the contributors, who have been extremely cooperative and patient.

INTRODUCTION

Manu Bhagavan and Anne Feldhaus

The release in 1982 of the first volume of the *Subaltern Studies* series is regarded as a watershed in scholarly inquiry of the South Asian past and present. Ranajit Guha, in the preface to the volume, stated that the

word 'subaltern' in the title stands for the meaning as given in the *Concise Oxford Dictionary*, that is, 'of inferior rank'. It will be used ... as a name for the general attribute of subordination in South Asian society whether this is expressed in terms of class, caste, age, gender, and office or in any other way .... There will be much ... which should relate to the history, politics, economics and sociology of subalternity as well as to the attitudes, ideologies and belief systems—in short, the culture informing that condition (Guha 1994: vii).

Subaltern Studies followed on the heels of the 1978 release of Edward Said's masterpiece, *Orientalism*, a work that linked knowledge, and its construction and dissemination, to power and exploitation, and the two methodological schools laced together over the following years to dramatically influence the way in which the study of South Asia is itself approached (Said 1994a). In 1994, Said released *Representations of the Intellectual* (1994b), in which he argued that the intellectual's true role was to 'speak truth to power', that is, to speak out against injustice and to stand morally with, and advocate for, the world's dispossessed and marginalized (1994b). All of this work represented innovative approaches in the academy and, at the same time, a harsh indictment of the academic establishment itself, for its role in maintaining and creating hierarchies of power.

Unquestionably the subaltern and Saidian methods came as shocks to the system, but there were, as Ranajit Guha acknowledges in his preface, others who had been 'equally unhappy about the distortions and imbalances generated by ... [the elitist] trend in academic work on South Asian questions' (Guha 1994: viii). Indeed, since the early 1960s, one of the pioneers of modern scholarship on South Asia had been doggedly working on bringing the condition of oppressed people in South Asia to the attention of elites in the region and the world. Eleanor Zelliot studied subalterns long before it was fashionable to do so. While the 'Untouchable' or Dalit ('the oppressed', literally, 'broken to pieces') movement in India has been the principal focus of her attention, she also foresaw Guha's insight that culture informs the condition of subalternity. Her research attempts to understand as much of the caste condition as possible, and encompasses diverse topics such as mystical devotionalism (bhakti), the practice of religion (particularly Buddhism) and its political implications, the goals of political leaders and movements (especially B.R. Ambedkar and the movements he started or inspired), and the power of poetry and literature to simultaneously resist and rejoice.

The essays in this volume and in its companion, *'Speaking Truth to Power': Religion, Caste, and the Subaltern Question in India*, are a tribute to the life and work of Eleanor Zelliot. Not only did Zelliot break new empirical ground, she also laid the foundation for methodological breakthroughs that occurred nearly two decades after she began her work. Importantly, Zelliot has avoided the pitfalls for which Said scathingly rebuked the institutional academy. In some measure as a result of her Quaker background, Zelliot has single-mindedly 'spoken truth to power'[1] through her work. That is, rather than seeking merely to study passively and objectively the 'others' who have been the focus of her work, Zelliot has sought to involve herself in their plight, their lives, their misery, and their hope, and she has used her position and her writing to advocate their cause. Yet Zelliot has also made considerable efforts to 'let the subaltern speak' for themselves. In this, she pre-emptively hewed to Gayatri Spivak's later words of warning for subaltern studies, that such a postcolonial scholarly project might, in recovering subaltern subjects, re-commit acts of violence against 'them', by eliding differences, speaking for the subalterns, and locating such a voice within a hegemonic, Western discourse.[2] Zelliot has chosen to work in both English and Marathi; she has collected and edited various 'subaltern' narratives in both languages, allowing her subjects to tell their own stories from their own perspective.[3] Elsewhere, she has added her own judicious and careful reading and analysis, making every effort to write or speak as often as possible within fora accessible to, or administered by, Dalits specifically and South Asians more generally. As the Association for Asian Studies noted in its citation naming her the recipient of the 1999 Award for Distinguished Service to Asian Studies, Eleanor Zelliot '"changed the paradigm" in the study of South Asia'.

All of the contributors to our two volumes have been touched by Eleanor Zelliot in some way. For all of them she has been a teacher, a mentor, a generous colleague, and/or someone whose scholarly writings have influenced their work. The pieces presented over the course of our two books have been brought together in each of the areas in which Zelliot has made major contributions, so that they build on and move forward from her earlier work. We have roughly arranged the chapters of the two volumes around the themes that Zelliot herself used in presenting her own work *From Untouchable to Dalit* (Zelliot 2001a), a collection of the most significant essays from the first three decades of her scholarly career.[4] The overall layout of the two volumes, thus, reflects the arc and coherence Zelliot herself saw as binding her publications together. '*Speaking Truth to Power*' focuses broadly on how religious manifestations inform social structure in India, refracting Zelliot's observations on the role of belief and practice in the life of marginalized people, 'subalterns', in the region. The essays in the present volume build explicitly on her far-reaching, path-breaking scholarship on the Dalit cause.

Eleanor Zelliot's most important contributions in this area may be roughly divided into two parts, politics and literature, though we must recognize that these are not mutually exclusive categories. Her essays in the first of these two areas focus primarily, but not exclusively, on the life and thought of Bhimrao Ramji ('Babasaheb') Ambedkar, a twentieth-century reformer and champion of caste justice in colonial and postcolonial India.[5] Years before Shahid Amin articulated the metaphoric construction of Gandhi as Mahatma,[6] Zelliot plotted out the ways in which Ambedkar configured a Mahar mythic past and, in turn, was configured within it (Zelliot 2001g). This was part of her larger interest in Ambedkar's overall intellectual vision. Zelliot also outlined Ambedkar's formative experiences in the United States, as he studied at Columbia University under legendary scholars such as John Dewey, Edwin Seligman, and Alexander Goldenweiser (Zelliot 2001b). The result, she spelled out in another article, was a thinker and politician often at odds with his famed contemporary, Mahatma Gandhi. The dispute between them, she argued, was somewhat akin to 'certain aspects of the Black Power movement versus "White Liberals" in America in the 1960s' (Zelliot 2001e: 151).

The chapters that follow concentrate on the political spaces in which Dalits operate, as well as on those that Dalits have created. We have interpreted the term 'Dalit' both literally and loosely here, and have included essays that specifically discuss caste, ex-Untouchables, and Ambedkar Buddhists, as well as intersecting configurations of 'the oppressed', including Muslims, women, workers, and the urban poor. As political history is the arena in which Eleanor Zelliot has made her most basic contributions, essays on this subject constitute the bulk of this volume.

Anupama Rao starts off the volume by drawing the consequences of Ambedkar's political work, as well as that of intellectuals who preceded him and literary figures who followed him, in creating the category of the Dalit—an 'inaugural political subject' in modern Indian political life. Specifically, she argues that the Dalit experience fashioned an alternate and important negotiation of modernity and democracy, one that departed significantly from other counter-colonial 'nativist modernities' that did not adequately engage with the concerns of caste.

Ramnarayan Rawat and Rajendra Vora focus on the politics of particular Dalit groups. Rawat examines the Chamars of Uttar Pradesh in the mid-twentieth century, especially the 1940s. Although many scholars have seen this as the period during which Dalit struggles were swallowed up in the Congress agenda, Rawat argues that the 1940s were the pivotal years in which Dalit identity was formed, along with a Dalit social and political agenda that continues to the present day. Vora draws our attention to the very recent past and adds another variable to the mix, trying to understand the position and politics of low-caste Muslims in the late-twentieth and early-twenty-first centuries. He shows how intercaste alliances are being forged to create a new Dalit Muslim identity that transcends the distinction between low-caste and outcaste groups. Since the Mandal Commission Report (1980) identified some Muslim communities as Other Backward Caste (OBC) groups, a number of Muslim OBC organizations have been formed. Vora describes in detail the first of these, one that grew out of a Marathi Muslim literary organization founded in 1989.

Sukhadeo Thorat explores Ambedkar's theoretical and policy positions on a range of issues that have affected the whole of India, including Dalits as well as others. Thorat sketches Ambedkar's principal contributions in economics, the academic field in which he received his PhD from Columbia University in 1925, and one of the areas in which he served as a policymaker in the 1940s and 1950s. Thorat examines Ambedkar's published views on agricultural and industrial development, planning, water control, electrical resources, and labour, as well as his thoughts on economic systems that offered an alternative to capitalism for newly-independent India.

Mani Kamerkar provides us with a case study of the economic policies of British colonialism in western India. These policies framed the context in which Ambedkar first rose to prominence, and they formed an important part of the background of the conditions he sought to change. Kamerkar discusses the taxation of peasants, an obviously repressive aspect of colonial rule, and shows how the land policies associated with taxation also constituted a form of 'oppression' of the peasants in the area of her study: Bassein Taluka, north of Bombay.

Maintaining the focus on the colonial period, Abigail McGowan studies a type of institution that would seem, in contrast to colonial land and taxation policies, to have had lower-caste, lower-class Indians' welfare at heart: industrial schools for artisan-caste boys. McGowan finds, however, that the schools were not well-attended, and that, although their aim was to modernize the Indian economy, they were not intended to disrupt the caste-based hierarchy on which that economy was built. They sought, instead, only to improve the efficiency of the artisans' work. Thus, far from being tools of revolutionary social change, these institutions actually helped secure and maintain class and caste structure. Shailaja Paik returns us to the present, and provides us with another angle on education. Her chapter highlights the viewpoint and aspirations of a little-studied category, that of the Dalit middle class. She studies the education of Dalit girls, who are now women, showing how difficult it was for them to get an education, and also the ways in which their lives have been, and are being, altered by schooling.

All these chapters remind us of the courage and grace of ordinary people in standing up to daily humiliations and violence. Yasmin Saikia goes one step further, literally into a war zone, to radically alter the very concept of the ordinary. She narrates the life and stories of common men and women from the 1971 Bangladesh war who were either victims or perpetrators of horrific acts of inhumanity and brutality brought out by the war. If these acts were merely the logical conclusion to the kinds of atrocities that go on even in times of 'peace', Saikia seeks a human 'language of understanding' that can yet be recovered from these gruesome spaces, so that we might all come to terms with our past.

Vijay Prashad's essay attempts to further this 'language of understanding', in this case by discussing the comparison of race and caste as a way of creating solidarity among the dispossessed in very different parts of the world. He warns, however, that to take the comparison too far, by conflating race and caste, could lead to another example of US global hegemony. Prashad spells out the history of race and caste in South Asia, concentrating on the ways in which they became intertwined in the colonial period, and surveys the legal and political moves intended to ameliorate discrimination against Dalits in independent India. He argues that, although race and caste are similar in their economic effects, the struggle against these two forms of discrimination must be waged on terms specific to their very different contexts.

Despite her intense interest in the life, thoughts, and works of Ambedkar, for Zelliot, as for the subaltern school many years later, an exclusive emphasis on the leader of a mass movement for the marginalized remains, to an extent, an elitist exercise if it is divorced from the stories and views of the ordinary people who comprised the movement itself. While she has tried to capture some of this sense in her politically focused essays (for instance, Zelliot 2001h), Zelliot has been sensitive to the fact that such treatment still tends to rely on the narratives of elites. The problem could only be circumvented, she concluded, by turning away from the formal political sphere to other facets of 'everyday life', most notably to the poems and writings that common Dalits celebrate. Her work on Dalit literature explores the whole range of the genre, from the militancy of Dalit Panther Namdeo Dhasal to the innovative, playful folk-poetry of Waman Kardak. Oral traditions hold a prominent place in the transmission of such work, as Dalit writer Daya Pawar points out:

In the Brahman house—writing
In the Kunbi House—grain
In the Mahar house—singing[7]

In her essays on this literature, Zelliot has added her voice sparingly, adroit enough to know that much Dalit writing literally speaks for itself. Impossible to miss is the sheer anger in many of the voices directed at the injustice of caste oppression, as in Tryambak Sapkale's poem 'Angulimal', in which the writer identifies himself with the legendary bandit who sliced off the fingers of his victims and wore them as a garland around his neck.[8] But this is a reasoned anger, marshalled to the cause of positive social change.

Many Dalit writers, in this quest for social justice, have seen and sought solidarity with other oppressed peoples and groups, while some, pre-emptively, in keeping with Prashad's analysis, have cautioned all of us to be wary of eliding real and significant differences between causes. Gangadhar Pantawane, for instance, linked the African-American and Dalit experiences:

There is no difference between the *place* of the Negro in America and the step or the level of the Untouchable in India.... Both were confined in the prison of fatalism. To prolong this imprisonment, the whites found authority in the Bible's myths and symbols, and the clean castes in the Vedas and Manusmriti (cited in Zelliot 2001c: 280–1).

Inversely, other Dalit writings have cautioned that such global unions of the dispossessed remain tenuous at best, if only because the Dalit cause as a whole failed to register with the worldwide Left, the political force with the way but not the will to intervene energetically. Sapkale was transparent in his criticism:

The other day I heard your speech—
you condemned America
for bombing Vietnam—
Workers of the World unite

you roared.
The next day your brothers
condemned Russia
and wept for the Hungarians
Gawai brothers lost their eyes.
not a tear I saw
In your eyes
No protest meetings.
Just a small news in a couple of dailies
and everything is so peaceful! Quiet! Quiet![9]

In keeping with Zelliot's work on the literary forms of resistance to injustice, we conclude this volume by presenting several new essays on Dalit literature.[10] Laura Brueck's contribution focuses on the Dalit Lekhak Sangh, an organization of Hindi Dalit writers based in Delhi. Brueck describes the activities of the Sangh and illustrates the kinds of issues that are debated in the members' literary discussions, then analyses a short story by one member of the group, Ajay Navariya. Throughout she points to the dilemma of attempting to bring Dalit literature into the mainstream of Hindi literature while at the same time maintaining its distinctiveness as a literary genre that by definition comes from the margins. Remaining in the realm of short fiction, Veena Deo explores the images of Dalit women in the short stories of a Marathi-speaking Dalit woman writer, Urmila Pawar. In the process Deo examines the issues that the stories, and the process of translation, raise about the politics of representation, the impact of the mass Dalit conversion to Buddhism led by Ambedkar, and the interactions of class, caste, and gender.

Dilip Chitre and Bali Sahota turn our attention to Dalit poetry. In keeping with Zelliot's insistence on letting the literature speak for itself, Chitre gives us his own translation of a fiery, political poem of the radical Dalit writer Namdeo Dhasal, preceded by a brief and sympathetic introduction. Sahota follows with an analysis and critique of contemporary Dalit literary aesthetics, including those of Dhasal, showing how this new work ambivalently aligns itself with the old spirit of the bhakti radicals (among others) on the one hand,[11] and with more neo-traditional ideologies of community on the other, including right-wing political parties, to fashion a new social order.

For Eleanor Zelliot, a historian by training and profession, the past was a means to confront the present and to imagine better moments yet to come. We thus end this volume with a poem that we think embodies this belief. Meena Alexander contributes an original poem that is, like Zelliot's scholarship, blunt and brutal in describing discrimination, but also 'incurably optimistic'[12] in hoping that we might still find our humanity and create a better way for all of us. Alexander's poem weaves together the concerns of many of our other chapters, including class, caste, race, and gender, with a hope for a transnational political space in which to imagine a brighter future.

NOTES

1. 'Speak truth to power' holds a prominent place in Quaker history, and is often associated with a meeting between George Fox and Oliver Cromwell in 1653.
2. Spivak 1988. See also a cogent synopsis at: *http://postcolonialweb.org/poldiscourse/spivak/spivak2.html*. Accessed 27 April 2007.
3. See Appendix of this volume.
4. While Zelliot 2001a serves as the source for all of Zelliot's works referred to in this introduction, in order to provide a sense of the chronology of her scholarship we also include in the bibliography the year each essay mentioned was originally published.
5. In line with her scholarly generosity and moral commitments, Zelliot has (only very recently) published her full biography of Ambedkar, the subject of her PhD dissertation submitted to the University of Pennsylvania in 1969, with a press that publishes only on Dalit subjects: Zelliot 2004.
6. Amin 1992. Compare Gopal Guru's essay in Bhagavan and Feldhaus (eds). 2008.
7. Daya Pawar, cited in Zelliot 2001d: 319. Kunbis are a peasant community in western India.
8. 'Angulimal', translated by Jayant Karve and Eleanor Zelliot, appears in Zelliot 2001f: 295–6. Angulimal, literally 'Garland of Fingers', is famous in Buddhist legend for eventually encountering the Buddha and repenting his actions. The Angulimal in Sapkale's poem is the pre-reformed, finger-stealing bandit, who sees no reason to repent such action in the face of the violent humiliation wrought on him and other Dalits by the oppressive world.
9. Sapkale, translated by Vidyut Bhagwat, cited in Zelliot 2001c: 289. The Gawai brothers were Buddhists who were blinded in a village dispute with upper castes.

10. See also the essay by Paula Richman in Bhagavan and Feldhaus (eds). 2008.
11. See Bhagavan and Feldhaus 2008, especially the introduction's discussion of Zelliot's work on bhakti, and Gail Omvedt's chapter on the bhakti radicals.
12. Zelliot claims this perspective in Zelliot 2001a: xx. Anyone who has ever encountered Eleanor Zelliot either in person or through her scholarship would, we are sure, concur with this self-assessment.

REFERENCES

Amin, Shahid. 1992 [1984]. 'Gandhi as Mahatma: Gorakhpur District, Eastern UP, 1921–2'. In Ranajit Guha (ed.). *Subaltern Studies III*. New Delhi: Oxford University Press, pp. 1–61.

Bhagavan, Manu, and Anne Feldhaus (eds). 2008. *'Speaking Truth to Power': Religion, Caste, and the Subaltern Question in India*. New Delhi: Oxford University Press.

Guha, Ranajit (ed.). 1994 [1982]. *Subaltern Studies I*. New Delhi: Oxford University Press.

Said, Edward. 1994a [1978]. *Orientalism*. New York: Vintage Books.

———. 1994b. *Representations of the Intellectual*. New York: Pantheon Books.

Spivak, Gayatri Chakravorty. 1988. 'Can the Subaltern Speak?' In Cary Nelson and Lawrence Grossberg (eds). *Marxism and the Interpretation of Culture*, Urbana: University of Illinois Press, pp. 271–313.

Zelliot, Eleanor. 2001a [1992]. *From Untouchable to Dalit*. New Delhi: Manohar.

———. 2001b [1977]. 'The American Experience of Dr B.R. Ambedkar'. In Zelliot. *From Untouchable to Dali*, pp. 79–85.

———. 2001c [1978]. 'Dalit: New Cultural Context for an Old Marathi Word'. In Zelliot. *From Untouchable to Dalit*, pp. 267–92.

———. 2001d. 'The Folklore of Pride: Three Components of Contemporary Dalit Belief'. In Zelliot. *From Untoucable to Dalit*, pp. 317–33.

———. 2001e [1972]. 'Gandhi and Ambedkar: A Study in Leadership'. In Zelliot. *From Untouchable to Dalit*, pp. 150–83.

———. 2001f. 'India's Ex-Untouchables: New Past, New Future and the New Poetry'. In Zelliot. *From Untouchable to Dalit*, pp. 293–316.

———. 2001g [1977]. 'The Leadership of Babasaheb Ambedkar'. In Zelliot. *From Untouchable to Dalit*, pp. 53–78.

———. 2001h [1970]. 'Learning the Use of Political Means: The Mahars of Maharashtra'. In Zelliot. *From Untouchable to Dalit*, pp. 86–125.

———. 2004. *Dr Babasaheb Ambedkar and the Untouchable Movement*. New Delhi: Blumoon Books.

1

WHO IS THE DALIT?
The Emergence of a New Political Subject

Anupama Rao

'**D**alit' means 'ground down', or 'broken to pieces', in both Marathi and Hindi. B.R. Ambedkar first used the term in 1928 or so, in his newspaper *Bahishkrit Bharat*, but the term gained new potency in Maharashtra during the 1970s, a period of literary and cultural efflorescence that saw the birth of Dalit *sahitya* (literature).[1] Today, the widespread currency of the term is also belated recognition of the Dalits' militant claims upon a history of humiliation and suffering.

In this short piece, I would like to suggest that the seemingly self-evident and obvious history indexed by the term 'Dalit' bears further scrutiny. Looking at the politics of naming allows us to more fully address 'Dalit' not so much as a name, but as a field of contestation and significance, that is, as a political category with a history. I therefore propose to examine how Dalitness was represented across the late nineteenth and twentieth centuries. I do so by exploring the emergence of the Dalit as a new political and ethical subject who challenged existing accounts of history, politics, and culture. In particular, I examine efforts by Jotirao Phule to address Dalits as part of a larger political and ethical community of non-Brahman Kshatriyas, who were defeated by wily Aryan-Brahmans; B.R. Ambedkar's argument about the Dalit as a political minority; and, finally, literary representations of the Dalit self. Each of these moments in the elaboration of Dalit identity suggests the long-standing presence of subaltern critiques of the caste-Hindu order, as well as the social, cultural, and historical contexts within which such critiques emerged. Thus, rather than focusing on movement-centric explorations of Dalit identity, I argue here that the emergence of the Dalit as a political-ethical subject is of profound importance for the ways in which we write broader histories of India's political modernity. The Dalit is an inaugural figure for understanding the specificity of Indian democracy, precisely because Dalits' experiences of humiliation and degradation forced them to rethink the relationship between modernity and democracy, instead of crafting a nativist modernity that countered the colonial masters but fell short of democratizing the illiberal economies of caste.[2]

This argument extends, even as it pays homage to, the pioneering scholarship of Eleanor Zelliot. Almost forty years ago, she acknowledged the centrality of a figure, B.R. Ambedkar, who is being recuperated today by academics and activists alike. This essay, in dialogue with those earlier efforts, attempts to indicate the theoretical transformation effected by Ambedkar's political thought, and argues for the significance of the Dalit as an inaugural figure of India's political modernity.

OUTSIDE HINDU HISTORY: NAMING AND THE CONSTITUTION OF COMMUNITY

Jotirao Phule's Satyashodak Samaj, established in 1873, brought non-Brahman and Dalit activists in western India together around a critique of caste as the *political unconscious* of Hindu society. Phule was uneasy with the novel alignments of secular and ritual power, that British colonization enabled. His unease coalesced around his representation of the 'new' Brahman, who was able to parlay his monopoly over ritual and scriptural knowledge into an exclusive claim upon western education and employment in the colonial bureaucracy. One of Phule's most significant responses to the colonial context, in which Brahmanical hegemony was both transformed and exacerbated in novel ways, was to make control over language and the politics of (re)naming a central element of anti-caste discourse. Naming was itself a way of critiquing ideology; it was a strategy of countering religious superstition and ideological indoctrination through rational thought, by taking control over the act of representation. The category of the *shudra-atishudra* was the end result of Phule's effort to produce a new ethical community, which would also be a political constituency that could be united in the struggle against Brahmanism.

If low-caste identity was defined through its fundamental antagonism to Brahmanism, its positive force derived from the courage and bravery of those autochthonous communities that had opposed the hegemony of the Aryan Brahman. In a typically brilliant move, Phule transvalued Orientalist as well as nationalist fascination with theories of Aryan conquest, to argue that a permanent and irreconcilable hostility between Brahmans and non-Brahmans characterized caste society from its inception. Phule's definition of history as the history of caste conflict further enabled his recuperation of a valiant pre-Aryan, Kshatriya history for the downtrodden communities.

Phule lauded the Untouchable communities of Maharashtra, the Mahars and Mangs, for putting up the strongest resistance against the Aryan-Brahman invaders. Arguing that the term Mahar meant *Maha-ari*, or the 'Great Enemy', Phule argued that the Maha-ari had been severely punished by the Aryan-Brahmans for their fierce resistance to them. It was to punish them for their resistance to Brahmanical domination that the Maha-ari were banished from society and condemned to poverty, to feeding on dead carcasses, and to wearing a black thread around their necks as a symbol of servitude.[3] Thus, Phule was the first to recuperate Dalits' history as a militant struggle against Brahmanical hegemony, which was met, subsequently, by their defeat and degradation.

Early Dalit activists such as Gopal Baba Valangkar and Shivram Janba Kamble drew on this narrative of a founding antagonism between the Brahman and non-Brahman communities. Like Phule, Kamble argued that the Mahars had been in the employ of virtuous Dravidian kings like Bali, Ravana, and Hiranyakashipu, who were defeated through trickery, and later castigated in Puranic literature as *asuras*, or demons (Kamble 1920). Valangkar, too, asserted the heroism of the Untouchable communities, and argued that the Mahars, Mangs, and Chambhars were Dravidian Kshatriyas who had fought the Aryan invaders twenty-one times, before they were finally defeated. In Valangkar's account, however, the identity of the Mahars as Dravidian Kshatriyas would be hitched to a new set of efforts, at the turn of the century, to highlight the martial past of the Mahars in order to lay claim to continued military employment in the British army. Valangkar privileged the repeated outcasting that the Untouchable communities suffered *after* their initial defeat at the hands of the Aryan Brahmans. Furthermore, in Valangkar's account, eating carrion was the most important symbol of the degradation of the Untouchable communities, and it was emphasized to a far greater extent than by Phule, to become a recurrent theme in explaining the root cause of the Untouchables' stigmatization.

Gopal Vithalnak Valangkar was a native of Ravadhul, about five miles from the town of Mahad. Valangkar had been an active member of the Satyashodak Samaj while in military service. In 1886, he retired as an army havildar and went to Dapoli, in Ratnagiri district in the Konkan, to take up a position as schoolmaster. Dapoli Camp was a unique settlement of Mahar and Chambhar military pensioners. A large population of Mahar and Chamar pensioners, including Ambedkar's father, Subedar Ramji Maloji Sakpal, were residents of Dapoli. Having experienced social mobility and relatively little discrimination in the military, these pensioners had created a community of their own near the town of Mahad. By 1892, however, they were to become victims of a decision by the British government to stop recruitment from the Untouchable communities.

Precisely because they had experienced the return to Untouchable status once they were refused military employment, this community of educated Mahars and Chambhars provided a ready-made political constituency that could be mobilized to demand civic and human rights. It was Valangkar who enabled their politicization. Valangkar was a crucial link between Satyashodak ideology and the emergence of a specifically Dalit critique of caste and untouchability. Valangkar had been educated up to the normal-school examination in Pune's Shri Ganesh School. More significant, however, was his exposure to the radical anti-Brahmanism of the Satyashodak Samaj. One member of the Satyashodak Samaj, Govind Ganpat Kale, recalled that Phule was a frequent visitor to Valangkar's home in the Maharwada in Bhavani Peth, where he would test members of the Samaj by seating them in the same *pangti*, or row, as Valangkar, while food was served (Patil 1927). Subedar R.S. Ghadge, a military pensioner who later became a member of the Poona branch of Vithal Ramji Shinde's Depressed Classes Mission, recalled that when he was stationed in Poona along with Valangkar, they had heard Jotirao Phule lecturing the Mahar regiment about the bravery of the Chambhars, Mahars, and Mangs who had valiantly fought the Aryan Brahmans in ancient times (see Ghadge 1981: 37).[4]

Valangkar was deeply influenced by Phule's critique of Brahmanical hegemony, and his efforts to craft a specifically Dalit critique of caste inequality were profoundly influenced by the rationalism and radical egalitarianism of Satyashodak discourse. In addition to founding the first Dalit organization in the Bombay Presidency, the Anarya Dosh Pariharak Mandali (Society for the Removal of the Misdemeanours of the Non-Aryans), Valangkar was a frequent contributor to the newspapers *Sudharak* and *Deena Bandhu*.[5] He was even nominated to the Mahad Local Board in 1895, though he was boycotted by the other members. In July 1894, Valangkar drafted one of the first petitions to the Bombay government demanding equal employment and civil rights for the Untouchable communities on behalf of the Anarya Dosh Pariharak Mandali.[6] In addition to his efforts to create an associational form through which to represent Dalit demands for employment in the colonial bureaucracy, Valangkar had written a *Vinanti Patra* in 1888, which was an extensive critique of caste exclusion that was structured in the form of a series of questions demanding that caste-Hindus defend the divine rationale for *jati* and *varna* distinctions and for the practice of untouchability.[7] In this text, as well as in his reply in 1894 to H.H. Risley's questionnaire regarding the origins and practices of various castes, Valangkar provided a genealogy of Dalit humiliation and suffering that demanded for rights and social recognition in the language of political liberalism and gave an alternative account of the Dalit past that emphasized the subordination of the Dalit communities.

Elaborating upon Phule's account of the defeat of the shudra-atishudras, Valangkar reminded the Maha-aris of their continued exploitation at the hands of the Aryan-Brahman invaders. He went on to incorporate a repetitive structure of degradation and humiliation into his narrative of defeat. Valangkar argued that the Mahar Kshatriyas had been outcasted after they had eaten meat to survive the Mahadurga famine of 1396. Again during the Peshwai, the lower-caste and Untouchable communities had found themselves facing severe religious exclusion under a Brahmanical state. In Phule's account, the abject position of the Dalit was historically produced through the foundational conflict between Aryan-Brahmans and the autochthonous Dravidian communities of western India. In Valangkar's account, however, this originary conflict was overlaid with an argument that the specific source of the Untouchables' degradation lay in the eating of carrion.

While this narrative of defeat and degradation remained a remarkably constant theme throughout the twentieth century, other aspects of this genealogy went through important emendation. Ambedkar's 1948 essay, 'The Untouchables: Who Were They and Why They Became Untouchables', challenged the racial theories both Phule and Valangkar had adopted to produce a powerful subaltern critique of caste domination. Ambedkar wrote partly in reaction to colonial accounts of the caste system as a hierarchical ordering (and assimilation) of racially diverse populations. This was an account he had challenged as early as 1916, in a paper presented to the Anthropology seminar at Columbia University, and published in the *Indian Antiquary* in 1917 as 'Castes in India: Their Genesis, Mechanism, and Development'. Ambedkar was also responding to the biological racism that characterized the discourse of National Socialism in Germany, with its horrific culmination in the Holocaust. Thus, unlike either Phule or Valangkar, Ambedkar consistently maintained that India was a nation with a common racial stock, and that castes were not racially distinct. Indeed, the animus between castes was the result of historical evolution, which culminated in the emergence of caste as a perverse and involuted form of class. Caste, Ambedkar argued, was the historical product of overlapping social, political, and economic antagonisms held in tension through the commandments of Hindu law. It was Hindu juridicality, as enunciated in the Sanskrit prescriptive texts such as the *Dharmashastra*, that legitimized, indeed rendered invisible, the violence of caste inequality. In Ambedkar's narrative, escaping Hindu history meant engaging with the defeat of Buddhism by Brahmanism as a world-historical event. Concomitantly, it involved addressing the *singularity* of the Dalit, instead of describing him or her as a member of the shudra-atishudra collectivity of defeated Dravidian Kshatriyas.

Buddhism, according to Ambedkar, was the forgotten agent of history that preceded Brahmanism and functioned as its most significant political and ethical adversary. In Ambedkar's account the Dalit was that singular figure who represented the forgotten history of Buddhism and its violent demise. The production of a separate genealogy for the Dalit fundamentally transformed existing narratives of a common origin for the shudra-atishudra communities. Indeed, Ambedkar's genealogy posits the Shudra as both within and without the caste order, an aggressor turned victim marked by a politics of resentment.[8] Thus, even though struggle against Brahmanical domination was at the very heart of the historical process, Ambedkar argued that the Shudras and the Untouchables were differently incorporated into the caste-Hindu order. Castes, Ambedkar argued, were divided according to a class principle: there was a crucial distinction between the Shudras and the twice-born castes, but more fundamental was that between the *touchable* Hindus, or *Savarna*s, and the *Avarna*s, that is, those without caste. Unlike Valangkar, Ambedkar altogether bypassed the necessity of arguing that the Untouchables had been stigmatized because they had, at some point in the hoary past, adopted degrading practices such as scavenging, or eating beef and carrion. Instead, Ambedkar argued that the Vedic Brahmans had been meat-eaters, and had adopted vegetarianism as a ploy to defeat Buddhism and to lay claim to its tradition of pacifism and non-violence. The Untouchables were a distinct group of Buddhists, the Broken Men, who belonged to a group of wandering tribesmen who had been defeated in battle as nomadic society gave way to settled agriculture. As a consequence, the Broken Men had become dependent on eating dead cattle for survival, for which they were later stigmatized. Ambedkar argued that the real reason for their stigmatization lay in their refusal to accept Brahman hegemony. Indeed, the Broken Men were the final vestiges of an alternative political and ethical community that had been destroyed by Brahmanism.

Rather than focusing on the Untouchables' changing position in the caste-Hindu order, Ambedkar's account emphasized the world-historical defeat of Buddhism by Brahmanism, as well as the Dalit's identity as a non-Hindu Buddhist, and thereby laid claim to a genealogy for the Dalit that lay *outside* Hindu history. The Untouchables were Broken Men who were degraded, homeless, and fated to inhabit the margins. A destitute, territorially dispersed community of suffering, they were history's detritus. Locked in an antagonistic relationship to Brahmanism from the start, the Broken Men were history's losers, even as they exemplified a crucial space of alterity.

Ambedkar's conversion to Buddhism in 1956 was thus a return to a religion that he described as an indigenous democracy that had included women, outcastes, and royalty alike. This was a complete rejection of Hindu inclusion, and simultaneously a critical effort to recreate Dalit selfhood by placing the Dalit outside the deforming narratives of Hindu history. Here Ambedkar's actions echoed earlier efforts to use the rewriting of history as one of the most potent weapons in a subaltern political–ethical critique of Brahmanism, even as it laid claim to a separate and distinctive genealogy for the Dalit as a non-Hindu.

WITHIN THE SPACE OF POLITICS: DALITS AS MINORITIES

Dalits were a territorially dispersed community of suffering. The critique of caste ideology as well as efforts to narrate the Dalit self had marked their exceptional status. What was the best mechanism for redressing a history of humiliation and discrimination? Is it possible to define a stigmatized and socio-economically marginal community as both equal to, yet different from, other political constituencies? That is, is it possible to equalize the status of unequal subjects even while maintaining their historic or cultural distinctiveness? Indeed, this is akin to the more global problem of recognition that feminists, as well as other minority groups, have encountered (see, for example, Povinelli 2002, Scott 1996, and Taylor *et al.* 1994). Let us trace the specific manner in which Ambedkar addressed this question as far as the Dalit community was concerned.

Ambedkar sought to democratize the community from within through the critique of political Hinduism, and to democratize it from without by changing the grounding principles on which 'minority' was defined. Both required working through politicized manifestations of community, or community-as-constituency.

During the 1920s, Ambedkar argued that the Depressed Classes ought to be recognized according to a new principle of minority, one capable of addressing the complex and multilayered nature of caste inequality, whose manifestations could not be neatly divided between religious or ritual and secular domains. Ambedkar's efforts to represent Depressed-Class interests as the class interests of a vulnerable and stigmatized community tried to move away from colonial definitions of religious communities as political actors. Rather, it was the material consequences of exclusion—destitution, poverty, illiteracy—that Ambedkar highlighted, in an effort to redefine the principle of minority. But it had become clear that the Untouchables' negative relationship to Hinduism was the crucial link in suturing together the distinct manifestations of caste inequality.

Ambedkar argued that untouchability was central to the caste-Hindu order. From his position as spokesperson for an exceptional community, degraded and yet possessing a latent political power, Ambedkar argued that the Untouchables formed the glue of the Hindu order although they were despised and marginalized. The principle of untouchability provided the single point of unification for the touchable but otherwise fragmented Hindu castes. In every other respect, differences of belief and practice fractured Hinduism irretrievably. To locate untouchability, that which was extraneous or supplementary to caste-Hinduism, as caste's secret, was perhaps the most powerful attempt yet by anyone to provide a systemic theory of caste. How could this negative principle become manifest, when it was precisely its misrecognition that reproduced the caste order? How to make the Depressed Classes visible as a 'separate element' whose interests were diametrically opposed to those of the Hindu community? We can use a Marxian analogy to argue that just as withdrawing labour power brings the economy to a standstill, what Ambedkar formulated for use as a political weapon, the demand for a separate electorate, was the caste equivalent of a general strike. Withholding consent to inclusion within the Hindu order was the only available mechanism for registering the position of the Dalit as structurally necessary to the caste order, though defined by sheer negativity. Indeed, the paradoxical position of the Dalit as both within and outside the caste-Hindu order was precisely what the separate electorate was meant to elucidate.

The separate electorate was a mechanism that had been used by the colonial state to define religious communities as political constituencies. As early as 1909, when Muslims had been granted a separate electorate with weightage in recognition of their status as a community of 'historic and political importance', the mechanism of the separate electorate had also served to numerically distinguish a Hindu majority from a Muslim minority. Instead, in the case of the so-called Depressed Classes, Prime Minister Ramsey MacDonald's Communal Award of 16 August 1932 allowed the Depressed Classes a double vote. They could vote for Depressed Class candidates through a separate electorate in areas where Depressed Class voters predominated, and they could also cast a vote in the general (Hindu) electorate. The Award thus marked the anomalous status of the Depressed Classes as a degraded Hindu minority, both as a part of, and apart from, the broader community of Hindus. Why indeed, we might ask, did Ambedkar demand a separate electorate for the Depressed Classes when other Depressed Class leaders, including Ambedkar's most significant political rival, M.C. Rajah, had shifted away from earlier demands for separate representation? Answering this question requires that we engage further with the political logic of the separate electorate.

The Round Table Conferences (subsequently RTC) of 1930 and 1931 saw an important shift *away* from Ambedkar's earlier advocacy of reserved electorates with weightage for the Depressed Classes. Why? Ambedkar realized that adult franchise was an impossible demand under colonial governance. But even more significant was the frustration with Congress leaders who refused to address the problem of the Depressed Classes as anything other than a problem of social and religious reform. The Nehru Committee, formed in 1928 as a nationalist response to the Simon Commission, extended invitations to formulate constitutional proposals to members of all the minority communities— Anglo-Indians, Christians, Muslims, non-Brahmans, Parsis, and Sikhs—except the Depressed Classes. The Committee noted that the Untouchables neither required nor wanted special political facilities, as theirs was a 'social problem' to be solved through education. Ambedkar bitterly criticized the Report for its recommendation to abolish community-based constituencies except for Muslims. '[W]hile separate constituencies for Muslims may threaten the nation separate constituencies for non-Brahmans threaten the Brahmans .... This is an effort to keep Untouchables and non-Brahmans away from power' (cited in Gore 1993: 116). He noted that reserved electorates would muffle Depressed-Class interests; separate representation was required.[9] As a consequence, dissatisfaction with Congress ran deep at the RTCs.

The second meeting of the RTC held from 7 September to 1 December 1931 found Ambedkar and Gandhi locked in conflict over the issue of separate electorates for the Depressed Classes. A meeting of the All India Depressed Classes Leaders' Conference held on 19 May 1931 in Bombay had endorsed the demand for a separate electorate as the 'right' of the Depressed Classes. But this was preceded by an inconclusive meeting with Gandhi in the spring of 1931, that left Ambedkar angry because Gandhi had failed to acknowledge him with the respect and importance he deserved. This was later confirmed by Gandhi's admission that he was unaware of Ambedkar's identity as a Mahar leader. Indeed, at the second meeting of the RTC, Gandhi characterized the separate electorate for Muslims as a 'gift', while arguing that a separate electorate for the Depressed Classes was impossible, as it would create an unbridgeable schism among Hindus.

The issue of separate electorates remained the most contentious issue at the second RTC. M.C. Rajah, for example, chairman of the Depressed India Association, who had earlier demanded separate electorates, now did an about-face; in a joint declaration with the Hindu Mahasabha, he demanded joint electorates with reserved seats for Depressed-Class candidates. Rajah noted that when he had demanded separate electorates it was assumed that the colonial government would continue to be the 'special protector of Minority interests'. Under changed political conditions, it was imperative that the Depressed Classes, which lacked an 'effective percentage', amalgamate themselves into the Hindu constituency with the provision of reserved seats.[10]

Ambedkar's efforts utilized the separate electorate to reveal the 'deadly antagonism' that existed between Dalit and Hindu. While this effort failed, with extraordinary consequences for the possibility of representing Dalit interests as such, it is important nonetheless to examine what Ambedkar sought to achieve through a separate electorate. Ambedkar understood Hindu ideology as justifying a complex form of inequality, characterized by secular and religio-ritual forms of exclusion. Thus, if Gandhi (and Congress nationalists) characterized untouchability as a problem of religious inclusion, Ambedkar politicized the putative split between these two domains and simultaneously questioned the terms of religious and political inclusion, to argue that the horizon of emancipation could not be contained within existing social relations. But how was this sophisticated theorization of caste society to be operationalized?

Since there was no single procedural mechanism or political form that could respond to the complexity of caste inequality, the separate electorate was an overdetermined political option from the start. By drawing attention to the Depressed Classes as a politically vulnerable non-Hindu community, the separate electorate would also position the Depressed Classes as politically consequential, since both Hindus and Muslims would recognize them as having 'the power to bring about a decisive shift one way or the other'.[11] The separate electorate endowed the Depressed Classes with political value by positioning them as an exceptional community on a par with both Hindus and Muslims. This mechanism could only succeed if the Depressed Classes could be defined as non-Hindus.

Ambedkar had repeatedly argued that the Depressed Classes were distinguished by material deprivation, physical vulnerability, and stigmatized status within the caste order. *They represented an altogether different principle of minority.* This was indeed the political conundrum of Depressed-Class identity; as Gandhi once noted, theirs was an identity to be transcended, not reified.[12] Gandhi's fast-unto-death and the ensuing Poona Pact, by reaffirming the identity of the Depressed Classes as degraded Hindus, also made untouchability an internal problem for the Hindu community.[13] There was no mechanism to democratize the community from within, however, as the perpetrators, the caste-Hindu majority, were the ones who were being asked to adjudicate their own behaviour! Gandhian reformism, with its focus on changing the hearts and minds of even the most orthodox Hindu, substituted penitence for procedural equality. It was not until after Independence that political citizenship was to be conflated with the reform and secularization of Hinduism.[14] We will not pursue this narrative of political representation into this period. Rather, we will examine the question of representation from another angle, through literary efforts to represent the existential aspects of Dalit life.

DALIT SELFHOOD AS LITERARY ARTEFACT

It was not until the 1970s that the problem of Dalit selfhood was staged as a problem of literary self-representation, one that overturned traditional ideas about literary form and content. An earlier generation of Dalit writers who had participated in Ambedkar's movement—for example, Shantabai Dani in her *Ratra Din Amhi ...* (1990); Vasant Moon, in his autobiography of growing up in a Nagpur slum, in *Vasti* (1995); or Narendra Jadhav's account of his father's life, *Amcha Baap Ani Amhi* (1994)—recalled the social and political upheavals of the 1920s–50s as consonant with new forms of self-making. Their accounts are so closely tied to Ambedkar's movement as to render self and community one, held together by the name 'Ambedkar'. Ambedkar is the protagonist of these narratives, who enables a profound transformation of the Mahar community by inaugurating a historic struggle for self-respect and social recognition that humanized a stigmatized and degraded community. In these accounts, his name accumulates a sort of fetish value; it is repeated, circulated, and made to represent the man, the movement, and the Dalit future.

Dalit *sahitya*, the literature that emerged from this transformative period in Maharashtra's politics in the 1970s, signalled a new phase in Dalit literary and political culture. Deeply identified with the neighbourhoods and working-class ethos of Bombay, Dalit sahitya came to be defined by the often-sexualized language of the Bombay slums and by a refiguration of literary Marathi. Namdeo Dhasal's famous collection of poetry, *Golpitha* (1972), focused on the red-light neighbourhood in which he grew up, comes to mind. As the progressive Brahman playwright, Vijay Tendulkar, noted, *Golpitha* is an object lesson in the desperate material circumstances and easy exchange of violence and intimacy that saturate Dalit life:

This is the world ... of the jobless, of beggars, of pickpockets .... Dhasal's *Golpitha* where leprous women are paid the price and fucked on the road, where children cry nearby, where prostitutes waiting for business sing full throated love songs ... (cited in Punalekar 2001: 228).

Indeed, for upper-caste Marathi readers of the time, autobiographical accounts came to predominate in their exposure to Dalit sahitya. Baburao Bagul's *Jevha Mi Jaat Corli Hoti* (1963), Daya Pawar's *Baluta* (1978), Mane's *Upara* (1980), and Shankarrao Kharat's *Taral Antaral* (1981) focused on narrating the painful histories of Dalit selfhood.

Baluta draws upon the quintessential symbol of the Dalit's humiliation, having to beg for leftover food as *baluta*, or his traditional village share for performing stigmatized labour. Understood more broadly as the Dalit's share or lot in life, *Baluta* historicizes the figure of the stigmatized Dalit by locating him within an economy of suffering. The narrator of *Baluta* undercuts the presumed veracity, the 'reality effect' of the autobiographical from the start, characterizing his story as a secret that must not be revealed, perhaps because of the shame as well as the pain of confronting the (collective) self of which he writes (Pawar 1993: frontispiece. The translation is mine):

Dagdu Maruti Pawar
Who carries as his portion [lit. *vatylya*, that which is apportioned]
This baluta of pain
Tied up in the folds [*padaraat*] of his clothes
Because of the condition [*vyavastha*] of Indian society

I am only the beast of burden
Who manifests his words

His desire was that
No one should be told [*konala sangu naye*]

I also feel
That we should not reveal this to anyone

Pawar plays on the relationship between secret and revelation instead of celebrating the autobiographical as an authentic act of self-representation. Indeed, Dagdu Maruti Pawar is both a character as well as a concept; he is the secret sharer of Indian society, whose shameful experiences cannot be related without disavowing the pact of caste-Hindu secrecy. The possibility of representing the Dalit self also requires challenging ideas of autobiographical interiority, individualism, and, most importantly, authenticity. As a negated, invisible figure, the Dalit's pain is literally unrepresentable; it is the secret that if revealed must also find expression through another kind of language.

CONCLUSION

History, politics, and culture—all were important sites where the problem of Dalit identity came to be posed. Yet each of these spaces reflects the insuperable challenges posed by the problem of Dalit inclusion. If defining 'Dalit' produced a crisis in each of these terrains, it was because Dalit activists and intellectuals, especially Ambedkar, posed the problem of equality not as an abstract thought experiment, but from within the embodied space of stigmatized selfhood. Doing this illuminated two intertwined issues: First, by questioning the terms of religious *and* political inclusion simultaneously, Dalit critique revealed that the horizon of emancipation could not be contained within existing social relations, and, second, though they took strategic recourse to the enumerative logic of the political majority and minority, as well as the ameliorative logic of a reformed Hinduism, anti-caste activists consistently maintained that the existential aspect of caste subalternity exceeded both sets of strategies. If caste, especially untouchability, is the deep structure of secular and religious configurations of community, as I have argued, and if, indeed, the Dalit is an inaugural political subject, then how is it possible to write an account of India's political modernity without engaging with the problem of Dalit freedom and emancipation?

NOTES

1. For good discussions of Dalit cultural politics in the post-Independence period, see the essays by Gopal Guru, Gail Omvedt, and Eleanor Zelliot in Shah 2001.

2. With regard to the content of nativist modernity, see Chatterjee 1986.

3. *Gulamgiri*, Phadke 1991: 160. Also see O'Hanlon 1985.

4. See also R.S Ghadge to P.S. Patil, Pune, 29 May 1930. P.S. Patil MSS, Shivaji University, Kolhapur, cited in O'Hanlon (1985: 272).

5. The first issue of *Deena Bandhu* (Friend of the Impoverished) was published in January 1877, with a circulation of 300 copies. By 1884, with a circulation figure of 1,650, the *Deena Bandhu* was second only to Tilak's newspaper, *Kesari*. (*Native Newspaper Report*, 6 September 1884).

6. The petition was not delivered until 1895, because the pensioners were afraid that their pensions would be suspended. *Deena Bandhu*, 7 April 1894.

7. This petition was published in *Purogami Satyashodak*, July–September 1979, as *Vithal Vidhvamsan*, or, 'The Destruction of Pollution'. There are doubts as to whether this text is indeed the *Vithal*, since Valangkar mentions a text that he had been unable to get published (*Deena Bandhu*, 10 May 1894). Valangkar is also supposed to have written another text, *Hindu Dharma Darpan* ('The Mirror of Hindu Religion'), about which no further information is available.

8. Ambedkar's critique of the Shudra should be seen in the context of the emergence, during the first two decades of the twentieth century, of especially powerful strand of non-Brahman politics that restricted Kshatriya identity for those Marathas from the original *shahannavkuli* (ninety-six) families. The entry of most non-Brahmans into the Congress Party by 1930 also gave Ambedkar a strong reason for critiquing the social and political trajectories of non-Brahmanism.

9. 'Nehru Committtee chi Yojana va Hindustanache Bhavitva' ('The Nehru Committee Recommendations and the Future of Hindustan'), *Bahishkrit Bharat*, 18 January 1929.

10. *Bombay Chronicle*, 24 March 1932.

11. *Bahishkrit Bharat*, 20 May 1927, editorial.

12. Gandhi had offered a powerful reason why the Untouchables did not constitute a community with the right to special political representation. 'Sikhs may remain as such in perpetuity', he pointed out, 'so may Muslims,

so may Europeans. Would "untouchables" remain untouchables in perpetuity?' (cited in Pyarelal 1932: 7).
13. For studies of the Poona Pact, see Dirks 2001, Nagaraj 1993, Rodrigues 1994, and Zelliot 1988.
14. See especially the essays by Marc Galanter and Partha Chatterjee in Bhargava 1998.

REFERENCES

Bhargava, Rajiv (ed.). 1998. *Secularism and its Critics*. New Delhi: Oxford University Press.

Chatterjee, Partha. 1986. *Nationalist Thought and the Colonial World: A Derivative Discourse?* London: Zed Books.

Dirks, Nicholas B. 2001. 'The Reform of Caste: Periyar, Ambedkar, and Gandhi'. In Nicholas B. Dirks (ed.). *Castes of Mind*. Princeton: Princeton University Press, 2001, pp. 255–74.

Ghadge, R.S. 1981. *Amhi Pahilele Phule* ('The Phule That We Saw'), edited by Sitaram Raikar. Pune: Mahatma Phule Samata Pratisthan.

Gore, M.S. 1993. *The Social Context of an Ideology: Ambedkar's Political and Social Thought*. New Delhi: Sage Publications.

Kamble, Shivram. 1920. *Nagpur Yethil 30 va 31 May ani 1 June 1920 Bahishkrit Bharat Parishadet Zhalele Ra. Shivram Janba Kamble Yanche Bhashan* (Shivram Janba Kamble's speech at the Bahishkrit Bharat Parishad of 30–1 May and 1 June 1920). Pune: Istralight Chapkhana.

Nagaraj, D.R. 1993. 'Self Purification and Self Respect'. In D.R. Nagaraj. *The Flaming Feet: A Study of the Dalit Movement*. Bangalore: South Forum Press, pp. 1–30.

O'Hanlon, Rosalind. 1985. *Caste, Conflict, and Ideology: Mahatma Jotirao Phule and Low Caste Protest in Nineteenth-Century Western India*. Cambridge: Cambridge University Press.

Patil, Pandharinath Sitaram. 1927. *Mahatma Jotirao Phule Yanche Charitra* ('A Biography of Mahatma Jotirao Phule'). Chikhali.

Pawar, Daya. 1993. *Baluta*. Mumbai: Granthali, 7th edn.

Phadke, Y.D. (ed.). 1991. *Mahatma Phule Samagra Wangmay* ('The Complete Works of Mahatma Phule'). Maharashtra Rajya Sahitya ani Mandal, Mumbai, revised 4th and 5th edn. First edition, Dhananjay Keer and S.G. Malshe (eds). Mumbai: Maharashtra Rajya Sahitya ani Sanskriti Mandal, 1961).

Povinelli, Elizabeth. 2002. *The Cunning of Recognition: Indigenous Alterities and the Making of Australian Multiculturalism*. Durham: Duke University Press.

Punalekar, S.P. 2001. 'Dalit Literature and Dalit Identity'. In Ghanshyam
    Shah (ed.). *Dalit Identity and Politics*. New Delhi: Sage Publications,
    pp. 214–41.
Pyarelal. 1932. *The Epic Fast*. Ahmedabad: Mohanlal Maganlal Bhatt.
Rodrigues, Valerian. 1994. 'Between Tradition and Modernity: The Gandhi-
    Ambedkar Debate'. In A.K. Narain and D.C. Ahir (eds). *Dr Ambedkar,
    Buddhism, and Social Change*. Delhi: B.R. Publishing, pp. 137–61.
Scott, Joan Wallach. 1996. *Only Paradoxes to Offer: French Feminists and the
    Rights of Man*. Cambridge, Massachuesetts: Harvard University Press.
Shah, Ghanshyam (ed.). 2001. *Dalit Identity and Politics*. New Delhi: Sage
    Publications.
Taylor, Charles, Kwame Anthony Appiah, Jurgen Habermas, and Stephen C.
    Rockefeller. 1994. *Multiculturalism: Examining the Politics of Recognition*.
    Princeton: Princeton University Press.
Zelliot, Eleanor. 1988. 'Congress and Untouchables: 1917–1950'. In Richard
    Sisson and Stanley Wolpert (eds). *Congress and Indian Nationalism:
    The Pre-Independence Phase*. Berkeley: University of California Press,
    pp. 182–97.

2

THE MAKING OF A DALIT PERSPECTIVE
The 1940s and the Chamars of Uttar Pradesh

Ramnarayan S. Rawat

Shankaranand Shastri's *Poona-Pact or Gandhi*, published in Hindi from Lucknow, Uttar Pradesh (UP) in 1946, and Nandlal Viyogi's *Ambedkar ki Awaz: Arthat Achhutoin ka Federation*, published in Hindi from Allahabad (UP) in 1949, are significant markers of the radical realignment that took place in Dalit politics in the 1940s.[1] These two authors tell of a new and unprecedented self-confidence and direction at this time among Dalit activists and politicians, in contrast to the earlier era of Dalit activism that spanned the first three decades of the twentieth century. As Shastri (1994: 76) asserts, 'these are different times, of 1946, not of 1932 [Poona Pact].' Shastri and Viyogi are united in asserting that Achhuts are separate from Hindus and that their liberation lies in acquiring political power to institute a programme of affirmative action. Both authors recognize the unique role of the Scheduled Castes Federation (SCF) in achieving these two goals.[2] In addition, they refer to the growing Achhut movement in 1946–8 in UP and other parts of India as evidence of their new strength, markedly different from 1932, when the Congress forced the Poona Pact on them.[3] These two authors, along with other Dalit writers and activists of the period, also offer a rounded critique of the Congress-led national movement. The most well-known work of this genre is B.R. Ambedkar's *What Congress and Gandhi Have Done to the Untouchables*. As Eleanor

Zelliot notes, 'it was during this period of the mid-1940s that Ambedkar launched his most vitriolic attacks against Gandhi', including the publication of his now-famous book in 1945 (Zelliot 1972: 89).

There are other events that underline the dramatic changes taking place in the character and tone of Dalit politics in the 1940s. The foundation of the SCF in July 1942 was followed by a period of intense agitational politics by the organization in 1946–7 in different parts of India, especially in the north Indian state of UP.[4] Further evidence of a new wave of radicalism in the 1940s comes from Jagjivan Ram's position towards Congress and Gandhi. At a news conference in Lucknow in 1946, Jagjivan Ram, the famous Dalit leader in the Congress, criticized Gandhi—for the first and only time.[5] He described Congress as a party of caste-Hindus and criticized Gandhi for not admitting the separate identity of Achhuts, despite the Poona Pact's explicit acknowledgement of this fact.

A brief discussion of Ambedkar's actions in 1948 will further illustrate the significance of the 1940s as a moment of departure for Dalit politics. In August 1947 Ambedkar joined the Congress government, as law minister. In the immediate aftermath of the SCF's popular agitation in 1946–7 and Ambedkar's crusade against what Shastri called Brahman-Baniya Congress, Ambedkar's decision to accept a position in the Congress government had a devastating impact upon rank-and-file members of the SCF. Shastri acknowledges this point when he writes, 'Ambedkar's entry into Congress' ministry created deep doubts in the minds of his followers' (1994: 147). Ambedkar addressed this concern in two meetings, one in Bombay and another in Lucknow. On 17 April 1948, in one of the most important speeches of his career, Ambedkar explained his decision to fellow Dalits in Lucknow. He justified his action by arguing that he had neither joined the Congress nor become its member, but had only joined the government. He claimed that this was the only way to ensure that the Dalit agenda would get incorporated into Congress policies, a goal for which he had been fighting for twenty-five years.[6] In addition, Ambedkar asserted that Dalits must transform their separate identity into a potential political force with its own distinctive agenda. This example illustrates that by the 1940s a clear sense of a Dalit agenda had emerged, one which could be implemented by joining the Congress government.

The title of Nandlal Viyogi's 1949 book, *Ambedkar ki Awaz arthat Achhutoin ka Federation* ('The Voice of Ambedkar or the Federation of Achhuts'), proclaims the key role of Achhut identity within the SCF's political strategy of the 1940s, a strategy that gave Dalits a new *awaz*, or voice.[7] Viyogi and Shastri's accounts, published in Hindi by Dalit-owned presses, have never been used or even acknowledged by mainstream Indian historians. Their assertions are at odds with widely held assumptions that dominate mainstream Indian historiography even today. The prevailing assumption is that in the 1940s Dalit struggles either lost their relevance or merged with Congress-led Indian nationalism, as opposed to an earlier period of isolation or opposition to the Congress in the 1920s and 1930s.[8] However, I believe that the 1940s was the decade in which the articulation of a Dalit agenda as we know it today first materialized, and for this reason more research is needed to fully excavate and reconstruct the lasting role of the Dalit struggles of the 1940s in shaping the perspective that still influences Dalit politics today.

In this chapter I will lay out the broad contours of a new Dalit perspective that was fashioned in north India in the mid-twentieth century. Drawing from my ongoing research on the history of Chamars in UP, I argue that members of the Chamar community played a significant role in constituting a broader Achhut politics and agenda, and in shaping the emergence of a Dalit perspective in UP. To emphasize the singularity of this moment, I will outline the main features of Dalit politics prior to the 1940s, and conclude by arguing that the core of Dalit politics as it developed in the 1940s has remained largely unchanged. Indeed, by the 1960s a commitment to the liberation of Dalits, a desire for social and economic progress, a sense of pride in their identity, and a firm resolve to resist domination by Hindu society had all become securely ingrained in the minds and actions of both Dalit activists and ideologues; these commitments are still evident today. The core issue of refashioning a pure, 'untouched' identity remained, but the most significant contribution of this new politics lay in the emergence of a Dalit identity as a foundational category for the social and political reorganization of ways of thinking and acting.

ORGANIZING DALITS THROUGH CASTE MAHASABHAS

Dalits questioned and rejected categories like 'Untouchables', 'Depressed Classes', 'Scheduled Castes', and 'Harijans' that were coined by colonial, Hindu, and/or nationalist discursive practices. This was not merely to contest dominant ascription of Dalits' identities but also, more importantly, to question the notions of impurity and pollution attached to their community, identity, and history. It was this that marked their struggle, so that from the very beginning Dalit activism took its own unique path. Various Dalit castes in different parts of India raised this issue independently by claiming that they had discovered a pure past and identity within Hindu religion. The more familiar examples of this kind of claim are the Balmikis of Punjab, the Satnamis of Chattisgarh, the Namasudras of Bengal, the Chamars, Pasis, and Bhangis of UP, the Shilpakars of Kumaon, and the Mahars and Chambhars of Maharashtra. I would characterize these initiatives as the first stage in the evolution of a Dalit perspective. Through a range of organizations and caste *mahasabhas* (associations), Chamars launched a struggle to contest the dominant colonial and Hindu narratives of their 'untouchable' identity by emphasizing the 'purity' of their lives and by demanding a status equal to that claimed by caste-Hindus.[9]

We have evidence from the CID files that in the 1920s Chamar mahasabhas mobilized their communities in urban and rural areas by organizing meetings and demonstrations to sustain and spread these ideas.[10] It was in the rural areas of the western districts of UP that the movement began to appeal to well-off Chamar peasants. Although Chamar protests were evident in many parts of the state, the most organized and sustained agitation took place in western UP. These protests were first noticed in 1922 in the districts of Meerut, Moradabad, Bulandshahr, Badaun, Bijnor, Bareilly, Pilibhit, Agra, and Aligarh. By 1923–4, evidence of Chamar protests came from other districts, such as Saharanpur, Etah, Etawah, Mainpuri, Mathura, Dehradun, Lucknow, Unnao, Kheri Sultanpur, and Partapgarh, as well as from districts in eastern UP such as Benares, Jaunpur, Basti, and Gorakhpur. To sustain the movement, a number of practices were promoted and adopted by Chamar organizations, such as abstaining from 'impure' practices like leatherwork and eating beef, giving up alcohol, maintaining a vegetarian diet, and engaging in specific Hindu religious and ritual practices. Additionally, Chamar groups also demanded access to schools and education, and protested against the practices of untouchability, numerous illegal cesses, and *begari* (unpaid labour) imposed on Chamar peasants by caste-Hindus.

In December 1927 the leaders of the Aadi-Hindu Mahasabha in UP made a claim for a more inclusive Aadi-Hindu identity and in the

process effectively challenged articulations of 'pure' Kshatriya identities
made by Chamar groups, similar to those made by other Dalit caste
mahasabhas like those of Pasis, Doms, Dhanuks, Koris, and Lal
Begis? The Mahasabha laid out the agenda in its conference on 27–8
December 1927 in Allahabad, an event that was widely reported and
discussed in newspapers in UP at the time.[11] The conference was
proclaimed the first All-India Aadi-Hindu conference and was attended
by 25,000 Dalits from UP. Another 350 delegates participated from
the Punjab, Bihar, Delhi, the Central Provinces, Poona, Bengal, Madras,
and Hyderabad. The Aadi-Hindu Mahasabha was described as a
movement of all Untouchables, and Swami Achhutanand was declared
their true leader. The struggle against social injustice was described as
their nationalism, social uplift as their religion, and self-respect as their
Home Rule, and the audience was advised to ignore Hindus who called
them 'traitors'. By emphasizing their Aadi-Hindu identity, the leaders
of the Mahasabha were hoping to build a new politics that would bring
all Dalit castes together.

In addition, the Aadi-Hindu Mahasabha raised these issues in a
petition it submitted to the Simon Commission during its tour of India
in 1928. The Simon Commission received similar petitions from Dalit
organizations in different parts of UP and India. They provide us with
useful material to understand the various facets of the Dalit agenda
that were being assembled around this time.[12] What is most striking
is that almost all the Dalit organizations that submitted petitions to
the Simon Commission were unanimous in claiming a separate Aadi-
Hindu identity, making this a marked feature of Dalit politics of this
time. Most of the ideas of the Aadi-Hindu movement were also widely
shared by other Dalit groups across UP, including the Ad Dharmis
from Dehradun, the Kumaon Shilpakar Sabha of Almora, the Jatav
Mahasabha of Agra, the Dom Sudhar Sabha of Garhwal, and the
Chamar Sabha of Kanpur.

Through their struggles in the 1920s and 1930s, Dalit activists and
organizations in UP laid out an agenda that addressed concerns of their
community. A more passionate and elaborate discussion of these
themes is evident in Chandrika Prasad Jigyasu's 1937 book *Bharat ke
Adi Nivasiyon ki Sabhayata* ('The Civilization of India's Original
Inhabitants'), published from Lucknow. By claiming that Achhuts were
the original inhabitants of India and descendants of the *dasas*, *asurs*,
and *dasyu*s mentioned in Brahmanical Hindu texts, Dalits were

challenging both colonial and Hindu interpretations of their identity. Aadi-Hindu was declared as the new identity of all 'Untouchables', distinct from the Hindu community. A core issue of the demands of this period was the desire for adequate safeguards for Dalits in various elective bodies through separate electorates, a demand that was to become the cornerstone of their struggle in the coming years. In addition, their demands included permanent rights over land by changing the Tenancy Acts, fixed wages for their agricultural labour including the removal and skinning of dead animals, rights to use public wells, abolition of begari, the right to convert to any religion, and rejection of the term 'Harijan'.

The characteristic feature of Dalit politics during this period was that it was fractured along caste lines in the form of Dalit caste mahasabhas, despite the efforts of the Aadi-Hindu Mahasabha to mobilize Dalits on the basis of their shared Aadi-Hindu identity with a distinctive non-religious political agenda. The breakthrough took place in the 1940s—organizationally and ideologically—with the formation of the SCF.

FORMULATING AN ACHHUT IDENTITY

'What I want is power—political power—for my people, for if we have power we will have social status,' stated Ambedkar in his inaugural address to the Dalits in the fifth Uttar Pradesh SCF conference on 24 April 1948.[13] He underlined the role of a separate Achhut identity as a necessary feature of Dalits' politics in their attempt to transform themselves into a political force under one leader, one party, one programme, one slogan, and one banner. The UPSCF demanded proportional representation for Dalits in government services and legislative institutions as an effective method for implementing the affirmative-action agenda. In addition, resolutions passed during the conference made the point that even though India had achieved independence, the position of Dalits had not changed and would not change unless the government guaranteed constitutional changes.[14] Affinity to such an agenda was not confined to radical Ambedkarite Dalit organizations; rather, it was shared across the spectrum, even by members of Congress Harijan organizations. In June 1946, the District Harijan Conference of Meerut and the District Harijan Uddhar Sabha of Saharanpur raised issues similar to those of the UPSCF, including a demand for proportional representation.[15] In their resolutions, they argued that the rights of Harijans are separate from those of caste-Hindus and that the Congress should recognize the differences.

A new feature of Achhut politics in the 1940s was the emergence of the SCF as a party that offered a political platform for all Achhuts. Indeed, the most significant development in Dalit politics in the 1940s was the dissolution of Dalit caste-Mahasabhas into the SCF's organizations. The formation of the SCF provided an organizational body for Dalits to come together under one political formation with a shared agenda. Leaders of the Aadi-Hindu Mahasabha from UP as well as leaders of other Dalit organizations from UP and other parts of India were present during the foundation of the SCF in Nagpur on 18 July 1942. In UP the SCF was considered a worthy successor to the Aadi-Hindu Mahasabha and rapidly replaced the branches of the Aadi-Hindu Mahasabha all over UP. According to Viyogi, the SCF also replaced Achhut organizations like the Ad-Dharm Mandal in Punjab, the Depressed Classes League of Namasudras in Bengal, and the Depressed Classes Association in the Central Provinces (Viyogi 1949: 9–12). The majority of the Dalit organizations that were attracted to the SCF were Chamars like the Jatav Mahasabha of Agra, the Raidass Mahasabha of Allahabad, and the Kureel and Chamar Mahasabhas of Kanpur. In addition to the Aadi-Hindu Mahasabha, non-Chamar organizations like the Kumaon Shilpakar Mahasabha also joined the SCF. By establishing district branches of the SCF these leaders in urban centres of UP were also attesting to its growing popularity among all sections of Dalits. District branches of the SCF were established in Agra, Aligarh, Allahabad, Etah, Etawah, Lucknow, Kanpur, Meerut, and Kumaon.[16] Thus, the merger of various Dalit caste-Mahasabhas with the SCF was one of the most significant developments in Dalit politics in the 1940s.

The Dalit confidence of the 1940s lay in the movements organized by the UPSCF from 1946–7. The satyagrahas by the SCF in 1946–7 were organized to protest against the Poona Pact, the Congress, and the Cabinet Mission Award for rejecting Dalits' demands for proportional representation through a separate electorate. There were other issues, as well, including the abolition of begari, the distribution of land to Dalits, free education and scholarships, and reservations of jobs within the government services. It took almost a decade for Dalits to recognize the full negative implications of the Poona Pact on electoral politics.[17] The Poona Pact was identified as the main evil by which the Congress and caste-Hindus had prevented Dalits from getting their leaders elected to Legislative councils at the State and Federal level.

By the 1940s Dalits had come to the conclusion that only through gaining political power could they implement a programme of affirmative-action in representative bodies, educational institutions, and government jobs. This was not merely the agenda of radical, anti-Congress Dalit organizations, but one that pro-Congress Harijan organizations had come to share. At the popular level, two Congress Harijan organizations, the District Harijan Conference of Meerut and the District Harijan Uddhar Sabha of Saharanpur, independently outlined similar positions in their meetings in 1946—asserting the principle that a separate electorate was the only way to secure political rights for Dalits. Even Jagjivan Ram argued that the only difference between Congress Harijan organizations and Ambedkarite organizations was that the latter wanted Dalits' separation from Hindus, but both shared the political and social agenda of Ambedkar.[18] It is this new sense of agenda shared across the political spectrum that makes the 1940s unique for Dalit politics.

The UPSCF organized satyagrahas against the lack of representative character of the Legislative Assembly in two phases—in July and August of 1946 and from March to May of 1947.[19] The first of these movements affected twenty-three districts of UP, out of which Meerut, Bareilly, Muzaffarnagar, Aligarh, Etah, Etawah, Kheri, Kanpur, Azamgarh, and Gorakhpur witnessed prolonged agitation from June to November 1946.[20] 'Poona Pact ko Wapas Lo' ('Scrap the Poona Pact') and 'our leader is Ambedkar' were two of the many slogans raised by the satyagrahis in Lucknow in 1946.[21] The UPSCF organized a series of daily satyagrahas in Lucknow in front of the Legislative Assembly to question the democratic credentials of this elected body in the absence of proportional Dalit representation within it. The satyagraha was held to coincide with the working days of the Assembly in July and August, beginning on 16 July and ending on 16 August 1946. This series of protests culminated in the arrest of nearly 400 Dalits. Tilak Chand Kureel, President of the UPSCF, along with other prominent SCF leaders such as Behari Lal Jaiswar, Piyare Lal Talib, and Shankaranand Shastri, courted arrest.

DALIT AS A FOUNDATIONAL IDENTITY

The formation of the Republican Party of India (RPI) did not represent an abandoning of Achhut identity and politics, nor did it represent a move to class politics, as a host of scholars have suggested. I have argued elsewhere that seeing the formation of the RPI as a shift from caste to class dangerously obscures the Dalit point of view, which sought to build up political alliances without losing the focus and power of a united Achhut identity (see Rawat 2004, chapter 5). The Republican Party's slogans sum up the mood of the times and reveal the ideological moorings of the party: '*Jatav-Muslim bhai bhai: Hindu kaum kahan se ayee*' ('Jatavs and Muslims are brothers: Where did the Hindus come from') and '*Thakur, Brahman aur Lala: Kar do inka munha kala*' ('Thakurs, Brahmans and Baniyas: Blacken their faces'. Cited in Duncan 1979: 271). If anything, these slogans indicate that Dalit struggles against domination by Hindu society were fought along caste, not class, lines, by emphasizing Dalits' separate Achhut identity. Rather than dissipating since the 1940s, the attractiveness of a shared Dalit identity has continued to grow.

Even before the formation of the RPI, Ambedkar had made a tactical move in July 1947 by joining the Congress government as a law minister. This was, indeed, a dramatic development, particularly given the popular movement against the Congress which the SCF had been leading for the previous two years. In UP as well, many Dalit leaders joined the Congress government and/or the Congress party. Ambedkar realized the disorienting impact of his decision and felt it necessary to clarify his stand. He chose to do so in UP (in Lucknow), because this had emerged as his most important base outside Maharashtra. His speech at the fifth conference of the UPSCF in April 1948, discussed earlier, emphasized his continued commitment to a shared Achhut identity and agenda, but stressed the usefulness of using the Congress government to implement this agenda, as he had done earlier with the British government. More recently, a similar dramatic move was made by the Bahujan Samaj Party (BSP), a Dalit political party with a strong following in UP. In 1995, the BSP strategically chose to form a government in UP with the support of the Hindu-right-wing Bharatiya Janata Party (BJP). Prior to this, in 1992, the BSP had walked out of its alliance with the Samajwadi Party (SP), described by the mainstream media as a secular and anti-BJP party. BSP leaders argued that as far as

Dalit priorities were concerned, there was no difference between the Congress, the BJP, and the SP. The BSP's refusal to have any alliance with the SP, and its electoral alliance with the BJP, were described by mainstream media and intelligentsia at the time as a politics of opportunism for refusing to join the secular forces. Both Ambedkar in 1947, as a leader of the SCF, and the BSP in 1992 made what appeared to outsiders a radical shift in their 'natural' political position. Only by understanding and analysing these actions from within a Dalit perspective can the continuity with both Ambedkar's and the BSP's larger agendas be recognized.

To summarize my argument, the agenda of a Dalit identity and politics laid out by the Aadi-Hindu Mahasabha in 1928, including a programme for defining a set of rights, seemed to have reached fruition in the 1940s. It was no longer an abstract idea of the Aadi-Hindu Mahasabha, but one that was shared by various Dalit organizations and worked out through the movements and struggles that emerged between 1928 and 1947 in UP. The 1940s provided an important transitional moment by bringing together under the SCF umbrella disparate Dalit organizations that embraced the vision of a shared Achhut politics and a commitment to rights that continues to define the lives of Dalits today. The idea of united interests across all castes of Dalits under the shared identity of Achhuts acquired a unanimous acceptability among diverse sections in the 1940s—sections which previously, in the 1920s, would not have recognized themselves as belonging to the same community. The title of Nandlal Viyogi's book is a good example of the emergence of the idea of Achhut or Dalit as a foundational category. It was this clear perception of his overarching agenda that convinced Ambedkar to join the Congress ministry in 1947.

The most enduring legacy of the Aadi-Hindu movement in UP was the conceptualization of a separate Dalit identity as not merely a political category but also a social and cultural category—a way of thinking not just about Dalit society but also about Hindu society. It is only by recognizing the history of the movement and the way of thinking that accompanied the movement that Chandrika Prasad Jigyasu and millions of other Dalits were able to describe the Congress as a *Hindu* party, or to criticize the Left polity for refusing to address issues of social inequity. The sense that the Dalits of UP had in the 1940s and 50s, and still have today, of having their own agenda, was made possible only through the history and political organization of these decades. The unmistakable feature of this struggle and its enduring legacy has been the conception of a clearly defined notion of Dalit politics and agenda. Through their struggles and writings, Dalits have forcefully articulated their vision and views by engaging with Congress nationalism, colonialism, the politics of Hindu reform organizations, and the communist movements. Today, 'Dalit' can be recognized not only as a powerful and effective identity, but also as a perspective that performs a foundational role in defining a world view for political action and everyday life.

NOTES

1. The second edition of Shastri's book (1965) was revised to include political developments up to 1956. The term 'Federation' in Viyogi's title refers to the Scheduled Castes Federation, or SCF.

2. The term *achhut* was used by Dalits in their struggles and writings in UP to mean 'pure' or 'untouched', giving it a new radical meaning and rejecting the Hindu interpretation of 'untouchable'. Because both Shastri and Viyogi use the term in their writings, I also use the term Achhut to specifically mark out the moment of the 1940s, while using the term Dalit more generally.

3. The Poona Pact was signed on 24 September 1932 between Dalit leaders and caste-Hindu leaders. Under the pact, Ambedkar gave up his demand for separate electorates in favour of a system of primary and secondary elections that allowed separate electorates for Dalits in the primaries and a joint electorate in the general elections. After the experience of the 1937 elections, radical Dalits viewed the Pact as a conspiracy to prevent Dalits from electing their true representatives, while Congress-backed candidates were easily elected. For a detailed discussion see Rawat 2003.

4. For an extensive discussion of agitations organized by the SCF in UP in the 1940s, see Rawat 2002.

5. *The Pioneer* (Lucknow) 21 February 1946. Shastri (1994: 50) also recognizes a shift in Jagjivan Ram's position.

6. Shastri (1994: 148). *The Leader* (Allahabad) 26 April 1948.

7. Viyogi (1949) and Shastri (1994) make this point repeatedly in their books.

8. A few examples of historians who make this argument are Lynch 1969, Juergensmeyer 1982, Zelliot 1988, Masayaki 1992, Vicziany and Mendelsohn 1998, and Bandyopadhyay 1997.

9. Chamar Sabhas, such as Jatav Mahasabha, Jaiswar Mahasabha, Jatiya Chamar Sabha, and many others, were formed at the village level. I discuss them in chapter 4 of Rawat 2004.

10. Officially known as Police Abstracts of Weekly Intelligence (PAI), Criminal Investigation Department (CID), UP (CID office, Lucknow, UP). The weekly CID reports provide detailed accounts of Chamar protests in UP. See various CID reports between 1922 and 1926.

11. Report of All-India Aadi-Hindu Mahasabha, 7 January 1928, submitted to the Simon Commission. Appendix: List of Memoranda, Evidence—UP/427; Report on United Provinces (3 volumes) Indian Statutory (Simon) Commission, Oriental and India Office Collection (henceforth OIOC), British Library, London, UK.

12. These representations are available in the private papers of John Simon. MSS. Eur. F. 77/Simon Collection, OIOC, British Library.

13. *National Herald* (Allahabad) 26 April 1948. The paragraph is based on the report of Ambedkar's speech published in this newspaper. At least 7000 delegates and activists attended the conference.

14. Ibid.

15. F. No. 41/4/47-R, Request from the scheduled castes of UP, Secretariat of the Governor-General Reforms (National Archives of India [hereafter NAI], New Delhi).

16. PAI (Police Abstracts of Weekly Intelligence) reports for the year 1946, of various weeks.

17. For a detailed discussion of the impact of the Poona Pact on Dalit politics and on the two elections of 1937 and 1945–6, see Rawat 2003.

18. *The Pioneer*, 21 February 1946.

19. These movements are discussed at length in Rawat 2002.

20. Based on the various weekly PAI reports for 1946.

21. This account is based on the reports from *The Pioneer*, 17, 18, 19, 23, 25, 29, and 30 July, and 16 August 1946, and on PAI, 5 and 26 July; 2, 9, 16, and 23 August; and 6 September 1946.

REFERENCES

Bandyopadhyay, Sekhar. 1997. *Caste, Protest and Identity in Colonial India: The Namasudras of Bengal, 1872–1947*. London: Curzon Press.

Duncan, R. Ian. 1979. 'Levels, the Communication of Programmes, and Sectional Strategies in Indian Politics with Reference to the Bharatiya Kranti Dal and the Republican Party of India in UP State and Aligarh District (UP).' PhD dissertation, University of Sussex.

Jigyasu, Chandrika Prasad. 1937. *Bharat ke Adi Nivasiyon ki Sabhayata*. Lucknow: Bahujan Kalyan Prakashan.

Juergensmeyer, Mark. 1982. *Religion as Social Vision: The Movement against Untouchability in 20th Century Punjab*. Berkeley: University of California Press.

Lynch, Owen. 1969. *The Politics of Untouchability: Social Mobility and Social Change in a City in India*. New York: Columbia University Press.

Masayaki, Usuda. 1992. 'Pushed Towards the Partition: Jogendranath Mandal and the Constrained Namasudra Movement'. In H. Kotani (ed.). *Caste System, Untouchability and the Depressed*. Delhi: Manohar, pp. 221–74.

Rawat, Ramnarayan. 2002. 'Partition Politics and Achhut Identity: A Study of the Scheduled Castes Federation and Dalit Politics'. In Suvir Kaul (ed.). *The Partitions of Memory: The Afterlife of the Division of India*. Bloomington: Indiana University Press, pp. 111–39.

———. 2003. 'Making Claims for Power: A New Agenda in Dalit Politics of Uttar Pradesh, 1946–48'. *Modern Asian Studies*. vol. 37, no. 3, pp. 585–612.

———. 2004. 'A Social History of "Chamars" in Uttar Pradesh, 1881–1956'. PhD dissertation, University of Delhi.

Shastri, Shankaranand. 1994 [1946]. *Poona Pact or Gandhi*. 11th edn, Lucknow: Bahujan Kalyan Prakashan.

Vicziany, Marika and Oliver Mendelsohn. 1998. *Untouchable: Subordination, Poverty and the State in Modern India*. Cambridge: Cambridge University Press.

Viyogi, Nandlal. 1949. *Ambedkar ki Awaaz arthat Achhutoin ka Federation*. Allahabad: Jagriti Press.

Zelliot, Eleanor. 1972. 'Gandhi and Ambedkar: A Study in Leadership'. In J. Michael Mahar (ed.). *The Untouchables in Contemporary India*. Tucson: University of Arizona Press, pp. 69–96.

———. 1988. 'Congress and Untouchables, 1915–50'. In R. Sisson and S. Wolpert (eds). *Congress and Indian Nationalism: The Pre-independence Phase*. Berkeley: University of California Press, pp. 69–95.

3

MULTIPLE IDENTITIES OF BACKWARD-CASTE MUSLIMS IN INDIA

Rajendra Vora

Muslims constitute the second-largest religious community in India, thirteen per cent (130 million) of the total population. Spread over the subcontinent, the Muslim community is, contrary to popular belief, internally highly heterogeneous. Apart from divisions based on sect, region, and economic class, Muslims in India are divided by caste-like structures, making it difficult to maintain a definition of Muslim identity based solely on religion. Empirical studies have brought to the fore two broad categories of Indian Muslims: Ashraf (noble or upper class) and Ajlaf (common or low class) (Ahmad 1966: 268–78). The Ashrafs usually include the descendants of immigrants and are known as Sayyids, Shaikhs, Mughals, and Pathans, while Ajlafs are mostly descendants of converts from Hindu lower castes: weavers, butchers, carpenters, oilmen, barbers, washermen, and leather-workers. Even though rigid caste distinctions are not found among Muslims, there does exist a caste hierarchy that supports inequality in the distribution of prestige, power, and status. The Islamic principle of equality, it is said, is observed only in the religious domain.

The political orientations of Muslims reflect these two broad divisions in more ways than one. The elite sections in the Hindi belt were in favour of Partition because they thought their privileged position in the bureaucracy would be lost in a united India, while the low-caste masses remained more or less neutral to the Partition (Engineer 2004: 3984). It was mainly the privileged class that migrated to Pakistan, while poor artisans and shopkeepers preferred to remain in India (Noorani 2003: 139–41). The difference between the attitudes of the masses and the upper strata is seen in their perception of such issues as Muslim personal law. A study conducted in 1998 shows that villagers see no reason why there should be a separate personal law, whereas Muslim leaders view the law based on Shariat as one of the bases of religious identity (Dyke 1999: 122). Voting-behaviour surveys have pointed out that relatively backward Muslims may support a party with a radical programme (Sanjaykumar 1996: 138–41). In the 1999 Lok Sabha elections in Uttar Pradesh (UP), the upper class generally favoured the Congress, while the majority of working-class Muslims, such as the weavers in eastern UP, went with Mulayam Singh Yadav's Samajwadi Party (Bhushan 1999: 29).

Backward-caste Muslims became aware of the gap between their viewpoint and that of upper-caste Muslims after 1990, when the Union government accepted the Mandal Commission's recommendation to extend job reservations to backward castes. As a consequence, a backward-caste perspective that challenges the establishment has emerged within the Muslim community. My essay analyses this new perspective and the distinct identity of Muslim backward castes it has produced, with an emphasis on Maharashtra.

The origins of backward Muslim consciousness can be traced to the colonial period. In the 1920s the Momins (a caste of handloom weavers) of Bihar, who form around twenty per cent of the Muslim population of Bihar, supported the Congress instead of the Muslim League (Brass 1975: 247–57). In that decade, Bihar Momins and those of eastern UP formed an all-India Momin conference. In the first decade after Independence, the Momins of Bihar floated the Bihar State Backward Muslim Federation, but the Federation turned inactive in later years (Khan 1997: 65–6). The Kaka Kalelkar Backward Classes Commission (1955) was the first to recognize the fact that there were backward castes among Muslims and that they were on a par with their Hindu counterparts (Mondal 2003: 4894). In the late 1950s Rammanohar Lohia, a Socialist leader from UP, made backward-caste politics a constituent part of his socialist model. Lohia claimed that backward castes, ex-Untouchables, tribals, women, and depressed

Muslims and Christians constituted around eighty-five per cent of the country's population, but their proportion in politics, the army, government jobs, and trade was less than ten per cent. The Socialist party, he held, should give at least sixty per cent of the posts in public life to these backward sections (Lohia 1964: 121–42). However, Lohia's backward-caste politics did not attract the depressed Muslims.

The Backward Classes Commission headed by B.P. Mandal was an offshoot of Lohia's project. Its report (1980) listed about eighty Muslim communities among the backward castes that became entitled for a twenty-seven per cent reservation in public jobs and educational institutions (Jenkins 2001: 32–50). The decision of the V.P. Singh government in 1990 to accept the recommendations of the Mandal Commission generated a new awareness among backward-caste Muslims, especially in the new middle class that was emerging within these castes. As a reaction to the growing consciousness and activities among backward-caste Muslims, Muslim elites started a movement to demand reservations in government jobs for all Muslims. In 1994 they floated an association for promoting education and employment for Muslims (Alam 2003: 4881–5). The association claimed that the entire Muslim community formed a backward class, and demanded that reservations be extended to Muslims in educational institutions and public jobs in proportion to their numbers and level of backwardness. Syed Shahabuddin, the founder of the association, argued that the cake would have to be cut not just horizontally, by caste and class, but also vertically, by religion, for the sake of an even distribution of opportunities. The Islamic Council of India and the All India Milli Council also pleaded for reservations for all Muslims (Jenkins 2001: 32–50). In 1994 Kerala, with a 23.22 per cent Muslim population and a Muslim party (Muslim League) as a partner in the ruling coalition, became the first state to accept this demand. Since coming to power in 2004, Andhra Pradesh's Congress government has fulfilled its electoral promise to provide a five per cent reservation for Muslims in educational institutions and public jobs.

Backward-caste Muslims are not swayed by these actions or arguments of the Muslim establishment. They see them as another attempt of the privileged sections to seek benefits in the name of the community, and point out that general reservations made on a religious basis will basically benefit the Ashrafs and will not reach the lower-

class or lower-caste Muslims (Engineer 2004: 3984–5). A recent survey
reveals that upper-caste, upper-class Muslims almost completely
control the institutions and organizations of the community. Out of
between ten and forty executive members and directors of the All India
Personal Law Board, the All India Milli Council, and the Imarat–i-Sharia
(Bihar and Orissa), only a couple come from backward classes or castes,
while their proportion of the total Muslim population is about ninety
per cent. The same is true in the case of waqf boards, mosques, darghas,
minority educational institutions, minority commissions, Urdu
academies, Hajj committees, and the Maulana Azad Foundation at
the regional and national levels. The disproportionate representation
of high-caste Muslims is also found in the class-one services of the
government bureaucracy (Alam 2003: 4882). A Bihar state study shows
that hardly any backward-caste Muslims are found among the Muslim
members of the legislature or parliament (Engineer 2004: 3984–5). This
is why backward-caste Muslims insist upon caste-based reservations,
whereby deprived sections will get the benefits that flow from reservation.

Backward-caste Muslims insist that the Muslim community in
India is not a homogeneous entity. The community is divided both
horizontally and vertically, with caste-like divisions being the most
decisive. There is a contradiction between the interests of the Ashraf
castes and those of the Ajlaf castes. The backward-caste perspective
demolishes the myth of a single collective Muslim mind and takes a
different view of the world than that of upper-caste Muslims. The
Muslim leadership, which basically comes from the upper castes, takes
up cultural and sensitive issues in order to mobilize the people. They
harp upon memories of Muslim power and the lost glories of the past
(Alam 2003: 4881–5). The traditional leaders concentrate on symbolic
and emotional demands such as maintaining the minority character
of Aligarh Muslim University, continuing a separate personal law for
Muslims, the status of the Urdu language, and the controversy over
the Babri Mosque at Ayodhya (which Hindu nationalists claim is the
birthplace of the god Ram). Muslim religious leaders have also been
criticized by backward-caste Muslims for being concerned about empty
ritualism, acting within the limits of their own little world, living off
donations given by ordinary Muslims, and doing nothing for the welfare
of the poor. Those who control such organizations as Jamaat-i-Islami

or Tablighi-Jamaat, as well as Sufi shrines, are accused of having betrayed the true teachings and spirit of Islam (Sikand 2004: 94–102).

The new leadership emerging from among backward-caste Muslims views Islam as a radical project of social liberation. The Hindu downtrodden castes embraced Islam in order to seek equal status, which was denied to them by Hinduism. But this emancipatory aspect of Islam was later forgotten and these converts were placed in a position analogous to their pre-conversion status. The new leadership perceives itself as a 'revolutionary' one concerned with regaining the egalitarian aspect of Islam. It aims to free Islam from the clutches of high-caste Muslim leaders and to revive the true spirit of Islam, which condemns all divisions and hierarchies. These backward-caste leaders stress education, jobs, and material well-being rather than symbolic or emotive issues. They look to the Hindu backward castes as their allies in the struggle for equality and justice.

By transcending differences among lower and Untouchable castes, the new leadership is assuming a Dalit identity. These leaders call themselves 'Dalit Muslims', a term that includes descendants of 'Untouchable' converts and lower-caste converts. Ejaz Ali, in fact, demands that Scheduled-Caste status should be extended to Dalit Muslims and calls for a non-violent Jihad to be fought by Dalit Muslims in alliance with non-Muslim Dalits and the secular forces in the country. Many of these 'Dalit Muslims' regularly write in *Dalit Voice*, a periodical devoted to the question of the human rights of persecuted nationalities in India. Rashid Salim Adil, a social activist and lawyer based in Delhi, goes beyond advocating mere unity between Dalit Muslims and non-Muslim Dalits; he pleads for non-Muslim Dalits to convert to Islam, which he holds to be superior. Adil holds that conversion to Islam will be a means of empowerment and liberation of the oppressed (ibid.: 110–28).

In order to promote their alternative perspective, the new leadership has developed organizations of Other-Backward-Classes (OBC) Muslims.[1] In 1993, Maharashtra became the first state to have a Muslim OBC organization. The next was Bihar, where Ejaz Ali established the All India Backward Muslim Morcha (AIBMM) in 1994. Another new organization in Bihar is the Pasmand Muslim Mahaz (PMM), formed by Ali Anwar. Recently a similar organization, the Uttar Bango Anagrasar

Muslim Sangram Samiti, has been started in the northern districts of West Bengal (Mondal 2003: 4895). In the next section I review the activities and ideology of the organization in Maharashtra.

MAHARASHTRA

It is in the literary movement of Muslims that we find the origins of the backward-caste perspective in Maharashtra. For Muslims in Maharashtra the medium of creative writing has always been Marathi, the regional language, rather than Urdu. The short stories and novels they produced gave them a Marathi identity that was a departure from the standard pan-Indian Muslim identity. In 1989 some of these writers came together to form a distinct literary association. It is an established practice among marginalized sections in Maharashtra to use a literary movement as a platform to express protest against unjust social structures and to put forward an alternative framework. The Dalit literary movement is typical in this regard. The most significant activity of such movements is to organize annual conferences, at which the issues debated go beyond mere literature and literary criticism. Therefore, when Muslim Marathi creative writers started organizing annual conferences, the topics that came up for deliberation and discussion included their experience of inequality and the injustice produced by the caste distinctions within the community. The medium of communication for most backward-caste Muslims living in villages and towns is basically Marathi, and they are usually educated in Marathi-medium schools. Creative writers from this social background were bound to express their anger about unjust social relations from a Marathi literary platform created specifically for Muslims.

The idea of a Muslim OBC organization as a means to agitate for social justice and to seek legitimate space for downtrodden Muslims was raised at the second Muslim Marathi literature conference, held at Nagpur in 1992. At the next conference, at Ratnagiri in 1993, a detailed plan for the Muslim backward-castes organization was finalized. The leaders of the Maharashtra OBC organization made important suggestions to the activists leading this endeavour (interview with Vilas Sonawane, 1 April 2006). The All India Muslim OBC organization (AIMOBCO) was thus established in 1993 by the founder members of the Muslim Marathi literary association. At the first convention of the Muslim OBCs, held at Jalna in the Marathwada region in May 1994, Shabbir Ansari, who belongs to a weaver caste, was appointed the

organization's president. During the next five months, the AIMOBCO
organized a number of district and regional level conventions and
conferences. The year ended with a huge rally at Solapur in September,
attended by delegates from different parts of Maharashtra.

The massive attendance at the rally indicated the unrest among
backward-caste Muslims. It was a public expression of grievance and
pain (*Lokmat*, 8 September 1994: 2). Sensing this, and taking into account
the fact that elections were due soon, the then Congress government
decided to apply the Mandal Commission's reservation provisions to
Muslim OBCs in Maharashtra. The second convention of the AIMOBCO
was held at Aurangabad on the eve of the 1995 assembly elections.
Chief Minister Sharad Pawar was expected to address the convention.
Although he did not turn up, he was honoured and profusely thanked
in absentia for extending reservations to backward-caste Muslims.
The convention demanded the inclusion of all Muslim backward castes
in the reservation list, extending reservations to different sectors,
education and financial facilities, a housing and development corporation
for Muslim OBCs, and so forth. The convention urged the government
to direct local revenue officers to give caste certificates to Muslim OBCs
and not to re-examine a certificate once it had been given (*Maharashtra
Times*, 16 January 1995).

The year 1995 saw the Bharatiya Janata Party–Shiv Sena alliance
come to power in the state. This alliance of Hindu militant parties
pointed out that the government resolution (GR) regarding reservations
for Muslim OBCs had never been issued. The government soon revived
the GR, probably believing that the reservations for backward Muslims
might divide the community (interview with Sonawane, 31 March
2006). If the September 1994 Solapur rally was a great success, the
national convention held at Delhi on 29 August 1996 was a spectacular
show. It was attended by important leaders of various secular parties
and by activists as well as journalists. Delegates from various backward-
caste groups from all states except Tamil Nadu, Kerala, and the north-
eastern states participated. The convention demanded extending the
Mandal provisions to all Muslim OBCs, scholarships, land reforms,
funding for small entrepreneurs from backward communities, and
restoration of concessions to Scheduled-Caste Muslims that had been
withdrawn in 1984 (*The Times of India*, 12 September 1996). The next
convention, held at Lucknow in 1997, was attended by Dilip Kumar, a
very popular Muslim actor from the Hindi film industry. The success

of the Delhi and Lucknow conferences produced disquiet and
nervousness among the Ashraf leaders of the north, prompting them
to organize two seminars of the Ashrafs at Aligarh Muslim University
and to float a platform to build their defences (interview with Sonawane,
6 April 2006).

After a steady growth for almost four consecutive years, in 1998
the Muslim OBC movement in Maharashtra started showing signs of
discord. The two founding fathers and ideologues of the movement,
Fakruddin Bennur and Vilas Sonawane, began to distance themselves
from Shabbir Ansari, the president of the organization, and also from
the organization's activities. They were not happy with the way Shabbir
Ansari was running the organization, especially with Ansari's move to
take the organization closer to party politics. At the time of the 1999
elections the distancing of Bennur, Sonawane, and their friends in the
organization from Shabbir Ansari culminated in nearly splitting the
organization. Shabbir Ansari approached Sharad Pawar (who had left
the Congress and had formed the Nationalist Congress Party) for
tickets. But Pawar refused to oblige him, because by that time Vilas
Sonawane had succeeded in getting Dilip Kumar to promise to support
to the Congress and to address public meetings during the campaign.
Ansari, therefore, appealed to the Congress and secured five tickets,
on which four Muslims and one non-Muslim contested the elections
to the assembly (interview with Sonawane, 6 April 2006). Of the four
Muslim candidates—Datture Hafij Hussain in Miraj, Sayyaid Ahmed
in Nagpada, Abdul Rashid Mohhamad Tahir Momin in Bhivandi, and
Shamim Ahmad Khan in Parbhani—the first three registered victories.

The split was formalized after the elections of 1999. Since then
two Muslim OBC organizations have functioned simultaneously in
Maharashtra—one led by Shabbir Ansari (based in Jalna) and another
led by Iqbal Ansari (based in Pune). The Pune organization strongly
believes that a Muslim OBC organization should not indulge in party
or electoral politics, even though caste groups associated with the
organization may take their own positions and support the parties of
their choice (interview with Iqbal Ansari, 21 March 2006). While refusing
to go Shabbir Ansari's way, the Pune organization led by Iqbal Ansari
engages in activism with respect to reservations for Muslim OBCs
(interview with Iqbal Ansari, 21 March 2006). It routinely looks after
locating GRs concerning Muslim OBCs, facilitating the process of
securing caste certificates from revenue officers, approaching the

Maulana Azad Minority Development Corporation (instituted in 2002 by the state government) to obtain financial help for members of occupation-based castes, and carrying out related activities for the betterment of the backward sections of Muslims in the state.

REGIONAL IDENTITY

The course the Muslim OBC movement in Maharashtra has taken, the way it has advanced from its inception, the issues the movement has raised, and the ideological positions its leaders have taken from time to time have been decided by the history, social structure, and politics of Maharashtra. Consequently, the Maharashtra movement has acquired a regional character while maintaining its all-India connection.

Bennur (2003: 1–4) observes that even though the term 'caste' is not used with reference to Muslims, the nature of the *Jamat* or *biradari* is almost the same as caste, as it possesses all the traits of the caste system— endogamy, dress-code, separate mosques, occupation-based groups, hierarchy, stratification, and so on. The Muslim masses are a mirror image of the Hindu masses. Practically all types of castes are found among Muslims—occupational castes, service castes, backward castes, criminal castes, and also tribal and nomadic communities. The Muslim caste system differs, again like that of the Hindus, from region to region. Castes that are considered unclean or almost untouchable in one region are treated as only backward in another. Dhobis (washermen) or Darjees (tailors) are treated as Untouchables in the north, while in Maharashtra they are categorized as OBCs. The Ashraf class in the north is characterized by memories of the Mughal empire, a sense of social superiority, and a feudal outlook (*nababiyat*). This class considers people engaged in manual work as inferior (*kamjat*). In Maharashtra, where factors like Muslim rule, zamindari, and feudalism were rather weak, downtrodden Muslim castes are not treated like Untouchables, although Mehetars (scavengers) or Quereshis (butchers) who do unclean jobs are ostracized.

The majority of Indian Muslims are converts from Hindu lower and occupational castes. Their conversion, Bennur points out (2003: 2–9), was a result of the Sufis' preaching of Islamic principles of equality and brotherhood, and was not motivated by either money or power. Islam gave them a respectable identity. They rejected the principle of purity and pollution and the concept of human inequality, but they could not renounce those features of the caste system that were entrenched in the psyche and social life of the people. The categories of Ashraf and Ajlaf are a result of this phenomenon. The conversion process could change the caste system but could not annihilate it. This is why caste distinctions operate not only among Muslims but also among Sikhs, Jains, and Christians. Bennur agrees with Klass's theory (1980) that caste is a special feature of the South Asian social system. The Mandal report, according to Bennur, has taken cognizance of this.

Bennur does not agree with the sociologists who view Muslims in India as having a kinship system rather than a caste system. He argues that such sociologists' perception is influenced by their social location and political ideology, and that they therefore refuse to look at the social reality. Bennur condemns historians for interpreting medieval Indian history as a history of conflict between Islam and Hinduism and for branding all Muslims as foreigners. He disapproves of the attempt to present religious community as nation or nationality. The colonial power, he says, contributed to this understanding of Indian history and nationalism by systematically following a divide-and-rule strategy. As a consequence, instead of caste, religion came to be seen as the foundation of social structure and began to occupy a central place in socio-political discourse, and Hindus and Muslims began to be conceived of as monolithic groups. According to Bennur, Muslim rulers, their ulema, and feudal lords used and distorted Islam to suit their interests and to continue their domination over the converted Muslim masses. They rejected the existence of a caste structure in the name of religion.

Bennur finds backward-caste Muslims in Maharashtra to be economically, educationally, and socially marginalized, suffering from poverty, illiteracy, unemployment, and homelessness. Middle-class Muslims and their Ashraf leaders do not interact with them. OBC Muslims who live in villages lead a pitiable life, and some, such as Hajams (barbers) and Mehetars (scavengers), experience a sort of covert untouchability (Bennur 1999a: 2).

The movement in Maharashtra, therefore, aims at organizing Muslim OBCs to strive for education (from primary to higher level), modernization, and protection of traditional skilled occupations; providing housing, hostels, and scholarships for boys and girls; availing the benefits of reservations in jobs and educational institutions according to the provisions of the Mandal Commission; appealing to the government to establish a development corporation for Muslim

OBCs; encouraging Muslim educational organizations to start Marathi-medium schools; and persuading the government to include all Muslim OBCs in the Mandal list. The movement also tries to persuade Muslims to break down caste walls and seeks to make them aware of inter-caste marriage as a need of the hour. The main objective of the movement is to put an end to the caste system by integrating all Muslim OBCs. Upper-caste Muslims are able to maintain their hold over the OBCs because the OBCs lack unity. The movements' leaders consider their struggle part of a larger struggle of all oppressed groups. For example, in the Solapur rally of September 1994 they invited Christian backward castes to join them.

Muslim OBCs in Maharashtra are inspired by the anti-caste radicalism of Mahatma Phule and Babasaheb Ambedkar. Phule, who belonged to a backward caste, started the Satyashodhak Samaj (Truth-seeking Society) for the emancipation of the backward and Dalit castes from the slavery instituted by the upper castes. Ambedkar, a Dalit leader, embraced Buddhism to liberate the Dalit castes from the clutches of high-caste Hindus. Sonawane highlights Phule's contribution to the ideological framework of the Muslim OBC movement, mentioning especially Phule's insights about caste-based slavery in *Gulamgiri* ('Slavery') and economic exploitation in *Shetakaryacha Aasood* ('The Farmer's Whip') (interview with Sonawane, 6 April 2006). Besides seeing their movement as a continuation of the struggle started by Phule in the nineteenth century, Muslim OBCs also draw inspiration from the egalitarianism of Islam. Bennur believes that Islam should be seen as a liberating force, propounded by the Prophet as an emancipatory ideology. Islam was originally meant to eradicate the hierarchical structures and distinctions in Arabian society. This radical and emancipatory content of Islam has been revived by leaders of the Muslim OBC movement in Maharashtra as it has been by Muslim OBC movements elsewhere in the country.

The movement is on principle opposed to religion-based reservations in government jobs and educational institutions. Religion-based reservations, it believes, are nothing but a continuation of the appeasement policy of the Congress party. Such a reservation policy does not benefit the backward or weaker sections in any way, for religion is not the cause of their backwardness. This policy will divide the marginalized sections, encourage communalism among them, and allow the BJP to use the resultant rift to capture power. Reservations based on religion, moreover, violate the secularism principle of the Indian Constitution. Bennur (2004b: 1–4) argues that the Congress party is violating the core principle of the Constitution for the sake of electoral politics. For instance, the Congress government's policy of giving a five per cent reservation to all Muslims in Andhra Pradesh (AP) in 2004 will benefit only the upper strata, while the marginal sections will remain deprived. The majority of Muslims in AP are socially and educationally backward, and many are very poor, but this does not mean that they should be given religion-based reservations. Reservations must be based on caste.

Sonawane and Bennur are very critical of the Dalit Muslim category used by north-Indian Muslim backward-caste leaders, such as Ejaz Ali of the AIBMM (interview with Sonawane, 6 April 2006; Bennur 2003: 9–11). Bennur argues that the Dalits converted to Islam to free themselves from slavery and an inhuman existence, so why should they be given the same Dalit identity in the name of radicalization, and why should their self-respect be shaken again? He points out that many Muslim castes are experiencing upward mobility. They are changing their occupations. Some are switching over to new means of livelihood and even discarding the practice of endogamy. Bennur found that many from the Muslim masses in Maharashtra were critical of the OBC movement because they wanted to get rid of caste labels. If this is their view about the term 'OBC', what would be their reaction to taking on Dalit identity? Converted Muslims have tried to renounce many features of Dalitness. The mere fact that there is a division between the dominant class of Ashrafs on the one hand and that of backward, illiterate, poor Muslims on the other does not call for a label of 'Dalit Muslims' for the latter. Bennur thinks that the category Dalit Muslim will not be helpful for Muslim backward castes in their efforts toward empowerment.

OBC Muslims in Maharashtra strongly believe that there is no one identity for all Muslims. This does not mean that they are against religious identity as such. What the leaders of the Muslim OBCs stress is that religious identity is only one form of identity. They hold that they belong to the backward castes among Muslims, and that they want to mobilize the backward castes against the domination of upper-caste Muslims. The OBC identity is the one that they project when challenging upper-caste Muslims and when uniting with non-Muslim OBCs. These leaders reject a pan-Indian identity because they hold that they are Marathi Muslims belonging to Maharashtra, a region with its own distinct character. Their movement was born out of the Muslim Marathi literary movement. An OBC Muslim living in a rural or semi-urban area realizes that Urdu is not his language. It is the language of Ashraf Muslims, the language of urban, metropolitan Muslims. For all practical purposes, Marathi is the language of communication for the majority of Muslims in Maharashtra. As in the case of Bangladesh, language sometimes acquires greater prominence than religious identity (Sayyad 2001: 7–12). Sonawane points out that, to begin with, Urdu is an Indian language and has no direct relation to Islam. Lower-caste Muslims in Marathwada, in some districts of Vidarbha, and in villages on the Maharashtra-Karnataka border speak Dakhani, not Urdu. Thus, Dakhani and Marathi play a more important role in the identity formation of backward-caste Muslims of Maharashtra than does Urdu (interview with Sonawane, 6 April 2006).

As in the case of the OBC mobilization, Muslims in Maharashtra also took the lead in organizing a social reform movement with an emphasis on unjust personal law. In 1972, Hamid Dalwai, a reputed Marathi author and a Socialist, established the Muslim Satyashodhak Mandal (MSM, 'Muslim Truth-Seeking Organization') to undertake social reform activity from a secular-rationalist standpoint. The OBC movement appreciates the contribution of the MSM in bringing to the surface the unjust treatment of women in Muslim personal law (Shariat) and in exposing the orthodoxy of the ulema. But the OBC movement argues that it is not Islam but the Shariat practices thrust on women by the ulema that are responsible for the injustice. The movement feels that MSM did not take into account the social reality of Indian Muslims. It never tried to understand the mental make-up of Muslims, and always believed that there is only one Muslim identity. The MSM did not realize that Muslim society in India is divided into multiple castes. By concentrating on social reforms with reference to women, the MSM neglected the question of the material well-being of the majority of Muslims. Because the Muslim OBC movement views Islam as a radical and emancipatory force, it does not agree with Dalwai's sceptical position. Although Dalwai was a Muslim, his perception of Islam basically remained Brahmanical, and he took positions that were more suitable to Hindu elites (Sayyad 2001: 28–30). The AIMOBCO's outlook on the application of personal law to cases of divorce is one of compromise and conciliation, not confrontation (interview with Iqbal Ansari, 21 March 2006).

As noted above, the AIMOBCO (Pune) has kept itself aloof from electoral or party politics, a factor that was one of the most important reasons for the split in the organization. Bennur takes the view that electoral and party politics will bring casteism, unfair competition, and selfish bargaining to the movement. In his view, the AIMOBCO as an organization should not take any position during elections, but the members of the organization and various communities may take part in elections on their own. In Maharashtra members of Muslim backward castes choose various parties according to their preferences and affiliations. Securing election tickets or getting power positions for a few does not lead to the development of marginalized communities. On the contrary, this type of power politics results in certain castes or communities having a monopoly. The movement gets into the hands of a few political manipulators and finally dissolves into power politics via electioneering; this is what happened in the case of the Dalit movement in Maharashtra (Bennur 1999b: 2).

CONCLUSION

The Muslim OBC movement is now twelve years old. The movement is a child of the Mandal Commission. Such a movement is not conceivable without the Mandal Commission report, which listed backward Muslim communities as OBCs eligible for reservations. The movement was born after 1990, when the V.P. Singh government at the centre accepted the recommendations of the Commission. The Mandal Commission constructed OBC identity for backward Muslims—the official category framed by the state generated a self-consciousness among backward-caste Muslims that finally resulted in their movement for social justice and equality. Earlier, Rammanohar Lohia's backward-caste politics had projected an alliance of backward castes and depressed Muslims in the 1950s, but there were no takers for his project among the depressed Muslims. When the Mandal Commission report was submitted in 1980, it did not produce awareness among backward-caste Muslims. Their movement was born only after 1990, probably because by that time a sizeable middle-class leadership had taken shape within the backward Muslim communities, and the goal seemed attainable. The demolition of the Babri mosque at Ayodhya in 1992 exposed both communal and liberal Muslim leaders, and created a vacuum in ideology as well as in leadership. Muslims were now receptive to fresh ideas and ready to listen to new leaders (interview with

Sonawane, 6 April 2006). This political atmosphere probably aided the movement of Muslim OBCs, which was taking a backward-caste approach. Thus, the failure of communalist politics provided the background for the rise of the OBC movement in the early 1990s.

The movement has passed through two stages. From its inception to the late 1990s is the stage in which the movement aimed to pressure the government to frame a reservation policy in accordance with the provisions of the Mandal Commission. The movement succeeded in this regard, since the government implemented the recommendation of the Mandal Commission and included Muslim communities in the OBC list. In Maharashtra, although the government accepted the AIMOBCO's demand to form a development corporation for Muslim OBCs in 1995, the Maulana Azad Minorities Development Corporation was constituted only in 2002. It covers all Muslims and not only Muslim OBCs. The second stage began after the main demands regarding framing of the policy were accepted. In this stage, the movement is engaged in the routine activity of monitoring the implementation of the provisions about reservations. In this respect, the Muslim OBC organizations in different states function basically like non-government agencies, playing the role of middleman between citizens and the bureaucracy.

The movement is not spread evenly in all states. In Bihar, for example, where the movement is in comparatively good shape, there are two organizations, one led by Ejaz Ali (AIBMM) and another led by Ali Anwar (PMM). Muslims of the northern districts of West Bengal have a small organization. In Maharashtra the movement is split into two organizations, while in Karnataka and Madhya Pradesh it is in a nascent stage. UP, with a Muslim population of around seventeen per cent, has not been able to develop a Muslim OBC movement, possibly because of the disorientation generated by the Samajwadi Party and the BSP, as both of them have a good base among Muslims. Thus, generally speaking, the Muslim OBC movement is gradually declining. It could be argued that the movement has reached a stage from which it can either decide to exist in the form of a non-government organization sorting out the problems of Muslim OBCs case by case, or plunge into politics by developing a political party. In the current era of coalitional politics, even the smaller parties are likely to gain a share in power. Muslim OBCs could enter into this competition, which has become more open in recent years. This would mean taking a risk in order to attain a share in power that they could use to liberate themselves from domination by the upper-caste Muslims and to establish the principles of social justice and equality enshrined in the teachings of Islam and the writings of Phule and Ambedkar.

Thus, the Muslim OBC movement has played a historic role. It is a politics that is rooted in the soil. It is true-to-the-ground reality, not something imposed from above by leaders unrelated to the masses. The movement has given rise to a new leadership that comes from the downtrodden sections that have experienced deprivation of the worst kind. The movement brings Muslims out of their so-called 'ghetto mentality' and brings them closer to backward communities belonging to other religions. It establishes solidarity across religious boundaries (Bidwai 1996: 2). By opposing religion-based reservations and by constructing an identity based on backwardness, the movement has successfully challenged fundamentalist designs on the one hand and Hindu extremism on the other. I have argued elsewhere that the best way for Muslims to get out of the minority trap is to join the caste-majoritarianism project, and that by doing so they will also be able to counter the Hindu majoritarianism of the BJP (Vora 2006). The caste-based mobilization of the Muslim OBC movement punctures the minoritism of the Muslim community and establishes links between the struggles of the Muslim and non-Muslim marginalized sections whereby a majoritarianism of the oppressed can forcefully emerge.

NOTES

1. The term Other Backward Classes (OBC) is used by the Indian Constitution for those backward groups which are not included in the Scheduled Castes. The Mandal Commission identified these OBCs in its report. The term 'classes' here is interchangeable with 'castes' for all practical purposes.

REFERENCES

Ahmad, Imtiaz. 1966. 'The Ashraf-Ajlaf Dichotomy in Muslim Social Structure in India'. *Indian Economic and Social History Review*. vol. 3, no. 3, pp. 268–78.

Alam, Anwar. 2003. 'Democratization of Indian Muslims: Some Reflections'. *Economic and Political Weekly*. vol. 38, no. 48 (12–21 November), pp. 4881–5.

Bennur, Fakrauddin. 1999a. 'Muslim OBCla Rajkiya Dawanila Bandhu Naka'. *Lokmat*, 14 June.

_____. 1999b. 'Nivadnukanche Rajkaran Aani Muslim OBC Chalwalichi Dasha'. *Lokmat*. 4 December.

_____. 2003. 'The Dynamics of Caste Problems of the Indian Muslims'. Paper presented at the National Consultation on Marginalisation of Dalit Muslims in Indian Democracy, Deshkal Society, New Delhi, 11–12 October.

_____. 2004a. 'Maharashtrache Rajkaran aani OBC Jatijamati'. *Samatanayak*. May, pp. 37–9.

_____. 2004b. 'Muslim Samaj aani Tyanchaya Aarakshanachi Samasya.' Unpublished paper, October.

Bhushan, Ranjit. 1999. 'Real Politick Casino'. *Outlook*. 18 October, pp. 28–30.

Bidwai, Praful. 1996. 'Age of Empowerment: Muslim OBCs Discover Mandal'. *The Times of India*, Mumbai, 12 September, p. 2.

Brass, Paul. 1975. *Language, Religion and Politics in North India*. New Delhi: Vikas Publishing House.

Dyke, Virginia van. 1999. 'The 1998 General Election: The Janus-faced Policies of the BJP and Religious Mobilization at the District Level in Uttar Pradesh'. In Ramashray Roy and Paul Wallace (eds). *Indian Politics and the 1998 Election: Regionalism, Hindutva and State Politics*. New Delhi: Sage Publications, pp. 105–28.

Engineer, Asghar Ali. 2004. 'Reservation for Muslims'. *Economic and Political Weekly*. vol. 39, no. 36 (4–10 September), pp. 3984–5.

Jenkins, Laura Dudley. 2001. 'Becoming Backward: Preferential Policies and Religious Minorities in India'. *Commonwealth and Comparative Politics*. vol. 39, no. 1, pp. 32–50.

Khan, Maulana Wahiduddin. 1997. *Indian Muslims: A Need for a Positive Outlook*. New Delhi: Al-Risala Books.

Khalidi, Omar. 2006. *Muslims in Indian Economy*. New Delhi: Three Essays Collective.

Lohia, Rammanohar. 1964. *The Caste System*. Hyderabad: Navhind.

Mondal Seik, Rahim. 2003. 'Social Structure, OBCs and Muslims'. *Economic and Political Weekly*. vol. 38, no. 45 (12–21 November), pp. 4892–7.

Noorani, A.G. 2003. *The Muslims of India: A Documentary Record*. New Delhi: Oxford University Press.

Sanjaykumar. 1996. 'Muslims in Electoral Politics'. *Economic and Political Weekly*. vol. 21, no. 2–3 (13–20 January), pp. 138–41.

Sayyad, Mahebub. 2001. *Muslim Marathi Sahitya: Ek Aaklan*. Yewale: Krantijyoti Savitribai Phule Prakashan.

Sikand, Yoginder. 2004. *Muslims in India Since 1947: Islamic Perspectives on Inter-Faith Relations*. London: Routledge Curzon.

Vora, Rajendra. 2006. 'The Hindi Heartland: A Region Sacred to Hindus and Muslims'. In Rajendra Vora and Anne Feldhaus (eds). *Region, Culture and Politics in India*. New Delhi: Manohar, pp. 317–52.

4

B.R. AMBEDKAR'S THOUGHT ON ECONOMIC DEVELOPMENT

Sukhadeo Thorat

From 1915–25, B.R. Ambedkar made significant contributions in the field of public finance and monetary economics, almost all being part of academic requirements for advanced studies at Columbia University and the University of London. After the 1920s, the main focus of his writings shifted to other disciplines.[1] Nevertheless, he continued to express views on economic issues not only as an academic economist but also as a policymaker, in the Bombay Legislative Assembly and the Constituent Assembly, as labour minister in the Central Cabinet from 1942–6, and as a member of Parliament and a minister until 1956. His writings on economics covered a wide range of inter-related issues, including economic development and planning, the capitalist system, alternative economic systems, and the economics of the caste system.

Ambedkar's three major writings on economic issues appeared in the 1920s. While they generally bear the mark of a neo-classical perspective, they also show both his identification with the working classes and a harsh critique of imperialism (Omvedt 1994). After 1930 there was a gradual change, and a heightening of economic radicalism in 1946. In this article I propose to highlight Ambedkar's views on economic development, economic planning, and the role of the state, including his focus on agricultural development, water and resource development, labour problem, and alternative economic systems.

ECONOMIC DEVELOPMENT

In 1918 Ambedkar participated in an academic debate on the problem of small holdings, to which he contributed a thought-provoking paper (Ambedkar 1979). Although this paper focused on the problem of small holdings, Ambedkar placed the analysis within the much broader theoretical framework of economic development. The paper began with a discussion of small holdings, moved on to an economic analysis of agricultural backwardness, and ended with industrial development as the solution to the problem of agricultural development in general and small farmers in particular. The paper thus laid out a theoretical and policy framework for general economic development.

The underlying assumption in academic discussion was that small and scattered landholdings were economically inefficient. The issue was how to consolidate small and scattered holdings in order to make them economically viable. The solution put forward by academic economists was comprised of two methods: the voluntary exchange of owned land to reduce parcelling and to increase the size of holdings; and compulsory consolidation of farms by the government, including restricted sale of the right of occupancy. The decision of whether the restriction should be compulsory or voluntary was to be based on the principle of 'economic holding', to be fixed on the basis on acreage of land owned. The lower land ceiling was to be 'a parcel of land necessary to keep fully engaged and support one family' (Ambedkar 1979: 460, quoting the Baroda Committee), or 'a holding which allows a man [the] chance of producing sufficient to support himself and his family in reasonable comfort, after paying his necessary expenses' (Ambedkar 1979: 466, quoting the Hon. G.F. Keatinge). The solution was to be a matter of administrative and legal measures and the consolidation of holdings was to be treated as a practical problem.

Ambedkar approached the issue differently. For him the issue was essentially economic, and not legal or administrative. He differed from others on two important grounds: the definition of economic holding and the economic principles determining the size of holdings (and hence the solution of their enlargement). While others viewed an economic holding from the standpoint of consumption rather than production,

Ambedkar looked at the issue of small holdings from the standpoint of the economics of production. He maintained that true economic relations could subsist only between total out-turn and investment. If out-turn paid for all the investment, no producer would think of closing his/her farm. The farm was thus a paying economic unit in terms of production and not consumption. Production in turn was not governed by land alone but was the result of a combination of land, capital, and labour. It was the proportion of other factors of production to a unit of land, and not only the amount of land, that rendered a piece of land economical or uneconomical. A small farm might be as economical as a large one.

According to Ambedkar, the problem of small holdings was not fundamental but derived from the parent evil of maladjustment in the social economy. A household with a small holding was unable to acquire and use some factors of production in the right proportion. While there was too little capital (in the form of capital goods and implements) and land, the supply of labour was in excess. Being in short supply, land and capital were relatively expensive compared to labour and hence became major constraints on population. The solution was to increase capital in the form of goods and implements and reduce the use of labour by siphoning off the surplus labour to non-agricultural production. This would at one stroke lessen the pressure on land in India. Besides, the remaining labour would be productively employed and would produce a surplus; and since surplus is capital it could be invested in agriculture. In short, Ambedkar saw industrialization as the most sound remedy for India's agricultural problems. Besides leading to an increase in labour productivity and capital investment in agriculture, it would create the economic necessity of enlarging landholding. By doing away with the premium on land, industrialization would leave few occasions for subdivision and fragmentation. As an indirect consequence of industrialization, the problem of agriculture could be curbed.

Thus, the problem of agricultural backwardness (of which the issue of small farms was a part) was essentially due to deficiency of material capital in relation to land and labour. Low capital accumulation was due to low capacity to save, which, in turn, was the result of low productivity and income from agriculture. The solution to agricultural development, according to Ambedkar, lay in improving the productivity of land and labour, increasing the farm income of cultivating households, and expanding the domestic capacity to save for productive investment. The way out was inter-sectoral transfer of labour from agriculture to industry. This was expected to increase productivity and hence the income of labour in both agriculture and industry. The reduced pressure of population would encourage the enlargement of farm size by reducing the premium on land. The availability of implements and a more flexible supply of land for cultivation could thus provide the opportunity for optimum use of resources in production.[2]

ECONOMIC PLANNING: THE POST-WAR ECONOMIC (RECONSTRUCTION) PLAN (1942–6)

Ambedkar's entry into the Central Cabinet as member-in-charge of the Labour (and also Irrigation and Power) portfolio in 1942 coincided with the formulation and implementation of the post-war plan for India's reconstruction and economic development. Such a plan was necessary to overcome some urgent post-war problems pertaining to the rehabilitation of defence personnel and the conversion of industry from the requirements of war to those of peace. Unlike the war-affected countries of Europe and Asia, in India the plan was not confined to measures for rehabilitation but included plans for economic development. In fact, this plan marked the beginning of systematic, all-India economic planning by the central government. Not only did the policies and plans conceived and implemented from 1942–6 have an impact on the type of economic regime that India adopted at Independence, but many of these plans continued and later became a permanent feature of India's economic development.

As a member of the Central Cabinet, Ambedkar also became a member of the Reconstruction Committee of Council, the highest body set up to decide the objectives and policies of the plan. In addition, he was the President of the Policy Committee set up to improve the condition of labour and develop irrigation and electric power. He contributed significantly to the formulation of the general objectives of the plan and the specific policies for labour, irrigation, and electric power development.

A perusal of Ambedkar's writings and discussions during 1942–6 allows us to understand his thinking about economic planning for India. Ambedkar argued:

The problem of post-war reconstruction in India is essentially different from the problem of reconstruction in other war-affected countries, because for them the problem of reconstruction is a problem of rehabilitation of industries which were destroyed in war. The problem of reconstruction in India, on the other hand, is mainly of the industrialization of India as distinguished from the rehabilitation of industry (Government of India, Reconstruction Committee of Council 1944).

Based on the theoretical framework developed in his paper of 1918, Ambedkar emphasized the need for industrialization for overall economic development as well as for the development of the agricultural sector. Poverty in India, according to him, was entirely due to dependence on agriculture alone. Agriculture failed to produce sufficient food to feed the people. The roots were to be found in the maladjustment of the social economy:

India is caught between two sides of pincers, the one side of which is progressive pressure of population and the other is limited availability of land in relation to its needs. The result is that at the end of each decade we are left with negative balance of population and production and a constant squeezing to standard of living and poverty. The population pressure is giving rise to an army of landless and dispersed families as well. It can be stopped when agriculture is made profitable. Nothing can open possibilities of making agriculture profitable except a serious drive in favour of industrialization. For it is industrialization alone which can drain away excess of population into gainful employment other than agriculture (Thorat 1993: 46; see *The Times of India* 1943).

Ambedkar thus emphasized the need for industrial development in order to gain increased agricultural productivity and income. The policy prescriptions based on theoretical formulations conceived in 1918 were restated in 1943 and eventually incorporated in the objectives of the post-war reconstruction plan. The section on general objectives, which relates to the sectoral dimension, reads:

Agriculture is and will remain India's primary industry but the present imbalanced economy has to be rectified by intensive development of the country's industries so that both agriculture and industry may develop side by side. That will enable the pressure of population on the land to be relieved and will also provide the means required for the provision of better amenities (Government of India, Reconstruction Committee of Council 1944b: 2).

Infrastructure such as roads, communication and transport services, irrigation, and electric power, in the development of which Ambedkar had played a pioneering role, was treated as a prerequisite for industrial development. It was believed that this infrastructure would bring a relatively higher (annual) rate of growth in industrial production and employment and help absorb the surplus labour from agriculture. In the Policy Committee on Public Works and Electric Power (25 October 1943), Ambedkar asked, '"Why do we want cheap and abundant electricity in India?" The answer is that without cheap and abundant electricity no effort for industrialisation of India can succeed' (Government of India, Reconstruction Committee of Council, 1944a: 26).

ECONOMIC PLANNING, LABOUR, AND THE DOWNTRODDEN

Aware of the limitations of a capitalistic economy under parliamentary democracy in ensuring economic security to the masses, Ambedkar argued for an important place for labour and the Depressed Classes in the planned economic development of the country. He was particularly concerned that the government should not only develop programmes but translate them into terms that the common man could understand: peace, housing, clothing, education, good health and, above all, the right to work with dignity. The State should not be content merely with securing fair conditions of work for labour but should strive to secure fair conditions of life as well. Great responsibility lay on the State to provide the poor with facilities for individuals to grow according to their needs. In order to do that, the government could not be laissez-faire, but would have to use a system of control.

Influenced by Ambedkar's views and facilitated by the Labour government in Britain during the 1940s, labour was accorded an important place in the post-war development plan:

the declared objective was to raise the standard of living of the people as a whole and to ensure employment for all. To that end the purchasing power of the people was to be increased by improvement in the efficiency and consequently the productivity of labour on the one hand and simultaneous development and reorganization of agriculture and industries and services on the other (quoted in Thorat 1993: 47).

Provisions to make labour more productive included free or subsidized education up to the age fourteen, medical relief, water supply, and other public utility services, including electric power. These measures were to improve the health and efficiency of labour. Other goals included fairer wages, maternity and sickness benefits, and holidays. Many of these schemes were undertaken by the Labour Department while Ambedkar was President of the Policy Committee on labour.

In Ambedkar's view, the Scheduled Castes and Depressed Classes needed to be treated as a separate entity in the planning exercise, and this provision was incorporated in the Plan's objectives. The Plan documents stated:

One of the objectives of the government would be to take steps to ameliorate the condition of the Scheduled Castes and backward classes. Care must be taken to see that social amenities such as education, public health, water supply, housing, which are meant to be provided under the plan, work especially for the benefit of such classes and that the handicap of ignorance and poverty under which they now labour is offset by special concessions in the shape of educational facilities, grant, scholarships, hostels, improved water supply and similar measures. It would be the special responsibility of the government to see that early measures are taken to remove the handicap of these classes and help them to raise their level to that of their more fortunate fellow citizens. The provision of full employment as well as various measures of social security contemplated under the section of labour would also automatically benefit the backward and the depressed classes.[3]

Besides labour, the Central government's irrigation and electric power policy of 1942–4 also reflected Ambedkar's views about the place of the poor in the country's development. He urged policymakers to incorporate measures in the irrigation development policy to benefit the poor and oppressed sections of society.

Ambedkar was in favour of improvement in production efficiency. But, like Jawaharlal Nehru, he was not merely a growth-maximizer (of national income). He did talk about letting the national income grow large enough before an adequate standard of living could be provided for all. At the same time, he was concerned about the distribution of national income to the common man. In 1943 he emphasized that:

It will not be enough to make industrial development of India as a goal. We shall have to agree that any such industrial development shall be maintained at a socially desirable level. It will not be enough to bend our energies for the production of more wealth in India. We shall have to agree not merely to recognize the basic right of all Indians to share in that wealth as a means for a decent and dignified existence, but devise ways and means to insure him against insecurity (Ambedkar 1943b: 105).

This view was emphasized while formulating India's irrigation and hydroelectric policy. In October 1943, in his presidential address to the Policy Committee on electric power, Ambedkar said:

Why do we want cheap and abundant electricity in India? ... Without cheap and abundant electricity no effort for the industrialization of India can succeed .... Why is industrialization necessary?... We want industrialization of India as the surest means to rescue the people from the eternal cycle of poverty in which they are caught. Industrialization of India must, therefore, be grappled with immediately (Ambedkar 1943a: 105).

He went on to add that India would have to tackle the problem of electricity in an earnest, statesman-like manner, thinking in terms of human life and not in terms of competing claims of the central and provincial governments.

A similar emphasis was to be accorded to the development of irrigation. In his presidential address to the Conference on Multipurpose Development of Damodar Valley, Ambedkar stressed that:

the Centre expects the Provinces to bear in mind the absolute necessity of ensuring that the benefits of the project get ultimately right down to the grass roots i.e., everyone living in the valley and some of those in the vicinity, all have their share in the prosperity which the project should bring. This, in my view, is essential and for this reason we want the establishment of some agency early enough so that that agency can set about planning at once in a manner in which its essential and ultimate objective can be secured (Ambedkar 1945a).

WATER AND POWER DEVELOPMENT

The Central government policy with regard to water resources and hydroelectric power development was evolved and given a definite shape under Ambedkar's tenure as Minister for Labour (and Irrigation and Power) between 1942 and 1946.[4] It began as part of the reconstruction plan and later on became a long-term policy of the Central government. These efforts by Ambedkar and the Labour Department resulted in the emergence of an all-India policy for the development of the country's 'water and electric power resources', the creation of an administrative apparatus and technical bodies at the centre to assist the states in developing irrigation and electric power resources, the initiation of such important present-day river valley projects as the Damodar River Valley project and the Hirakund project, and, for the first time, the development of electric power policy. The key elements of the new water policy were a multipurpose approach to water resources development on the basis of river basins, the concept of a river valley authority, and the creation of technical expert bodies at the Centre to promote the development of water and power resources.

In a conference on the development of Orissa rivers, Ambedkar expressed his views about the conservation and use of water resources. Criticizing the recommendations made by various committees, from the first one in 1872 to the Orissa Flood Advisory Committee of 1945, he observed:

With all respect to the members of these committees, I am sorry to say that they did not bring the right approach to bear on the problem. They were influenced by the idea that water in excessive quantity was an evil. That when water comes in excessive quantity, what needs to be done is to let it run into sea in an orderly flow. Both these views ... are now regarded as grave misconceptions, as positively dangerous from the point of view of the good of the people (Ambedkar 1945b: 304).

Man suffers more from lack of water than from excess of it, Ambedkar said. Nature is not only niggardly in the amount of water it gives but also erratic in its distribution, alternating between drought and storm. This could not change the fact that water is wealth. Water being the wealth of the people and its distribution uncertain, the correct approach was not to complain about nature but to conserve water (Ambedkar 1945b: 304–6).

Earlier, since excess water was considered a major problem, the remedy suggested had a single purpose—to control floods. Ambedkar differed with those who believed in this approach. He observed that 'if conservation of water was mandatory from the point of view of public good, then obviously the plan of embankments was a wrong plan. It was a means which does not subserve the end, namely conservation of water, and must therefore be abandoned.' The appropriate approach, according to him, was the one adopted by some developed countries: 'to dam rivers at various points to conserve water permanently in reservoirs' and put it to multipurpose use. Besides irrigation, such reservoirs could be used for generating electric power and navigation. Ambedkar particularly emphasized the use of rivers for navigation. In the Conference on Orissa Rivers (8 November 1945), he observed:

Navigation in India has had a very chequered history. During the rule of the East India Company, provision for internal navigation occupied a very prominent part in the public works budget of the Company's government. Many of the navigation canals we have to India today ... are remnants of that policy. Railway came later, and for a time the policy was to have both railway and canals navigation. By 1857, there arose a great controversy in which the issue was railway versus canals. The battle for canals was fought bravely by the late Sir Arthur Cotton .... Unfortunately supporters of railways won (Ambedkar 1945b: 693).

Ambedkar added:

I am not quite happy about this victory of railway over canals. Much more annoying is the opinion of supporters of railways that canals must go because they do not pay without knowing that if the canals do not pay it is because their capacity to pay has been terribly mutilated by leaving them uncompleted. I am sure that internal navigation cannot be neglected in the way in which it has been in the past. We ought to borrow a leaf from Germany and Russia in this matter and not only revive reconstruction of our old canals but make new ones also and not to sacrifice them to the exigencies of railways (Ambedkar 1945b: 693).

The storage scheme that Ambedkar proposed would provide not only irrigation and electricity but also a long line of internal navigation. He believed that the multipurpose use of water would convert the forces of evil into powers of good. He subsequently emphasized this perspective for projects on the Damodar, Mahanadi, Sone, and other interstate rivers. The Sone Valley Project, for example, was a multi-purpose river management scheme. Its purpose was not only canal irrigation and perennial hydroelectric power, but also increased utilization of such power for agricultural development (such as for pumping from tube wells), increased fertility achieved by de-watering waterlogged areas, cheap power for industrial development, and improved flood control. Opening the Conference on Sone Valley in March 1945, Ambedkar highlighted the scheme's importance to the economic development of UP, Bihar, and parts of other states. He emphasized that for the possibilities of the scheme to be fully exploited the approach must be regional rather than local. In the conference on the Mahanadi river as well, Ambedkar urged the participants to adopt a regional approach.

In the conference on the River Sone, Ambedkar emphasized that the necessity of taking a regional rather than a local approach meant that ultimately there must be an agreement to set up an appropriate organization with the authority to supply the bulk of electricity and water for irrigation and navigation.[5] The systematic steps towards the introduction of the concept of a River Valley Authority for projects on interstate rivers and the creation of two technical-expert bodies at the Centre, namely the Central Waterways, Irrigation and Navigation Commission and the Central Technical Power Board, were attempts to provide technical advice for the multi-purpose development of water resources on a regional basis. Ambedkar made this clear in the Calcutta Conference of 3 January 1945:

As a preliminary step for securing the best use of water resources of the country the Government of India have created a central organization, called the Central Technical Power Board, and are contemplating to create another to be called the Central Waterways, Irrigation and Navigation Commission. The objects which have led to setting up of these two organizations are to advise the Provinces on how their water resources can be best utilized and how a project can be made to serve purposes other than irrigation (Ambedkar 1945a).

At the same conference, Ambedkar expounded the nature of the new water policy:

It is not far from true to say that so far there has been an absence of positive all-India policy for development of water resources. There has not been enough realization that our policy for waterways must be a multipurpose policy so as to include the provision for irrigation, electrification and navigation. Government of India is very much alive to the disadvantage arising from the present state of affairs and wishes to take steps to evolve a policy which will utilize the water resources to the purposes which they are made to serve in other countries (ibid.).

Multi-purpose use of water resources for the regional development of the entire river valley basin was the key element of the new water policy. The adoption of the concept of a River Valley Authority (to overcome the jurisdictional problem on interstate rivers) and the creation of two technical-expert bodies at the Centre were means to achieve this objective.

LABOUR POLICY

In addition to the water and power policy, significant measures were taken to deal with the problems of labour during Ambedkar's tenure as labour member. Ambedkar's labour policy goals were threefold: (1) providing safeguards and social security measures to workers; (2) giving equal opportunity to workers and employers to participate in formulating a labour policy, and strengthening the labour movement by introducing compulsory recognition of trade unions; and (3) establishing the machinery for enforcing labour laws and settling disputes. The mechanism evolved to achieve these purposes included: setting up the Indian Labour Conference and Standing Labour Committee; enactment of labour laws; establishment of the Chief Labour Commissioner's organization; appointment of the Labour Investigative Committee; machinery for fixing minimum wages; standing orders in industrial employment; and recognition of trade unions. These efforts to protect and promote the interests of labour and the working class made a significant impact on the labour movement and industrial relations in India.

THE LIMITS OF CAPITALISM, ALTERNATIVE ECONOMIC FRAMEWORKS, THE ROLE OF THE STATE

The preceding sections cover the period until the late 1940s. During that period, Ambedkar attributed a key role to industrialization, and favoured economic planning (particularly in infrastructure and the social service sector), progressive labour laws, and a focus on labour and the downtrodden. The theoretical arguments for industrialization were developed within the framework of mainstream economics, assuming a private economy or capitalist organization. Prior to the 1940s Ambedkar emphasized industrialization as a progressive agenda but said nothing about its being organized under the public sector, except for his insistence on state or public ownership and/or distribution of electric power and social services.

Between the mid-1930s and the late 1940s, Ambedkar's position changed, to an economic radicalism that criticized capitalism and advocated a dominant role for the state, the abolition of feudalistic land tenure systems like Khoti and Mahar Vatan, distribution of land, cultivation by cooperative and collective farms, and production and distribution of electric power under State ownership and control. Again, Ambedkar proposed these measures assuming the inevitability of capitalist organization (although occasionally he showed a preference for socialism). There was no serious alternative economic framework during these years. The precise statement of an alternative radical economic and political framework making a departure from the earlier position came in *States and Minorities*, written as a memorandum to the Constituent Assembly (Ambedkar 1947). This book calls for 'State Socialism': nationalization of basic and key industries, insurance, and agricultural land, the land to be worked in collective farms by peasants treated as tenants of the state. For the first time Ambedkar explained his preference for having industrialization and agriculture under the State. He also explained the need for economic planning, a stronger role for the state, and special safeguards to prevent social and economic discrimination against socially deprived classes. Providing a justification for State Socialism, he stated:

The main purpose behind the clause is to put an obligation on the State to plan the economic life of the people on lines which would lead to highest point of productivity without closing every avenue to private enterprise, and also provide for the equitable distribution of wealth. The plan set out in the clause proposes State ownership in agriculture with a collectivized method of cultivation and a modified form of State Socialism in the field of industry. It places squarely on the shoulders of the State the obligation to supply capital necessary for agriculture as well as for industry .... State socialism is essential for the rapid industrialization of India. Private enterprise cannot do it and if it did it would produce those inequalities of wealth which private capitalism has produced in Europe and which should be a warning to Indians (1947: 30–1).

In the case of agriculture, unlike the 1930s and 1940s, when Ambedkar argued for land distribution and tenancy rights, he now argued that:

Consolidation of holdings and tenancy legislation are worse than useless. They cannot bring about prosperity in agriculture. Neither consolidation nor tenancy Legislation can be of any help to the 60 millions of Untouchables who are just landless labourers .... Only collective farms on the lines set out in the proposal can help them (1947: 31).

Ambedkar's criticism of capitalism was mainly drawn from Marx, with whom he was in basic agreement. Writing in 1956, Ambedkar observed:

What remains of the Karl Marx is a residue of fire, small but still very important. The residue in my view consists of four items:
  (i) The function of philosophy is to reconstruct the world and not to waste its time in explaining the origin of the world.
 (ii) That there is a conflict of interest between class and class.
(iii) That private ownership of property brings powers to one class and sorrow to another through exploitation.
(iv) That it is necessary for the good of society that the sorrow be removed by the abolition of private property (1987: 444).

Taking the surviving points from the Marxist creed, Ambedkar built up a clear case for socialism. He agreed that in a social economy based on private enterprise and personal gain, both the unemployed and the employed must relinquish their rights and subject themselves to being governed by a private employer:

[For an unemployed person, t]he fear of starvation, the fear of losing a house, the fear of losing savings if any, the fear of being compelled to take children away from school, the fear of having to be a burden on public charity ... are factors too strong to permit a man to stand out for his fundamental rights. The unemployed are thus compelled to relinquish their fundamental rights for the sake of securing the privilege to work and to subsist (Ambedkar 1947: 32).

Writing about the safeguards suggested by the constitutionalists, Ambedkar observed that:

They argue that where the State refrains from intervention in private affairs—economic and social—the residue is liberty .... But .... To whom and for whom is this liberty? Obviously this liberty is liberty to the landlords to increase rents, for capitalists to increase hours of work and reduce rate of wages .... In other words what is called liberty from the control of the State is another name for the dictatorship of the private employer (1947: 32–33).

Ambedkar was critical of most democratic governments, which impose arbitrary restraints in the political domain and invoke the power of the legislature to restrain more powerful individuals from imposing arbitrary restraints on the less powerful in the economic field. Ambedkar favoured an economic system where not only the power of the government to impose arbitrary restraints was limited, but also that of more powerful individuals. This could be achieved by minimizing their control in the economic life of the people.

In responding on 17 December 1946 to the resolution related to the 'aims and objectives' of the future constitution of India moved by Jawaharlal Nehru on 13 December, Ambedkar (as a member of the Constituent Assembly) argued for a socialistic economic framework for India:

I should have expected ... the Resolution to state in most explicit terms that in order that there may be social and economic justice in the country, that there would be nationalisation of industry and nationalisation of land. I do not understand how it could be possible for any future government which believes in doing justice socially, economically and politically, unless its economy is a socialistic economy.

However, Ambedkar was aware of the constraints on the acceptability of the proposal to the Constituent Assembly. He therefore pushed only as far as he could. He continued, observing, 'therefore, personally, although I have no objection to the enunciation of these propositions, the resolution is, to my mind, somewhat disappointing. I am however prepared to leave this subject where it is with the observations I have made.' As on several other occasions, such as the Poona Pact, Ambedkar had to adjust his position on this issue as well.

NOTES

1. B.R. Ambedkar's principal academic works on public finance and currency between 1915 and 1925 included his MA dissertation (1915), his PhD dissertation (1925), and his DSC dissertation (1923).
2. The underlying causes of structural backwardness were, first, an acute deficiency of material capital, which prevented the introduction of more productive technologies; second, the low capacity to save, which could be raised by means of suitable fiscal and monetary policies; and, third, the fact that agriculture was subject to diminishing returns. Industrialization would allow surplus labour, currently underemployed in agriculture, to be more productively employed in industries that operated according to increasing returns to scale. (Chakravarty 1987: 40).
3. (i) The 10th meeting of the Reconstruction Committee of Council held on 11 September 1944, which discussed the objective of the plan, recorded that there was a case for treating the Scheduled Castes and Depressed Classes as a separate entity for the purpose of planning. Honourable member of Labour, Dr Ambedkar said that he would like suggest certain amendments on these lines. (Minutes of the 10th meeting, 11 September 1944, Reconstruction Committee of Council, 2/10/121, 1945.8.). (ii) Reconstruction Committee of Council, Post-War Development Policy, Draft Report, 1944, File No. 1(4)P-45, Finance Department, Planning Division.
4. Between 1943 and 1945, Dr Ambedkar addressed conferences on Post-War Development of Electric Power in India, 25 October 1943; Damodar Valley Scheme, First Calcutta Conference, 3 January 1945; Post-War Electric Development, 2 February 1945; Multi-Purpose Development of Damodar Valley, Second Calcutta Conference, 23 August 1945; and Multi-Purpose Plan for Development of Orissa Rivers, 3 November 1945.
5. Proceedings of a meeting held on 10 March 1945 to discuss certain proposals regarding the development of Sone Valley, File No. D.W./IRI/336-p/45, Finance Department, Planning Branch.

REFERENCES

Ambedkar, B.R. 1915. 'Administration and Finance of the East India Company'. MA dissertation, Columbia University.
_____. 1923. 'The Problem of the Rupee'. DSC Dissertation, University of London (School of Economics). London: King and Sons Ltd.
_____. 1925. 'The Evolution of Provincial Finance in British India'. PhD Dissertation. London: King and Sons Ltd.
_____. 1943a. 'Post War Development of Electric Power in India'. *Indian Information*, 15 November.

_____. 1943b. 'First Session of Plenary Labour Conference: Dr Ambedkar on Social Security'. *Indian Information*, 15 September, pp. 143–4.

_____. 1945a. 'Multipurpose Development of the Damodar Valley'. 3 January and 23 August 1945. *Indian Information*, 1 October, pp. 345–50.

_____. 1945b. 'Multi-Purpose Plan for Development of Orissa Rivers'. Presidential speech, 8 November 1945. *Indian Information*, 15 December, pp. 692–6.

_____. 1945c. 'Dr Ambedkar on Social Security'. *Indian Information*, 15 September.

_____. 1947. *States and Minorities: What are Their Rights and How to Secure Them in the Constitution of Free India*. Bombay: Thacker & Company. Reprinted in *Writings and Speeches of Dr Ambedkar*. Vol. 1. Vasant Moon (ed.). Bombay: Education Department, Government of Maharashtra, pp. 381–449.

_____. 1979. 'Small Holdings in India and their Remedies. In Vasant Moon (ed.). *Writings and Speeches of Dr Ambedkar*. vol. 1. Bombay: Education Department, Government of Maharashtra, pp. 453–79. (Originally in *Journal of the Indian Economic Society*. vol. 1 [1918], pp. 78–88.)

_____. 1987. *Dr Babasaheb Ambedkar: Writings and Speeches*. vol. 3. Bombay: Education Department, Government of Maharashtra.

Chakravarty, Sukhamoy. 1987. *Development Planning, The Indian Experience*. New Delhi: Oxford University Press.

Government of India, Reconstruction Committee of Council. 1944a. First Report on the Progress of Reconstruction Planning, 1 March 1944. Delhi: Manager of Publication.

_____. 1944b. Second Report on the Progress of Reconstruction Planning. Delhi: Manager of Publications.

Omvedt, Gail. 1994. *Dalits and the Democratic Revolution: Dr Ambedkar and the Dalit Movement in Colonial India*. New Delhi: Sage Publications.

The Times of India. 1943. 'Urgency of Industrialisation of India'. 26 October.

Thorat, Sukhadeo. 1993. *Ambedkar's Contribution to Water Resources Development*. New Delhi: Central Water Commission.

5

COLONIAL OPPRESSION OF THE PEASANTRY IN THE BOMBAY PRESIDENCY

Mani Kamerkar

I have chosen the Bassein *taluka* as an example of the British revenue system and its effects on the peasantry. Bassein is a part of the Thana district. It lies along the Arabian Sea north of Bombay and is bounded by the Vaitarna creek in the north and Bassein creek and Salsette in the south. During the nineteenth century it became an important part of the Bombay hinterland, next to Salsette. The development of Bombay was accompanied by the revival of trade and commerce in the Bassein ports. In the nineteenth century Bassein taluka consisted of ninety-two villages (Government of Bombay 1898: 6), which were situated along the coastal belt and inland on the hill slopes. The soil is rich and red, and the flat belt was, and is, used for garden cultivation, giving a rich yield. Part of the land is salty and yielded a poor quality of rice. However, the salt pans were a prized feature of Bassein's economy.

The small but intensively cultivated acreage devoted to garden cultivation was confined to a narrow belt of land skirting the coast and extending for two or three miles inland. The soil was rich and alluvial, of the most fertile kind. Water was available very near the surface, so that regular wells were not even required. Small tanks and water holes, a few feet deep, were sufficient. The principal crops of these areas were plantains, betel vines, sugarcane, sweet potatoes, pumpkins, and various kinds of market produce required in Bombay. New varieties of plantains were grown here, the best being the red plantains. The 'Rajeli' variety of plantains was dried, and was a flourishing industry in the villages of Agashi, Valar, Bilinj, and Kophrad, where it was sold wholesale at competitive rates. Unripe bananas, which were sliced and dried for sale, were also profitable. Sugarcane was another important crop grown in the garden lands; it yielded a rich harvest, and the *gur* (jaggery) extracted from it found a ready market. The gur was of very good quality, had a good flavour, and was long-lasting, as it did not become soft.

The majority of garden landowners were Christians; they were credited with having turned the light sandy country of Bassein into an evergreen area. In addition to the Christians, Kunbis were seen as knowledgeable and hardworking, and they formed the bulk of the agricultural class (Government of Bombay 1882: 300ff.). Bassein certainly became an important agricultural area. Its trade and commerce increased along with its agriculture, but this did not always bring prosperity to the inhabitants in general.

In 1862 the government sought to raise a cess of Rs 6 per acre that was already in existence to a maximum of Rs 8–12 (eight rupees and twelve annas).[1] The lands were graded according to soil and arranged in four categories, with the less fertile lands paying revenue ranging from Rs 3 to Rs 4. A total increase of 31.2 per cent was being proposed. The majority of farmers were rice growers, and 83.13 per cent of the land was rice-growing land. The peasants who paid these revenue dues had already been over-assessed since 1820, when the British revenue system came into existence (Kumar 1984: 184). British revenue demands were harsh, and to add to the peasants' difficulties, throughout the nineteenth century this area suffered from famine and other natural calamities, which reduced the average earnings of the general peasantry. The great famine of 1790 held back progress in Bassein and Salsette for years. This was followed by a failure of crops in 1802 due to the failure of the monsoon. Again in 1824–5 a failure of rains was followed by a scarcity of crops. Within less than fifteen years, in 1837 and 1838, another failure of crops occurred, again due to scarcity of rains, and yet another such calamity overtook the area from 1853 to 1855, when for three years the crops again failed. Two decades later, in 1877, the same problem arose, to be followed by two bad years at the end of the century. By its own admission, the government gave only very small remissions during this period.

In 1895, in order to justify a demand for an increase in land revenue ranging from 33 per cent to 118 per cent, the revenue officials claimed that Bassein had prospered enormously between the 1830s and the 1890s, and therefore could easily bear the burden of the increase (Government of Bombay 1898: 15). This supposedly favourable material prosperity was in fact marginal, except in the case of a favoured few. The British claimed that the population had increased from 44,784 in 1862 to 61,089 in 1872, a growth of 26.69 per cent, and in 1895 a special census gave the figure as 72,103, a further increase of 15.27 per cent—that is, over a forty-year period there was an increase of 41.95 per cent. In an overwhelmingly agricultural community (60.59 per cent of the population were agriculturists), such an increase would have resulted in putting pressure on the land, as there was an increase of only 10.75 per cent in the land under cultivation, from 41,786 acres to 46,278 acres (Government of Bombay 1898: 15). The wealth produced by an increase in the demand for Bassein goods was offset by the number of people per acre of land, and scarcely justified an increase in the rate of assessment.

Due to the proximity of Bombay and the increase in demand for rice, coarse grains, and garden products, the peasants were able to continue their livelihood. That there was a certain degree of stability cannot be denied, in view of the fact that only 2.2 per cent of the land was either mortgaged or sold (Government of Bombay 1898: 14). The prosperity, however, claimed by the British administrators was mainly reaped by the garden cultivators, whose crops had a ready market and constant demand in Bombay. This is proved by the fact that the garden villages never leased out their land but cultivated it themselves (Government of Bombay 1898: 15). The garden produce definitely benefited by an increase in the communication network, both roads and railways, along with the traditional sea routes. According to the British authorities, 'enormous' capital had accumulated; they wanted to tap it, and therefore the revenue officials were proposing an increase of 118 per cent in the tax (Government of Bombay 1882: 329).

The idea appears to have been one of bleeding the cultivator dry and not allowing him any benefit of his labour or of the infrastructure. Ultimately, a hue and cry was raised at this inequity and callousness. Vernacular newspapers took up the cause of these peasants, and between 1893 and 1896 a vigorous anti-tax campaign took place. The *Maratha* asked whether the government intended the peasants to hand over everything to it, leaving them nothing for themselves beyond the bare necessities of life. The article goes on to say that 'the most rack renting Irish landlord would, we imagine, blush for sure if he were asked to emulate our liberal and refined government in this respect' (1 January 1893).

Thus, the usurious rates proposed were based on the idea of extracting the maximum possible from the land. Land revenue sustained the British administration. Finally the government decided to levy an increase ranging from 25 per cent to 33 per cent (Government of Bombay 1898: 91); this increase was extremely hard on the average farmer and could reasonably be borne only by garden farmers and those, like Kolis and Bhandaris, who carried on other crafts and trades along with their rice farming, both sweet and salt. From the reports of the local officers, the coastal Agris, Kolis, and Bhandaris were the most prosperous among the 'middle-class' Hindus. The grass from their waste lands fetched high prices in Bombay, their salt rice fields did not require ploughing, or manuring, or planting. Besides growing rice, these groups made salt, fished, and built boats both for their own use and for sale (Government of Bombay 1882: 306–7).

An examination of the indices of growth in the thirty years from 1862 to 1895 also shows the type of development, if any, in Bassein. As already stated, the acreage increase of cultivated land did not keep pace with the increase in the population, and therefore the burden on the land increased. Some of the increase in population was, of course, absorbed in the growing trade and commerce, but not proportionally. The number of dwellings increased from 7,890 to 11,478—that is, by 45 per cent (Government of Bombay 1898: 12). Most of these dwellings were single-room huts made of rough poles with walls of karvi[2] stem, plastered with mud, and the roofs were covered with grass or palm leaves. Only in the village proper, in the coastal areas, were the roofs tiled (Government of Bombay 1882: 307). A very small section of the population could afford houses made of brick and mortar, with tiled roofs. Agricultural cattle meant for pulling carts and ploughs increased by a mere 284 (Government of Bombay 1898: 12), a number that scarcely speaks of agricultural prosperity. Carts increased by just eighty-six (Government of Bombay 1898: 12), and this was in spite of the fact that a few new roads were built in the district.

During this period, other actions of the British administration in the villages and forest lands of the district also had a considerable impact on the life of the average villager. The peaceful and cooperative life of the village people was greatly disturbed by depriving the villages of common *varka*s (waste) lands. These common lands had been an integral part of the village economy from time immemorial. Before this, varkas land had never been hereditary or proprietary. The farmer had been allowed to cultivate the land on payment of rent to the government, who was the sovereign owner of the soil (Jervoise 1878: 1). In the early part of the century, the British government had accepted this traditional arrangement to some extent. In a minute of the governor of Bombay, dated 5 January 1828, the claim of the government to the occupation of 'wasteland' is accepted as secondary to the claim of the common ryot.[3] Up to 1852 the government also accepted the fact that varkas lands of this region were nowhere divided into fields or properties with recognized limits.[4]

By a common understanding, village cultivators used various parts of the varkas hillsides or localities, cultivating only a small part of the varkas at a time. The same spot was not used regularly by one person but would be changed every two or three years, and thus no single person could establish a claim. The varkas land was also used for grazing and preparing '*rab*'[5] for the rice fields. Some of this land was also used for dry crops. The area that farmers used for these purposes was not in the least defined, and thus the concept of common ownership of these lands was maintained: they belonged to the village as a whole. Often varkas lands had a number of valuable trees, such as *ain* and teak, which were the common property of the village; no one could cut them for individual profit or use.

In the beginning the British followed the practice of measuring annually the area of varkas that was cultivated, and collecting assessment as so much per *bigha* (a measure of area) according to the type of crop being raised on the land. However, the British found this unsatisfactory and proposed a new scheme. As there were no 'properties' on the varkas lands, and as no individual could be assessed as holding a certain area of varkas land at a certain rate per acre, they resorted to a method fraught with danger for the future. Since most farmers of rice fields used varkas lands for making rab or to grow dry crops or grass, the British proposed that the varkas be cultivated 'free' of assessment, and in consideration of this privilege, they proposed imposing a higher rate of assessment on owners of rice lands, who used the varkas lands. By this plan, in 1854–5 each cultivator made payment dependent on and proportionate to the value of his rice holding (Jervoise 1878: 8). This was the beginning of ultimately dividing the varkas land into proprietary holdings. The owners of rice fields who paid a higher rate gradually laid claim to varkas lands, and their claims were ultimately accepted in 1874–5.

Until then, the varkas lands had never been measured or defined as assessed by the British survey officers, but the fact of this extra assessment was the thin edge of the wedge that entered into the only free, common property left in the villages. The farmers interpreted this extra assessment as giving them proprietary rights over portions of the varkas lands. They now began to claim that those portions formed a necessary part of their rice fields. These claims over the years became accepted by the British, and slowly the villagers lost all the free privileges of making rab, getting grass for their cattle, and growing dry crops. This especially affected the poorest sections in the village, particularly those without any fields for cultivation. Its deleterious effects on the villagers were manifold and caused widespread misery and poverty. The landless could no longer keep cattle or even grow marginal crops. Life became more difficult, instead of adding to any sort of prosperity.

Until 1874, the villagers had been allowed to cut common wood— not teak, black wood, or ain—on varkas land for domestic purposes but not for trade. To compound the mischief, and destroy an important ecological and economic necessity of the villages, the proprietors of rice lands were given proprietorship over the varkas lands they were cultivating, and revenue settlements were made with reference to those lands in 1874–5. At this time the varkas lands were surveyed and ownership of individuals over them accepted, thus destroying the age-old practice of cooperative usage in the villages and leading to further distress of the population at large.

In the revenue surveys of 1874–5, the British defined and allotted distinct holdings to individuals instead of allowing the villagers to use the whole of the varkas lands in common under arrangements made by themselves. This total right of proprietorship given to individual farmers was now extended to the trees on the varkas lands. The landholders laid claim to them, and thus another source of common wealth was grabbed by individuals who were only too willing to take advantage of the opening given to them by the British. They rapidly began to strip the varkas lands, in spite of the general laws against felling trees, especially teak. Such laws had been in existence since 1839, when the government had passed orders against cutting down teak and other big trees (Jervoise 1878: 8). In November 1847 the government had issued a notice whereby areas covered with numerous teak and other valuable trees were to be specially entered into the records as forest rights and reserved. However, where a few such trees grew on a landowner's acreage, they were to be valuated and offered for sale to the proprietor. If he refused to pay for them, they were to be cut down and sold (Jervoise 1878: 10). Thus, in its greed for extra revenue, the government itself became a party to the destruction of trees.

The Collector of Thana reported that the cultivation of varkas lands after the British assessments was responsible for the destruction of forests.[6] After these measures took effect, rice farmers felled many of the trees on varkas lands for sale or destroyed them for manure, even though no right of any kind on trees on varkas lands had been acknowledged in any survey settlements. Nearly all the varkas lands were covered with bush and tree jungles. It was estimated in 1882 that there had originally been twenty times as much varkas land as rice land.[7] But by 1895 the proportion of varkas lands had been reduced to 30 per cent of the rice lands through encroachments resulting from the settlement policies of the British.[8]

In addition to these inequities, the prices of essentials were rising and the cost of living was getting higher and higher. The population seems to have understood this, as recorded by R.H. Davis in 1867. They felt that their toil was greater, that nature was more niggardly, and that the battle of life was harder. The agrarian mind attributed the change to foreign rule, to the remittance of money to England, and to the decay of native manufactures.[9] Another official, A. Roberts, was more discerning and closer to the truth when he said:

The tenants, and farm labourers, artisans, domestic servants and others earn no more in British territory than elsewhere and sought but a bare subsistence for themselves and their families. The price of food and of all the necessities of life has risen so enormously within the last few years that I doubt whether the masses are so prosperous as they were before the mutiny or as they used to be under native governments.[10]

Another imposition on the population was the introduction of income tax. This was imposed by the government to meet their own financial emergencies. It affected certain sections of both the agricultural and the non-agricultural population. The rate charged was four paise in the rupee for income up to Rs 2,000 per year (Kumar

1984: 924–5). Thus, the agricultural population was burdened with a double taxation to which others were not subject.

The people of Bassein, as elsewhere, reacted very unfavourably to what they considered an extremely inequitable demand, and they made several demonstrations against this. On 5 December 1860, a crowd of about four thousand Kolis, Agris, Pandarpeshas, Vanis, and other farmers assembled in Bassein to meet Mr Hunter, the Deputy Collector. Half the crowd were Kolis, which indicates that they were the most affected. In typical imperial style, the official refused to listen to the grievances. When the crowd became restive, he tried to escape by the rear door, but as he crossed the creek he was caught, brought back, and more or less '*gheraoed*'. Even the police who were present refused to arrest the leader, Govardhan Gangadas. Even after that, as Mr Hunter was being escorted by other officials to the ferry, he was assaulted (Joshi 1957: 26–8). The agitators showed a degree of political maturity and resolution which really surprised the British.

There were similar agitations over these impositions in other parts of the Presidency and the country. As a result, the income tax was withdrawn in 1865. It was reintroduced in 1869 for three years, when it met with similar resistance. However, in 1886 the income tax was introduced once again, this time to stay, but with the provision that agricultural incomes were to be exempted (Kumar 1984: 928). This brought a certain amount of relief to the population at large.

In spite of the proximity of Bombay and its growing needs, the mass of the peasantry remained at a more-or-less static, bare-subsistence level, which was further aggravated by British land policies. That the British policies on land and other taxes had led to widespread distress was acknowledged by their own officers, except those concerned with extraction of maximum revenue. On the proposals of the revision of revenue made by several officials in 1895, the Collector of the district stated:

The statement that the agricultural populations are in comfortable circumstances is not correct. The Agris and the Kunbis are mostly debtors, and cultivate land as tenants and not as proprietors. Gold and Silver ornaments among their ladies are very few. Their poverty is brought on by their uneconomical habits and partly by the exactions of the Pandarpeshas. The Majority of the cultivators are servants of the Brahmans and other landholders.[11]

The Collector was also not happy about the proposed increase in land-revenue rates, but nevertheless accepted them, presumably in the interest of imperial needs.

NOTES

Editors' note: Professor Kamerkar died soon after she wrote and submitted this piece for our volumes in honour of Eleanor Zelliot. We are publishing the chapter here with some minor changes, which Professor Kamerkar did not have the chance to approve.

1. One anna = 1/16 rupee.
2. A medicinal plant (*Strobilanthes callosus*).
3. Minutes of the Government of Bombay, dated 5 January 1828 and Government order 565, in Jervoise 1878.
4. Report of Captain G. Wingate, Revenue Survey Commissioner, dated 11 August 1852, in Jervoise 1878.
5. '*Rab*' means wood-ash manure, prepared by burning cow dung, grass, or wood and branches.
6. Report of Captain G. Waingate, Revenue Survey Commissioner, dated 11 August 1852, in Jervoise 1878: 183.
7. Collector of Thana to Commissioner, North Konkan Division, 25 February 1895, in Government of Bombay 1898: 200.
8. Ibid.
9. Select Committee on East India, 1871: 717.
10. Ibid., p. 718.
11. H.F. Silcock, Collector of Thana, to Commissioner Northern Division, 25 February 1875, in Government of Bombay 1898: 201.

REFERENCES

Government of Bombay. 1882. *Gazetteer of the Bombay Presidency*. vol. XIII. *Thana District*. Part I. Bombay: Government of Bombay.

_____. 1898. *Revision Settlement of the Bassein Taluka of Thana Collectorate*. new series, no. 293, of 1896. Bombay: Government Central Press.

Jervoise, A. Clarke. 1878. *Memorandum of the Defense in the Suit of Vasudev Bhasker Pendse vs Collector of Thana*. Bombay: Government of Bombay.

Joshi, Govind Babaji. 1957. 'Majha Pravasachi Hakikat'. In *Source Material for a History of the Freedom Movement in India*. vol. I. Bombay: Government Central Press, pp. 26–8.

Kumar, Dharma (ed.). 1984. *Cambridge Economic History of India*. vol. 2. Bombay: Cambridge University Press.

6

EDUCATING ARTISANS AS COLONIAL MODERNITY
Industrial Education in Late Nineteenth-century Western India

Abigail McGowan

As many scholars have noted, the myriad social, economic, and political changes of late nineteenth-century colonial India affected communities unevenly. Some benefited, fighting for higher status, entering education, and taking up more lucrative professions. Others saw their positions decline, losing economic and cultural capital as they struggled to adapt. Artisans were among those who fared badly. Competing against both European imports and Indian mill products, handloom weavers, dyers, block printers, paper-makers, brass workers, blacksmiths, carpet weavers, and cotton spinners faced declining markets, shrinking profits, and growing debts. Not all suffered; some made new transportation and communication structures work to their advantage, developing larger, centralized workshops that supplied ever widening markets. But, as a class, more artisans faced decline than experienced expansion. In rural areas, as traditional patronage dried up, artisans turned to agriculture or left for the cities. In cities, semi-independent household production gave way to poorly-paid wage labour for others. Wherever they lived, artisans rarely used the technologies that made European products so successful. As the president of the 1910 Indian Industrial Conference, R.N. Mukerjee, argued, Indian artisans were 'universally illiterate and thus shut out from knowledge of any improved methods in their respective trades'. As a result, 'they make no advancement or progress throughout their lives and are content to continue working on lines that for generations have become obsolete' (quoted in Kale 1911: 77).

In honour of Eleanor Zelliot's work on oppressed peoples in India, I explore educational efforts aimed at those at the bottom of colonial industrial hierarchies: illiterate, technologically-backward artisans. In the late nineteenth century a string of schools sprang up in the cities and up-country towns of western India which aimed to revolutionize artisanal industries. These schools all operated independently under the authority of local municipal boards or missionary groups. But all shared a similar approach, combining instruction in traditional industries—usually carpentry and blacksmithing—with new standards of disciplined workmanship and a new orientation towards the emerging demand for westernized furniture, carriages, and decorative items. The hope was that such instruction would modernize methods and improve labour, not just in wood and metal but across crafts—a sector whose endemic poverty and technological backwardness seemed to demand outside leadership.

These industrial schools reflected the growing politicization of industrial development. On the one hand, the colonial state was trying to render its territory more productive, extending its reach farther into local communities in order to reform all aspects of the economy, from agriculture to labour to finance to industry (Ludden 1992; Goswami 2004). On the other hand, Indian intellectuals like Romesh Chandra Dutt, Mahadev Govind Ranade, and Ganesh Vyankatesh Joshi were using the colonial state's failure to spur development to define the problems with British rule (Chandra 1966). Both sides hoped to bring Indian industries to new life, but they diverged widely in how, when, and by whom that should be done. The native press, for instance, regularly blamed government reluctance to fund expensive technical institutes on the British desire to monopolize top industrial and scientific jobs. And yet, for all their differences, both sides agreed on at least one thing: the need for a new kind of education for artisans. British and Indian activists alike portrayed artisans as hopelessly backward and conservative, thereby legitimizing their own authority to intervene. At the same time, they argued that industrial schools had helped make possible the rapid industrialization of Germany, the United States, and Japan, and claimed that such schools could play a similar role in India (see, for instance, Mudholkar 1909; Clibborn *et al.* 1903). Consequently,

British and Indian activists came together to demand a new kind of education to bring India's artisans into the modern age.

Industrial schools offered artisans an entrée into the colonial educational system. Previously ignored in educational initiatives that favoured upper castes, low-status artisans now found themselves targeted by schools which even paid students scholarships to attend. Yet, this was not an emancipatory educational project. The education offered in the industrial schools aimed to modernize artisans as labour and nothing more. The goal was to turn illiterate, impoverished artisans into disciplined workers *without* encouraging them to aspire to non-industrial employment. This attempt to limit change was hard to maintain in practice. Some artisans rejected the whole project as too disruptive; already engaged in their own experiments with new technologies and product ranges, few of them enrolled in industrial schools, preferring instead traditional instruction. Others set their sights higher than was allowed at the schools, agitating for access to the general educational system necessary for non-artisanal careers.

It is this problematic modernity promised by industrial education that I explore here. In recent years, scholars have focused on how colonial education used literature and science to 'civilize' native populations according to western values and knowledge, implicitly promising that this would put Indians on a par with their rulers (Viswanathan 1989; Prakash 1999). Yet Indians who made it to the top of the colonial educational system found the promise to be false; the liberal ideal of empire was always compromised by a countervailing insistence on essential racial differences (Metcalf 1995; Bhabha 1994; Sinha 1995). The liberalism of late nineteenth century India, however, was not just confined to education for the elites, or to the agency of the colonial state. Instead, as Veena Naregal (2001) has argued, Indian elites themselves saw schools as a means by which to promise and then deny parity to the lower classes. Echoing Naregal, I trace here both how industrial education was used to reinforce colonial hierarchies and how artisans themselves tried to find their own alternatives.

INDUSTRIAL EDUCATION: OBJECTIVES AND EXAMPLES

There had been some scattered attempts to provide a more practical, manual type of education in the Bombay Presidency in the middle of the nineteenth century, starting with the Bombay School of Industry in the early 1850s. It was not until the 1870s, however, that these efforts really took root, resulting in the creation of some six new schools in that decade, with perhaps thirteen more in the 1880s and another twelve in the 1890s. Not all these schools survived; many, in fact, closed down within two or three years of opening, usually due to high costs on the one hand and failure to market the finished goods on the other. Still, the numbers of schools and students did grow: whereas in 1885–6 there were only seven industrial schools with 755 students in the whole of the Bombay Presidency (Government of Bombay 1886: cxx–cxxi), by 1898–9 the total had risen to sixteen schools with 1,343 students within the Presidency proper, plus several more in nearby princely states (Government of Bombay 1899: 55). In 1939 the presidency boasted some thirty-two officially-recognized industrial schools teaching things like carpentry, metal work, leather work, book binding, tailoring, and handloom weaving; another thirty institutions offered courses for girls in lace making, needlework, and other skills (Government of Bombay 1939: 20, 37). Most of these schools were small, training boys—or later girls—in one or two crafts.

Not all these schools offered precisely the same training. Indeed, given the variety of sponsoring bodies—ranging from missionary groups to local municipalities, princely states, and nationalist-oriented political groups—it would have been surprising if it had been otherwise. Some schools set out to create or develop new industries or crafts, including the manufacture of pen nibs, buttons, and brushes in Baroda, and carpet weaving in Ahmednagar.[1] Others, like the Sir Jamsetjee Jeejeebhoy School of Arts in Bombay and the School of Arts in Bhuj, tried to improve the quality of Indian art industries. Still others—the most popular by far—taught basic skills in existing, common consumer-oriented crafts.

In theory, this latter type of school was concerned with the state of labour in general, rather than with any one particular craft. As one of the government's top industrial officials, Alfred Chatterton, put it, industrial schools should seek 'to educate the hand and eye, to form habits of observation, judgement and accuracy, to cultivate the sense of proportion, to make the pupil ready, resourceful and self-reliant' (Chatterton 1904: 136). But not all artisanal industries were considered appropriate for forming these useful habits. Indeed, most industrial schools focused on just two: woodworking and blacksmithing (Buck 1901: 15). Only rarely did schools take up other industries, like handloom weaving, dyeing, leather work, or pottery; then, too, these crafts were usually offered in addition to wood and metal. To some degree the choice to encourage woodworking and blacksmithing was pedagogical: school officials saw these two crafts as particularly useful for teaching accuracy, precision, and other general skills (see Clibborn *et al.* 1903, Part II: 107). The choice was also probably driven by changing consumer desires: both these crafts were central to new consumer demands for furniture, buildings, gates and railings, and metal fittings.

THE DHARWAR SCHOOL OF INDUSTRY: PRINCIPLES IN ACTION

One of the many industrial schools of the period was the Dharwar School of Industry, which opened in 1873 to train boys for work in wood and metal in connection with a local saw mill. Typical of the industrial schools in the Bombay Presidency in terms of size, longevity, and type of instruction, the Dharwar school tried to improve local labour as a means to building new industries. Located in a small district headquarters in the southern part of the Presidency, the school perhaps had more limited access to markets and materials than others located in larger cities. But, like its counterparts in Poona, Bombay, Surat, or Ahmedabad, it struggled with common issues of attracting and retaining students, finding outlets for their work, and maintaining its long-term viability in the face of critical scrutiny. Thus, while the particular expression of such problems may be specific to Dharwar, the school there helps to illustrate the promises and limitations of industrial schools more generally.

Boys at the Dharwar school spent half their time in the classroom reading, writing, and simple arithmetic in the vernacular language, and half in the workshop, developing practical skills in carpentry and blacksmithing. The entire course lasted five years, during which boys moved through a sequence of progressively difficult levels of their crafts. In the first standard, for instance, students were expected to be able to plane and square a piece of wood; by the third standard they were supposed to have mastered the construction of simple door frames and desk-boxes and the basics of iron work; by the fifth and final standard they were required to be able to do any carpentry work assigned to them and to fit up a small working model steam engine (Government of Bombay 1875: 149–50). As they advanced through the standards, the boys were also supposed to master more general principles of efficiency, accuracy, precision, and diligence.

For K.M. Chatfield, the Director of Public Instruction for the Bombay Presidency, Dharwar was the perfect site for industrial education. Due to the existing saw mill, the school started with good buildings and a cheap supply of the best timber. Perhaps most importantly, it also started in 'a large and rich district requiring trained artisans for special industries, and little to no competition in t[he] local market due to dearth of skilled labour'.[2] In trying to supply that skilled labour, Dharwar officials targeted boys from artisanal families to be its students. As in other industrial schools in the Presidency, the Dharwar school hoped to modernize existing artisanal skills and technologies. The point, as John Wallace, editor of the *Indian Textile Journal* in Bombay, articulated later at the 1907 Indian Industrial Conference in Surat, was 'to improve the efficiency of the native craftsman so that he may turn out more and better work and get a better return for his labour' (Indian Industrial Conference 1908: 53). Regular examinations every six months ensured timely progress towards these lofty goals. And indeed they did make progress. In his annual report for 1880, Dharwar school superintendent H.W. Lewis noted success rates at all levels of instruction: four out of five had passed in first standard; four out of four in second; nine out of ten in third; six out of six in fourth; and five out of five in the fifth and final standard.[3]

As they passed their exams and mastered more advanced skills, students were to leave old artisanal methods behind in favour of a more modern way of production. For, along with their manual skills, the Dharwar school tried to teach its students better use of tools, more rigorous quality standards, and the value of time. As Lewis' students in 1880 worked on furniture, carts, carriages, railings for a new tank, boxes, and frames, they were subject to strict cost accounting and close supervision.[4] Through school efforts, boys were to become more efficient and disciplined, capable of meeting new demands for complicated furniture and household fittings. It is important to note, however, that they were not to aspire to much more than that: for all the talk of developing artisanal prospects, Dharwar school officials carefully avoided disrupting the existing caste-based division of labour by which lower castes were supposed to do the labouring and upper castes the thinking. Indeed, theoretical principles, advanced book study of any kind, and the English necessary for advanced studies were all explicitly left out of the curriculum at Dharwar in favour of classes in the vernacular that taught hands-on techniques and provided the most rudimentary literary education (Government of Bombay 1875, Appendix C: 149). This was entirely in keeping with the thrust of industrial education, which was conceived as quite distinct from the primary education that led to secondary school and non-manual employment. Indeed, industrial education as a whole was supposed to keep boys out of that other track. As the Government of India put it in 1904, industrial education for an artisanal boy aimed at 'giving him a general education which will enlarge his prospects as a craftsman *while preventing him from falling into the clerical groove*' (Clibborn *et al.* 1903, Part II: 6. Italics added). Too much literary education would, as Government of India Revenue and Agricultural Department Secretary E.C. Buck put it, 'make boys dissatisfied with an artizan's [*sic*] careers; that they would ... "get their heads in the air"' (Buck 1901: 20).

THE DHARWAR SCHOOL OF INDUSTRY: ARTISANAL REACTIONS

For officials at Dharwar, their school represented the perfect solution to the problems and needs of local artisans; rigorous instruction and regular examination would teach students more efficient practices and better work discipline—both necessary for the improvement of local industries. Local artisans, however, apparently saw things somewhat differently. Indeed, artisans in Dharwar and elsewhere seem to have had little to do with industrial education, only rarely enrolling their boys in industrial schools. In 1879 H.W. Lewis reported that out of the total of thirty-six boys actively enrolled, only five were officially of artisan or carpenter castes.[5] Two years later—the last year for which the caste composition of the student body was provided—the proportions were roughly similar, with only seven artisans out of the thirty-eight boys then attending school.[6] In Dharwar as in other parts of the Presidency and beyond, the school seemed to serve the lower classes generally, rather than artisans particularly.

Dharwar school officials insisted that the entire course was essential for achieving the skill levels needed for personal profit as well as industrial advancement, and tried out a variety of ways to force or encourage students to attend regularly and to stay for all five years. Unlike their instructors, however, students had no such commitment to the fixed terms of instruction. Attendance was sporadic at best: in 1880 the average attendance was only twenty-seven out of a total of fifty-two students officially on the rolls.[7] Those who did come rarely stayed for very long, with many dropping out after only one or two of the prescribed five standards.[8] Taking the positive view, some students seem to have been able to derive benefit from relatively limited schooling. As one member of the school's advisory board noted, once boys made even a small amount of progress in the school, they found they could earn more elsewhere, and so quit their studies for more remunerative employment.[9] From a more critical perspective, however, other students seem to have dropped out because they saw little benefit in the skills taught. This was a problem shared generally across industrial schools. In a highly critical resolution on the state of industrial education in 1904, the Government of India itself noted that 'the teaching given [in industrial schools] does not provide a training of a sufficiently high standard to enable them to hold their own with artisans who have learnt their craft in the bazaar.'[10]

If, as the government admitted, boys could learn as well or better through ordinary instruction in the bazaar, there was little incentive for artisans to embrace industrial education. Indeed, there were serious financial *disincentives* to sending boys to the Dharwar school. If a boy learned at home or in the workshop of a family member, he could begin contributing to family income immediately, whereas sending a boy to industrial school meant foregoing his earning potential during the period of instruction (Clibborn *et al.* 1903, Part II: 6; Nath 1906: 290). Not that boys earned nothing as students. The Dharwar school tried to make instruction more appealing by offering stipends, ranging from Re 1 a month for beginners to Rs 6 a month for the most advanced students.[11] For those at the higher levels, however, those stipends could not compete with wages available outside the school, which, for carpentry work, were estimated in 1882 at between Rs 10 and Rs 25 a month.[12] In times of economic uncertainty, as officials readily admitted, the opportunity cost of keeping boys in school was simply too high. For artisanal families, the poor instruction offered at industrial schools provided no real compensation for the financial sacrifice incurred.

Of course, economics was never the only influence on decisions about whether or not to send boys to industrial schools; there were strong cultural factors as well. As Nita Kumar has noted in her study of education in Banaras, colonial educational systems represented a threat to a community's ability both to define its own vision of the world and to socialize its youth into the ideals and skills of a particular profession (Kumar 2000: 13–37). There is no direct evidence of how local artisans perceived the offerings of the Dharwar school; we can only glean those perceptions through official reports on student composition and retention. It is not hard to imagine that many may have resented outside attempts to seize control over artisanal knowledge and practice. Nor is it unreasonable to think that parents may have feared that exposure to colonial education—even within the strict limits of what was offered in industrial schools—would tempt their sons away from familial professions. Given that very few boys who graduated from industrial schools did use their education in manual callings, those parents may well have been right.

This emphasis on artisanal reluctance to embrace industrial education is not meant to imply that artisans as a class were conservative or resistant to new opportunities. In the late nineteenth century, as Roy and Haynes have documented, artisans in western India were in the midst of sweeping changes, with people moving geographically in search of work, taking up new crafts, shifting out of household production into workshops, experimenting in diverse product lines, and adopting new materials and technologies (Roy 1999; Haynes 2001). Focusing on the craft at the heart of instruction at the Dharwar school—wood working—it is difficult to determine the precise nature of the changes in the region of the school. But elsewhere in the Bombay Presidency, the emergence of large-scale high-end furniture factories in Bombay and the proliferation of cruder varieties of furnishings provides evidence of adaptation and innovation among producers. Yet, it was precisely these artisans who, by and large, stayed aloof from carpentry classes offered in industrial schools.

Far from rejecting such schools for pushing too much change, some artisans may have rejected them for not offering enough. One of the few public groups to emerge in this period purely out of artisanal initiative, the Deccan Artisans' Association, was formed in Bombay in 1890 in order to improve the status of artisan groups through religious practice and secular measures including ensuring community access to 'technical and liberal education'. Run by representatives of the blacksmith, carpenter, coppersmith, mason, and goldsmith castes, the group hoped that by joining together they could better assert artisanal rights in the face of Brahmanical domination. As S.V. Kulkarni, the association's honorary secretary, put it, the group aimed to ameliorate 'the condition of the artisan class in general which, when compared with that of the self-opinionated and self-conceited so-called foremost races of the present day, owing to their having possessed manifold opportunities and diverse means to keep us back by the exercise of legal repressive—rather oppressive—measures at their command, socially, intellectually, politically and in various other ways'.[13] What these artisans wanted was not better training in manual skills and labour diligence but access to the full range of education by which they could move up the social ladder into positions of social, intellectual, and economic prominence. That the association was primarily interested in professional as opposed to craft advancement is suggested by the fact that its top office bearers were all in non-manual fields: the president, Bapuji Krishnarao Trilokya, for instance, was a retired government clerk, while Kulkarni was a sub-postmaster in Bombay.[14] Through their association, these men hoped to help other artisans get access to professional jobs; they demanded not industrial education but primary and secondary literary studies to prepare artisans to become leaders of industry and society.

INDUSTRIAL SCHOOLS: ASSESSMENT

The Dharwar school closed in 1883, after only ten years of operation. After years of high costs the government decided the educational needs of the district could be better and more cheaply served by training boys as apprentices at a new government railway workshop. The problems that plagued the Dharwar school—low attendance, failure to attract and retain boys from artisan castes, and high costs—were common to many of the industrial schools opened in western India.[15] Indeed, although some schools survived into the 1920s and beyond, many others closed much earlier. Makrand Mehta has estimated that the failure rate of industrial schools was more than 70 per cent, with government schools faring not much better than those operated by missionary or private initiative (Mehta 1992: 147–9).

Despite these evident problems, however, most observers called for *more* industrial education—albeit on improved lines—not less. Why invest so much time, money, and energy in such schools, for such poor returns? Why did government officials and nationalist activists alike continue to support the ideal of industrial education when the reality proved so disappointing? Two factors seem to have been central: elite concerns about crafts as a crucial but underperforming sector of the economy and elite understandings of the problems in crafts.

Representing 95 per cent of overall Indian industrial output in 1900, crafts were far too important to be ignored in late nineteenth century conversations about how to move the economy forward (Roy 1999: 6). Not that there was much agreement on the future of crafts. Nationalist activists like Ranade and Joshi argued that India's future lay in heavy, modern industry: crafts would and should give way to factory production along the lines of the West. As the Marathi newspaper *Kesari* put it in July of 1900, 'India cannot depend very long upon manual industries. Government should teach them [*sic*] to turn out industrial products, which are at present imported into India from abroad, by means of the latest inventions of science' (quoted in Government of Bombay 1900: 25). Others, however, argued that crafts had a more positive role to play. Figures as diverse as E.B. Havell, Alfred Chatterton, Aurobindo Ghose, and ultimately M.K. Gandhi argued in their own different ways for a cultural, spiritual, and economic revival of India on Indian terms; instead of building heavy industries, India should develop cottage industries, taking into account their dominance of overall production in the subcontinent and their suitability to Indian conditions. Whatever the future of crafts, though, all agreed on the need to develop them in the present, whether as a stop-gap measure to prevent unemployment or social dislocation while awaiting the inevitable transition to modern industry, or as the only sensible investment in India-specific development. In the late nineteenth century, the needs of crafts were thought to be better training and technologies for artisans. Vigorous industrial modernizers and go-slow traditionalists alike, most saw artisans as impediments to change, and schools as a means of inspiring progress.

Descriptions from the late nineteenth and early twentieth centuries almost always characterized artisans as stubbornly conservative and resistant to change. Author after author—from contributors to Indian reformist magazines like the *Buddhiprakash* (Ahmedabad) and *The Indian Review* (Madras), to top officials in the India Office in London— complained that, even when shown new technologies that would improve the quantity or quality of products, artisans refused to change, preferring to cling to their time-honoured, traditional ways (see, for example, Wardle 1890). Prem Behari, for instance, a delegate from the United Provinces to the first Indian Industrial Conference in Banaras in 1905, declared that all Indian artisans 'are averse to invention and reform, they will not move a step beyond the limits to which their grandfathers and great grandfathers advanced'. To prove this, he narrated the story of a low-caste weaver in Agra who, 'when he was asked to work on the imported Serampore loom, replied that he could not work on the loom, and if he did, he would be excommunicated from the caste. Such are the traditional training and religious prejudices of the illiterate class'. Behari's conclusion was that it was, 'therefore, extremely desirable that at least primary education should be given to the masses' (Behari 1906: xxxiii).

At its core, Behari's demand for outside education was based on a denial of artisanal change and initiative. In this he was not alone. Even though it was in the 1870s that Dutt, Ranade, and others began formulating their critiques of the imperial economic system, neither they nor those arguing for colonialism's economic benevolence saw artisans as in any way produced by the colonial setting. Instead, as Chandavarkar argues, elites in the late nineteenth century sought to deny labour's modernity, preferring to see artisans as traditionalist relics from an earlier time (Chandavarkar 1998: 1–29). Thus government industrial official Alfred Chatterton could offer the following description as late as 1906: 'As their forefathers worked, so do the artisans of today; without capital, without organisation, without machinery or mechanical assistance, and with only the tools and appliances in common use before the modern manufacturing era began' (Chatterton 1906: 23; for similar views see Nath 1906: 288–9).

For those like Behari and Chatterton who assumed that artisans resisted change, responsibility for the main problems of artisanal production lay with the artisans themselves, not with the colonial conditions that denied them capital and limited their access to modern machinery. For Behari, only outside education could disrupt 'traditional training and religious prejudices' and open artisans up to new ways of working. Ignoring all evidence of artisanal innovation, adaptation and initiative, late nineteenth- and early twentieth-century elites assumed that school officials were the only possible agents of change. British officials shared this assumption with many of the most committed Indian nationalists of the time. Indeed, what is striking about the commitment to industrial education is its essentially elite—rather than racial—nature. Whether at the heart of the government or agitating from outside, elite British and Indian industrial activists agreed that traditional industries were too important to leave in artisanal hands. From this perspective, the concern for industrial education was less about creating artisanal opportunities than it was about sectoral improvement—hence the conservative nature of that education in trying to limit occupational change or disruption.

CONCLUSION

The movement to found industrial schools did not emerge from a precise understanding of artisanal practices or how they were changing in response to developments in the colonial economy. School founders rarely seemed aware of the new industrial information emerging at the time in government gazetteers, which indicated artisans had access to new materials, faced competition from imports, and enjoyed wider opportunities for regional trade. Nor did school officials seem to have undertaken their own surveys of artisans to assess local needs around which to design school curricula. Instead, industrial education was based on assumptions that artisans were backward and needed new technologies and practices, that they could not manage to modernize on their own and so needed outside help, that schools would be an ideal way of imparting new information, and that artisans should be educated to be better labour but no more.

The failures of the Dharwar school suggest some of the limitations of those assumptions. The school did try to introduce modern methods and technologies, including new tools, perspective drawings, and western standards of measurement. Yet, since few artisan boys enrolled, the school could hardly claim to wholly re-fashion existing practices. Artisans preferred traditional means of instruction for financial as well as cultural reasons. When they did attend institutions like the one in Dharwar, school lessons seem to have complemented rather than replaced other sources of knowledge and training, which remained rooted in socially and culturally defined relationships of family, caste, and community. Other problems with the assumptions become visible through evidence from elsewhere in the Bombay Presidency. Developments in furniture production point to successful artisanal initiative both in the organization of the industry and in continual product development. The Deccan Artisans' Association, for its part, suggests that not all artisans were content with the limitations of industrial education, but aspired to move well beyond manual labour into the comfortable position of government employment.

Industrial education for artisans aimed to transform traditional industries. But it aimed to do so in an essentially conservative way, both in terms of educational goals and in terms of educational vision. Thanks to the skills and technologies imparted, artisans were to improve, but within existing lines of occupational division and power. That change, in turn, was to come only from the outside, from the benevolent interest of elite leaders, both British and Indian. Industrial education as such was to support and perpetuate the existing divisions within colonial society.

NOTES

1. Baroda State 1903: 19; for carpet weaving in Ahmednagar, see the records of the American Board of Commissioners for Foreign Missions, Houghton Library, Harvard University: see in particular Unit 4, vol. 31, Reel 425 (1901–9, letters M-W from the Marathi mission).
2. K.M. Chatfield, Director of Public Instruction, to Chief Secretary to Government, Educational Department, 11 November 1879. Maharashtra State Archives (hereafter MSA): Education Department (hereafter ED) 1880: v. 19, c. #8: 14.
3. H.W. Lewis, Superintendent, School of Industry at Dharwar, to Educational Inspector, Southern Division, 22 April 1880. MSA: ED 1880: v. 19, c. #8: 125.
4. Ibid.
5. See H.W. Lewis, Superintendent, Dharwar School of Industry, to J. Elphinston, Collector of Dharwar, 20 September 1879. MSA: ED 1880: v. 19, c. #8: 87.
6. Report from J.R. Middleton, Acting Collector at Dharwar, included in Arthur Crawford, Commissioner, Southern Division, to C. Gonne, Chief Secretary to Government, 5 September 1881. MSA: ED 1882: v. 31, c. #37: 227.
7. H.G. Pollisen, Executive Engineer, Irrigation Department, to J. Elphinston, Collector of Dharwar, 23 September 1879. MSA: ED 1880: v. 19, c. #8: 45.
8. See K.M. Chatfield to C. Gonne, Secretary to Government, Educational Department, 24 November 1876. MSA: ED 1876: v. 25, c. #50: 137, and Clibborn *et al.* 1903, Part I: 8–9.
9. H.G. Pollisen, Executive Engineer, Irrigation Department, to J. Elphinston, Collector of Dharwar, 23 September 1879. MSA: ED 1880: v. 19, c. #8: 46.
10. In the Government Resolution on Education Policy, 11 March 1904, quoted in Nurullah and Naik 1951: 696.

11. K.M. Chatfield, Director of Public Instruction, to Chief Secretary to Government, Educational Department, 11 November 1879. MSA: ED 1880: v. 19, c. #8.

12. Arthur Crawford, Commissioner of Southern Division, to C. Gonne, Chief Secretary to Government, 5 September 1881. MSA: ED 1882: v. 31, c. #37: 191.

13. S.V. Kulkarni, General Secretary, Deccan Artisans' Association, Bombay, to W. Lee-Werner, Secretary to Government of Bombay, 22 February 1893. MSA: ED 1893: v. 27, c. #313.

14. Commissioner of Police, Bombay, to W. Lee-Werner, Secretary to Government of Bombay, 17 March 1893. MSA: ED 1893: v. 27, c. #313.

15. For a general overview of the problems with industrial education in the Bombay Presidency in particular, see the report by E. Giles, A.W. Thomson and Cecil Burns, to Secretary to Government, Educational Department, 13 January 1902. MSA: ED 1902: v. 62, c.# 7: 98–100.

REFERENCES

Baroda State. 1903. *Report on the Administration of the Baroda State for the Official Year Ending 31st July 1901*. Baroda: Government Press.

Behari, Prem. 1906. 'Industrial Development of India'. In Indian Industrial Conference 1906, pp. xxx–xxxv.

Bhabha, Homi. 1994. 'Of Mimicry and Man: The Ambivalence of Colonial Discourse'. In Homi Bhabha. *The Location of Culture*. New York: Routledge. 1994, pp. 85–92.

Buck, E.C. 1901. *Report on Practical and Technical Education*. Calcutta: Office of the Superintendent of Government Printing.

Chandavarkar, Rajnarayan. 1998. *Imperial Power and Popular Politics: Class, Resistance and the State in India, c. 1850–1950*. Cambridge: Cambridge University Press.

Chandra, Bipan. 1966. *The Rise and Growth of Economic Nationalism in India*. New Delhi: People's Publishing House.

Chatterton, Alfred. 1904. *Agricultural and Industrial Problems in India*. Madras: G.A. Nateson & Co.

———. 1906. 'Industrial Work in India'. In *The Congress and Conference of 1905, Being a Collection of all the Papers Read and Submitted to the First Industrial Conference at Benares*. Madras: G.A. Natesan & Co., 1906, pp. 22–7.

Clibborn, Lieutenant-Colonel J. *et al.* 1903. *Report on Industrial Education, Parts I and II*. Calcutta: Superintendent of Government Printing.

Goswami, Manu. 2004. *Producing India: From Colonial Economy to National Space*. Chicago: University of Chicago Press.

Government of Bombay. 1875. *Report of the Director of Public Instruction in the Bombay Presidency for the Year 1874–75*. Bombay: Government Central Press.

———. 1886. *Report of the Director of Public Instruction in the Bombay Presidency for the Year 1885–86*. Bombay: Government Central Press.

———. 1899. *Report of the Director of Public Instruction in the Bombay Presidency for the Year 1898–99*. Bombay: Government Central Press.

———. 1900. *Report on Native Papers Published in the Bombay Presidency for the Week ending 28th July 1900*. Bombay: Government Central Press.

———. 1939. *A Compendium of Art, Arts and Crafts, Technical, Industrial, Commercial, Agricultural and Veterinary Institutions in the Province of Bombay*. Bombay: Government Central Press.

Haynes, Douglas. 2001. 'Artisan Cloth-Producers and the Emergence of Powerloom Manufacture in Western India, 1920–1950'. *Past and Present*. vol. 172 (August), pp. 170–98.

Indian Industrial Conference. 1906. *Report of the First Indian Industrial Conference Held at Benaras on Saturday, the 30th December, 1905*. Allahabad: The Indian Press.

———. 1908. *Report of the Third Industrial Conference Held at Surat on the 30th December 1907*. Madras: Indian Industrial Conference.

Kale, B.G. 1911. 'Small Industries in India'. The *Indian Review*. vol. 12, no. 1 (January), pp. 74–8.

Kumar, Nita. 2000. *Lessons from Schools: The History of Education in Banaras*. New Delhi: Sage Publications.

Ludden, David. 1992. 'India's Development Regime'. In Nicholas Dirks (ed.). *Colonialism and Culture*. Ann Arbor: University of Michigan Press, 1992, pp. 247–88.

Mehta, Makrand. 1992. 'Science Versus Technology: The Early Years of the Kala Bhavan, Baroda, 1890–1896', *Indian Journal of History and Science*. vol. 2, no. 27, pp. 145–69.

Metcalf, Thomas. 1995. *Ideologies of the Raj*. Cambridge: Cambridge University Press.

Mudholkar, R.N. 1909. 'Presidential Address'. In Indian Industrial Conference, *The Industrial Conference Held at Madras, December 1908*. Madras: G.A. Nateson, pp. 48–9.

Naregal, Veena. 2001. *Language Politics, Elites and the Public Sphere: Western India Under Colonialism*. London: Anthem Press.

Nath, Lala Baji. 1906. 'On Some of the Leading Industries of Upper India'. In Indian Industrial Conference 1906, pp. 302–21.

Nurullah, Syed and J.P. Naik. 1951. *A History of Education in India During the British Period*. Bombay: Macmillan & Co.

Prakash, Gyan. 1999. *Another Reason: Science and the Imagination of Modern India*. Princeton: Princeton University Press.

Roy, Tirthankar. 1999. *Traditional Industry in the Economy of Colonial India*. Cambridge: Cambridge University Press.

Sinha, Mrinalini. 1995. *Colonial Masculinity: The 'Manly Englishman' and the 'Effeminate Bengali' in the Late Nineteenth Century*. New York: Manchester University Press.

Viswanathan, Gauri. 1989. *Masks of Conquest: Literary Study and British Rule in India*. New York: Columbia University Press.

Wardle, Thomas. 1890. *Tissue or Textile Printing As an Art: A Lecture Delivered at the Manchester Municipal School of Art Museum on Wednesday, March 15, 1890*. Manchester: Marsden & Co.

7

BEY EKA BEY, BEY DONI CHAR (TWO TIMES ONE IS TWO, TWO TIMES TWO IS FOUR)
Dalit Women's Schooling

Shailaja Paik

You see, really and truly, apart from the things anyone can pick up (the dressing and the other proper way of speaking, and so on), the difference between a lady and a flower girl is not how she behaves, but how she is treated. I shall always be a flower girl to Professor Higgins, because he always treats me as a flower girl, and always will; but I know I can be a lady to you, because you always treat me as a lady, and always will.

> Shaw's summary of *Pygmalion* (Rosenthal and Jacobson 1992)

In this chapter we will listen to the voices of Dalit girls and women[1] who have struggled against all impediments to intrude into fortresses of knowledge that were under the hegemony of Brahmans. We will pursue some formidable questions about the role of Dalit parents in the lives of these women. I will chart the 'matrix of domination' (Collins 2000: 251), complicating it further by uncovering the interplay of caste, class, and the educational system on the one hand, and patriarchy and matriarchy on the other, attempting to unearth how this matrix of domination results in a renewed oppression of Dalit girls. For Dalits in general, education represents a quest for a liberating modernity. For women, this quest creates spaces where they can contest male domination or at least pursue their own interests and inclinations (Sangari and Vaid 1989: 12).

The findings presented here are based on interviews with 180 women conducted in Pune during 2000–2 and from June–November 2004. Most of the women I interviewed were first-generation learners, the first people from their community to enter schools. The teacher was usually Brahman and the phenomenon of a mixed-class, mixed-caste classroom was a new experience for the girls. Interviewed now, as grown women, they remembered their schooling as a very troublesome process, with the hurdles multiplying and the oppression becoming more complex the farther they went in school. Caste, gender, and class were accompanied by the often insidious play of educational institutions, which tried to suppress these new entrants. Social structures, cultural forces, and the education system operate synchronously to constrain the thoughts and actions of Dalit girls. Despite these impediments, significant numbers of Dalit girls have successfully completed their education at various levels. I will focus first on their problems in gaining admission to educational institutions, then on their experiences in education, and finally on the caste-based discrimination that they faced in school.

ADMISSION TO SCHOOL

Most of my respondents who were first-generation learners stated that their parents put them into the nearest available school for the sake of convenience, regardless of its quality. The parents were happy that they could at least send their children to a school. The exuberance of 'entering' the citadels of schools so long denied to them was a strong motivating force. Kamal Jadhav remembered, 'There was a co-ed school that was a little far away. There was another school only for girls, but that was too far. So we went to this government school in the police quarters. This school was close to our house, and had the added benefit of classes till HSC [Higher Secondary Certificate].'

It was generally necessary to travel a long distance to a town for further studies. This created great difficulty for girls. Shantabai Kamble's autobiography states:

I passed Class 6. For Class 7, I had to go to Pandharpur or join the technical school with the boys. I had no money to go to Pandharpur and Patil Master doubted how I could cope with the boys. However, after a few months, Kamble Guruji enquired about me and made me join the technical school. I was the only girl in the school. I felt left out. I engaged in all the jobs done by the boys. At the end of the year, I had to go to Pandharpur to appear for the exams. When the results were out, my cousin and I had cleared the exams (Kamble 1986: 36).

Shantabai was the only girl—Dalit or non-Dalit—in this technical school. Such schools focused on agricultural skills that were seen to be male preserves, such as using agricultural implements, ploughing, sowing, reaping, and carpentry, and girls were discouraged from attending. Upper-caste girls generally went to the regular high school in Pandharpur town.

Distance made a great difference in the towns and cities also, as travel on public transport was often both expensive and considered unsafe for girls. Urmila Pawar described her school days as follows:

Ratnagiri was a very small district and had small schools and colleges in the heart of the jilha [district]. Our school was about twenty minutes away. The school was in the taluka place and most of the parents did not allow girls to travel that far. They were *scared*. My case wouldn't have been different as my mother was all alone after my father passed away. However, my case was different as my father was a teacher and my mother religiously followed his last instructions of sending all of us to school. I could study ahead ....

In most cases, such considerations resulted in town-dwelling Dalit girls' education coming to an end after class 4 or 7.

This was an obstacle that girls faced even in a big city like Pune. Pune's social cartography caused Dalits to be distanced from the major educational and cultural facilities. The heart of the city, Sadashiv Peth, is the 'social polis'—the cultural capital—of Pune, replete with prestigious high schools and colleges, as well as research institutes, medical colleges, music schools, and well-known theatres. It is dominated by middle-class Brahmans and other upper castes. Other, lower communities, who have no space here, live in small, cramped quarters in the surrounding neighbourhoods. As in villages, the lower castes are clustered around a section with superior buildings and facilities that is inhabited by the high castes. The Dalit areas are even more peripheral, right on the margins of the city. Educational space has not been devised with the Dalits in mind. They would have to travel long distances to get to the better schools, and they lack the time or resources to do this. In effect, they are denied access to the superior educational institutions of the Sadashiv Peth area. Dalits often speak longingly about these schools in the heart of the city.

Though the municipality provides schools free of cost, they are of very low quality, characterized by absent teachers, bad teaching, easy progress from one class to the other, few or no facilities for students or teachers, and poor teaching aids. Dalits send their children to such schools because they lack the money, the time, the influence, or the knowledge to send them to better schools. Although the municipality even provides some educational accessories—bags, shoes, uniforms, books, and meals—free of charge, very few of my informants knew about these facilities and even fewer had availed them.

Along with proximity, parents also preferred to send their children to schools where other Dalit children went. The child was supposed to be 'safe' in the company of these other children. Meera's slum was home to most of her relatives, and all of them went to the same school together. 'We had two schools, but all my cousins went to one school, the nearest one available .... My mother used to work all day, and our great-aunt kept watch on us.' Girls in general, and pubescent girls in particular, were subjected not only to the schools' Foucauldian surveillance, but also to that of their parents and relatives. Hence, proximity of the institution was a requirement.

Another important reason for selecting the nearest school is that many mothers have to rear children in the absence of fathers who earn a living away from home. The uneducated mothers probably do not know much about other institutions; furthermore, they fear for the safety of their daughters if they have to travel long distances on public transport each day. For example, Kamal, whose father was absent most of the time, was still upset that her mother did not send her to high school on the grounds that the school was too far from their home. Her mother was handling all the private and public affairs of the family and did not want any added bother about the daughter's physical safety while travelling. She therefore discouraged Kamal's higher education. Sandhya also remembered her mother's indifferent attitude towards her higher education:

She was all right when I went to school. But, when the college was far she said that I should not travel by bus that far, as it was *dangerous*. So, I lost the first few months of college due to that. But later on I insisted on going to college and started making small beginnings. I started taking the bus and did it confidently. *She* then allowed me to travel when *she* found it comfortable. However, I pursued my Masters.

We thus find that the mothers acted as matriarchs, dominating and restricting the girls. These girls now had to fight matriarchy plus patriarchy. Sarah Lamb (2003) writes insightfully about the position of the wives when their husbands are away for jobs. Women shoulder all responsibilities of the household in the absence of men. However, the mother's overprotection not only bounded the physical space of the girls but also led to their self-abasement (cf. Steedman 1986: 106). It had a psychological impact on the girls, and it obstructed their fight for further education. The mothers' projection of fears and anxiety led to a growing diffidence among the Dalit girls and restricted their interaction with other groups in society during school and sometimes even during higher education. The triple oppression of caste, class, and gender made the mothers chain their daughters.

Grinding poverty, increased unemployment, and community distress all served to restrict the kind of support and recognition that parents could allocate to their children's education. School-going Dalit girls were highly privileged to go to school, whatever the circumstances and whatever the quality of the school. Kamal Jadhav commented, 'The standard and medium of the school did not matter at all. We could attend school, that was more than enough.' Sarita Bhalerao poignantly remarked:

We went to the nearest available school and were *privileged to get whatever we could*, compared to our cousins in the village. They remained illiterate and continued with small farming. At least we could study a little and get our children educated. My father could afford to send me to school, as there were no fees and may be if there were, I wouldn't have been there. In those times nobody knew about education or the benefits of education.... If a child was registered in school but did not attend, then the peons used to come and take that child to school.

Draupadi seconded this and added, 'If our parents were to pay fees, only boys would have been sent and girls would have never seen the school gates'. These women are aware of the concession they procured and also of the gender discrimination they were subjected to. These were exceptional cases: the large majority of Dalit women knew nothing about schools, fee concessions, or any other benefits that were available to them.

EXPERIENCES AT SCHOOL

After Independence, the Government of India allocated considerable resources to make education available to the masses. The Constitution spoke of the duty to provide for the depressed sections of society. The Five-Year plans allocated a good percentage to the education sector. The government framed various policies to open government schools that provided free uniforms, books, bags, meals, milk, and cost-free education. A few of my informants had taken advantage of these schemes. Snehlata said that her school, run by the district authorities, went up to class 7, and that later she went to the Gram Shikshan Sanstha. 'I got a uniform, meals, milk, and books till the class 4 only. We did not have to pay any fees.' Sometimes these facilities provided by the government have proved to be the only way to increase attendance. 'We went to the school just to get the sweet powder,' said Meera. Most of my informants, however, said that they knew nothing of any such facilities. It seems that in most cases they existed only on paper. It is possible that the funding was appropriated in a corrupt way.

Urmila reported that she got free textbooks until class 4, and that after that her parents had to buy them:

We always bought third- and fourth-hand books, whatever we could get for studies, with whatever we could understand before, after, under, and amidst the graffiti. All this was bought at the cheapest available rates, as my mother didn't give much money. There were all kinds of pictures in the books: animals, humans, trees, glasses, goggles, names of girls and boys, messages of love, poems, criticisms, filthy language ... all kinds of things were written there.

Urmila also remembered how she used old exercise books and text books: 'I used exercise books made of old papers and did not trouble my parents for newer ones,' she said. Champabai mentioned that she did not have exercise books:

I used a slate till the 7th class. Most children of our caste had only text books. We didn't know exercise books, a pen, or a pencil at all. I scribbled all my homework and even the class room study on one slate. And I remember we used to write everything in just one book; all subjects in one book. My mother bought books very rarely and father didn't pay much attention. He didn't know much about my school or my schooling. He never bothered to enquire about it. This was the case with most of the parents of the lower castes.

This was one reason why some of the girls kept away from school. Another issue was clothing. In some cases, Dalit parents could not afford to buy the necessary uniforms, or they could not replace them when they became worn out. It was common for teachers, peons, and others to comment on the students' lower-caste backgrounds, their poverty, and their threadbare uniforms in a way that reproduced stereotypical images of 'dirty' Dalits. For example, Bharati's teachers and fellow students mocked her mercilessly because she did not dress well for school. 'I used to also feel ashamed of my dress and got a lot of beatings from my teachers. He said *our* clothes were always dirty.' This provides another instance of the way the education system reinforces wider forms of social discrimination.

The prevailing ethos in the schools was that of Brahmanical respectability, and this inevitably affected Dalit girls. The dress code associated with Brahmans, such as their style of draping a sari, and their supposed standards of hygiene were considered to be superior. Kamal stated, 'We liked to dress up like them. We wanted to drape saris like the Brahmans did.' The Dalit girls made minute observations of Brahman life: food habits, vegetarianism, consumption of ghee, and cooking practices. They tried to imitate the 'pure' (nasal toned) Marathi spoken by Brahmans. They preferred to wear the sober colours associated with the dress of the Brahmans, avoiding jazzy colours and 'vulgar' fashions.

The teachers and upper-caste students crippled the identity of the Dalits to such an extent that these women were left with a reinforced sense of their cultural unworthiness, even if they themselves at times did not consider the dominant culture legitimate. This is reflected in the everyday lives of many Dalits, who tend to disparage their own medicinal knowledge, art works, traditions, culture, and crafts, and to imitate 'purer' forms of language, dress, food, occupation, culture, and pedagogy. Some have shed a last name that signifies their Dalit origin and have taken the kind of village name with the suffix 'kar' that is associated with upper castes. For example, some members of the Nagare family have changed the name to Nagarkar. A few have discarded their traditional drums, singing, and so on. Sandhya's son, who is studying genetics, underscored, 'things can be learned only from the Brahmans. They tell you how to live, how to fight and progress in life'. He said that he would marry only a Brahman girl.

Many Dalit respondents complained that they received very little moral support for or input into their education at home. According to Meera:

My father was a drunkard and beat up my mother. My mother used to run to her aunt's place along with her children to protect herself from the drunkard husband. It was difficult to attend school. I never studied at home. There was no space at home. Whatever was taught was only at school. I also did not like to study at home because of some comments made. Our relatives used to visit us sometimes. If they ever saw me with a book, they used to ask me what future I had with those books. We were to sell glass, tin, and rags, they said. Why study then? They also told my mother that I should not be educated much and suggested that she stop my schooling. But my mother did not listen to them.

Few uneducated Dalit parents had any understanding of what education entailed. This was a grave handicap to their daughters and sons in their education. In fact, the different values that were inculcated in schools could cause problems for the children at home.

Many Dalits, in common with people in general in India, feel that higher studies or certain professions are fit only for certain castes. This is seen in a number of popular Marathi proverbs. For example, 'Shikshan, vyapaar karava tar Brahmananich/marwadyane, Maharani nahi ('Education is for the Brahmans; business is to be done only by Marwaris [Banias] and not by a Mahar.') or, 'brahmana ghari ved-purana, kunbya ghari dana, ani mahara ghari gana' ('Education is the arena of Brahmans, agriculture is for the peasant, and singing and dancing are for the Mahars.'). Some of the parents of the women I interviewed held this attitude about their daughters. Poonam's father, for example, had very low aspirations for her, disrespecting her abilities and her own aspirations, despite her brilliant performance in school. He did not want to spend money on science education for her and demanded that she take up arts or commerce, which was cheaper. He also thought that science and engineering were for men, and not good for girls. 'What are girls going to do with science and engineering?' he asked. In this unique case, Poonam's mother supported her daughter's decision to take up the subject of her choice.

In my observation, lower- and middle-class men of the lower castes generally have very low aspirations. They think that they themselves and their children are mediocre and do not possess the ability or resourcefulness to strive for or attain greater heights. The effect of this is much less pronounced in families in which the second or third generation of getting educated, and mothers are able to groom their daughters for educational success. Manini, Malavika, and her brother were thus under constant pressure to perform better. Both the sisters emphasized that their parents made them study science against their will, as they wanted them to be doctors. When I asked their mother about this, she said:

There was no doctor or any other professional of that high rank in my house. Most of them were in clerical services or were teachers. [My husband and I] were both earning and we thought that we could afford good education for our children. We had no facilities or choices, but we could bestow them upon our children. Hence we did not take into consideration the children's choices. Also we did not think about their non-English background and how they would have to fight the English world. Those were different times; we acted in a craze and pushed them towards these disciplines.

English represented a particular problem for many Dalit girls, particularly for those whose parents had the means to send them to English-medium schools. These schools were invariably private schools charging high tuition fees, and they were prestigious. Dalits for the most part had no access to such education, but where they did, they struggled due to the lack of any culture of speaking and reading English at home. Most of them suffered from an inferiority complex because of their deficiencies in this respect. Brahmans in particular have long been renowned for their abilities in English, and the Dalit girls inevitably compared themselves to them. Alaka stated:

Yes, I did find the English language difficult. It was my father who wanted me to study in English medium. I took up English literature as a challenge. There was a good job market for English teachers. My teachers in school and one in college taught English by explaining it in Marathi. Funny, isn't it? I was good at writing, but I couldn't speak. I couldn't clear some interviews as I could not speak fluently in English. However, I gradually picked it up on my own and today I teach English literature at a junior college.

Another problem for Dalit girls was that they were expected to carry out housework in addition to their studies. When I interviewed Bharati, she was cooking while her parents sat in another room with the door closed. She suffered from defective eyesight but was still made to work very hard. She lowered her voice and told me that at times she had been made to work from a very small age, as she was the eldest. She had to do all the housework and also take care of her siblings. She complained that she was harassed like a step-daughter. Housework was for girls alone; fathers and brothers hardly contributed to it at all. If their mother was ill, these daughters were expected to handle all the household responsibilities. Most of the time it was the mother who expected and made these girls serve the household. Many fathers did not interfere in these 'private' affairs.

Again and again, housework was pinpointed as a major problem for girls in education. They were left exhausted after school and housework, and hence could not complete their homework. Then they were afraid that if they attended school the next day they would be beaten for failing to do their homework. If anything, this problem was more pronounced among the better-off Dalits who had aspirations to join the middle classes, as they sought to impose a particular middle-class notion of female domesticity. Not only were the girls expected to perform mundane domestic tasks, they were also expected to do them well. Many middle-class Dalit parents want their daughters to fit into a 'middle-class' gruhini ('lady') mould. Mothers would, therefore, insist that their daughters engage in housework, cleaning utensils, washing clothes, rolling 'round' chapattis, decorating the home, and learning arts and crafts to please their future husbands. Alaka laughed when she remembered her mother's training: 'She asked us to do housework first and study later. We had to get up early mornings to study and do housework, which was equally important. She wanted us to be equally capable on all fronts.'

Not all parents acted like this. Manini and Malavika were never given any work at home. Swati Waghmare was busy in school and in playing cricket rather than doing housework. Prakshoti Pawar hated her house due to her parents' strictness and rebelled against any housework. These parents took immense interest in their children's work and inquired about their studies. Dr Harsha talked about her school days:

My mother taught us initially. Later father took over. He made me sit late in the nights solving arithmetic problems and I remember an incident in class 7. I used to just work out the easy problems, without paying attention to the difficult ones. I did not want any bother. My father sat with me the night before the exams. He started with all the tougher ones and beat me up till I found the logic of solving the problems. The exam went very well and to my surprise I scored full marks in my algebra paper. It was after that beating that I started to look at the root of any problem. This training has gone a long way in making me what I am today. The teachers could not do what my father did.

Informants often complained that teachers did not teach them well. Snehlata said:

I disliked geometry. It was in the 8th or 9th class when we had some geometric theorems. The teachers just copied them from the books to the board, one after the other, and told us to copy.... Nobody asked how the teacher derived the proof. Nobody dared to ask questions. I did ask once, but, with the response I got then, I never dared to ask anything after that. They did not reply properly, and only insulted us. We learned everything by heart. We just scraped through most of the time.

Jyotsna, who had attended a prestigious high school, added: 'Sometimes, if they were new, they were not able to teach properly. Some were not bothered if the class was understanding their lessons or not. Some of the college teachers were irresponsible. They sometimes did not complete the recommended syllabus for a subject. They also did not know much, could not explain well. So we had to join [extra coaching] classes.'

The teachers—who were commonly from a Brahman or upper-caste background—generally adopted an authoritarian manner, and were minutely sensitive to anything that might be taken as a challenge to their power. No questions could be asked or comments made. If somebody gathered enough courage to ask a question, she or he was trampled in an uncouth manner. This was a monologic form of pedagogy. No dialogue was entertained. Some scholars have argued that teachers may unconsciously treat low-caste children differently from other children or have reduced expectations of them (Khan 1993: 226).

The evidence for the Dalits shows, however, that the teachers often discriminated consciously.

Nonetheless, not all teachers act like this. A significant number of them have played a positive role for Dalits. Ambedkar's Brahman teacher, who gave Ambedkar his last name, is just one example. Poonam Rokade, an engineer, praised her teacher:

My teacher did help me in mathematics. He spent some extra time on my coaching and did not charge me any fees. The engineering syllabus was tough and I felt like dropping out at times. I repeatedly failed in one particular subject and I couldn't figure out the reason. I thought it was caste discrimination. However, one day I gathered the guts to face the teacher of that subject and asked him the reason for my failure in his subject alone. He was a Maratha.... He was good to me. He explained that my method of writing answers was faulty. I followed his advice and succeeded.

A few teachers took a keen interest and advised the students about their further opportunities. Sandhya Meshram said that when she told her teacher about her social work interests the teacher advised her to pursue a Masters in Social Welfare; Sandhya is happy with that decision. Occasionally teachers were innovative and implemented changes to interest and benefit low-caste students. Such tendencies were nonetheless exceptions rather than the rule. These rare teachers must have constantly faced the pulls and pushes, the tensions of their position in the social ladder and in the classroom, while wanting to bring about the best in their committed Dalit students.

Parents often complained about insecurity for girls attending schools. Instances of abduction, rape, and molestation of girls dampen the enthusiasm of both parents and girl students in pursuing education beyond a certain age; thereafter the girls remain bound to their homes. There have been numerous incidents in colleges and universities in Mumbai and Pune in which girls have been sexually abused. Newspapers are replete with such stories. Publicity by feminists has at least brought this to light, whereas before it was almost completely concealed. In my project, eve-teasing was found to be a particular problem in the slums. The only informant who was prepared to talk about this was Meera, who told me how she was abused by one of her teachers at a private mathematics class:

When I was in class 7 I used to attend 'Yash' classes [a pseudonym] for maths. We had a teacher who liked me very much. I didn't like him at all. He used to hold me close wherever I was. He bit me on my cheek once. I told my mother .... And my mother complained to the higher authorities and that person was then suspended. After that I did not go to any class.

CASTE DISCRIMINATION IN SCHOOLS

Some of my Dalit informants denied that they had faced caste discrimination at school. When the majority of their fellow pupils were from a Dalit or lower-caste background this was no doubt the case. Suvarna Kuchekar reported that her Marathi-medium corporation school was a haven for her, as most pupils were of low caste:

I did not face anything in school as it was a corporation school dominated by backward children. The teachers also even if from the open category [not in jobs reserved for Dalits or other low-caste people] did not trouble as such. My friends also know my caste and are fine with me. They come home and I go there and we are quite close. I have never hidden my caste.

In several cases, those who had attended schools with many high-caste children also denied that they had faced any discrimination. Nonetheless, from the expressions that I saw on their faces, I feel that they may have been blanking out humiliating memories.

Others were more frank. Bharati complained, 'Children teased me a lot. They said that I was from a "dirty caste" and so should stay away from them. They hid my bag and stole my only pen. So I did not like to go to school.' Mrs Kuchekar remembered how a Brahman teacher treated her in the 7th class: 'He was really harsh. He asked me, "What are you going to do with education?" He further continued, "These people will never improve. You will never understand this maths; it is not meant for you."' Monica Tapase said that although she used to obtain higher grades, her teachers encouraged and praised the 'others' (Brahman students), not her. 'In my case,' she said, 'they never acknowledged that I was doing well. I did not like it; however, I continued to study well to prove myself.' Kumud Pawde reported that Dalits were not allowed to touch the drinking utensils at school:

We had to drink water at the corporation tap, which was very far away. Then I wondered why should I do it, and I started to rebel. However the attendant

abused me badly and took me to the teacher. The teacher lady beat me with a
stick. Gadgil Sir taught us English in Class 5. He knew that I was good at English.
He always said that 'a Mahar girl was going ahead and you [others] are the
stones of the Narmada [river]'. I gradually progressed to class 8.

Sadhana Kharat, a teacher, said that the 'other' girls used to put
their skirts tucked in properly so that they would not touch hers when
they sat on the benches. 'They had separate groups also and stayed
away. I never had friends from the upper castes as such.' School friends
tended to be of the same caste. Jyotsna Rokade, Hira Kharat, and others
mentioned these impenetrable caste groups. Sudha Bhalerao, who
attended a Brahman-dominated college in the heart of Sadashiv
Peth, said, 'I preferred friends from my caste as they have a similar
background and that caste bond makes the relation stronger. The others
keep asking our background, our customs, our caste, gotra, and so on;
it becomes difficult to answer boldly.' Once again, Dalit students were
humiliated for not having this cultural capital.

Some Dalit girls pretended to be of a higher caste. Meena Mahajan
recalled that her name did not reveal that she was a Mahar. She said:

In school I told my friends that I was a Maratha. I had a terrible complex. I
thought that they would not talk to me if I revealed my caste. I saw how their
faces fell. Once when I was in Class 10, one teacher loudly asked me, 'You are
a Hindu-Mahar, right?' I felt so bad I stood with my head down. I was the
only one in that class. Further, I never told anyone my address in Mangalvar
Peth. The name itself reveals our Mahar *aali* [ghetto]. I don't tell my caste
openly even today. Why tell if it is not required? I declare that I am a Brahman.

In a few cases, Dalit girls deliberately courted high-caste friends.
Lalita Randhir, for example, said:

I have always preferred Brahman friends. My brother always had Brahman
friends. They came to our home but my brother never went to their place. He
picked up a lot from them. I also liked Brahman friends, because my mentality
and the mentality of the other Backward Caste students did not match, I did
not like their thinking, behaviour. [I looked down upon them.] In my school
and college I had some 'other' friends who liked me, as I was clean.

Thus these Dalit girls (including me once upon a time) thought that Dalits, including Dalit girls, were 'backward' and not good company to keep with. Caste and race are vicious phenomena in that they often cause one to look down on one's own brethren.

Champabai Bhalerao, a first-generation Mahar learner from Mumbai, said that she did not face any caste discrimination at all. She responded, 'I don't remember anything really significant when it comes to caste. My teacher was an Israeli. We were at her house the whole day. The other castes were also there, but there was nothing like caste discrimination. At that time Ambedkar's struggle was going strong and everybody was aware of it. So may be they knew that it would be very harmful if they behaved in that manner'. Champabai's teacher was a foreigner and, therefore, not likely to enforce Indian caste prejudices. In addition, most of the second- and third-generation learners who were in cities did not face caste discrimination.

CONCLUSION

Prakashachya Vatewar (On the road to enlightenment)[2]

The dark has only just turned	But to travel this road
The road seems clearer	One must get used to
I agree of course	Holding poison in
Religion, customs, traditions,	Let the throat turn blue!
Still cloud and obscure the view	We too will then know how to open the third eye.

The statements of the women I interviewed describe in vivid terms an important aspect of the Dalit struggle to enter the middle class. They were pursuing their education determinedly, as they believed it to be the remedy for all ills. These women's experiences raise thorny questions about Dalit patriarchy. Dalit girls are in 'quadruple jeopardy'. They are not only 'doubly bound' (Gay and Tate 1998: 169–84), like African-American women, but 'quadruply bound' by 'outsiders'— caste, class, and the education system—and 'insiders', their parents. However, this is not true in all cases. Some liberal-minded parents allow their daughters freedom, understand their aspirations and their struggle, and support them.

NOTES

1. I shall use the terms 'girls' and 'women' interchangeably. This is because, although the informants I interviewed included a few adult women, they were transported into their girlhood when they reflected on their school life.
2. 'Knowledge is Potent', a poem by Ravindra Pandhare, published in *Asmitadarsha* and translated by Eleanor Zelliot and Veena Deo in the *Journal of South Asian Literature*. vol. 29, no. 2 (Summer/Fall 1994), pp. 41–68.

REFERENCES

Collins, P.H. 2000 [1991]. *Black Feminist Thought: Knowledge, Consciousness and the Politics of Empowerment*. New York: Routledge.

Gay, C and K. Tate. 1998. 'Doubly Bound: The Impact of Gender and Race on the Politics of Black Women'. *Political Psychology*. vol. 19, no. 1, pp. 169–84.

Kamble, Shantabai. 1986. *Mazhya Jalmachi Chitrakatha* ('The Narrative Depiction of My Life'). Mumbai: Popular Prakashan.

Khan, Shahrukh. 1993. 'South Asia'. In Elizabeth M. King and M. Anne Hill (eds). *Women's Education in Developing Countries: Barriers, Benefits and Policies*. London and Baltimore: Johns Hopkins University Press.

Lamb, Sarah. 2003. 'The Beggared Mother: Older Women's Narratives in West Bengal'. In Gloria Goodwin Raheja (ed.). *Songs, Stories, Lives: Gendered Dialogue and Cultural Critique*. New Delhi: Kali for Women, pp. 54–75.

Rosenthal, Robert and Lenore Jacobson. 1992. *Pygmalion in the Classroom: Teacher's Expectation and Pupil's Intellectual Development*. New York: Irvington Publishers.

Sangari, K. and S. Vaid (eds). 1989. *Recasting Women: Essays in Colonial History*. New Delhi: Kali for Women.

Steedman, Carolyn. 1986. *Landscape for a Good Woman*. London: Virago.

8

BODIES IN PAIN
A People's History of 1971

Yasmin Saikia

E leanor Zelliot's scholarship must be understood as an 'emancipatory' discourse aimed at recognizing and voicing the 'oppressed' to bring about change in practices and institutions that limit human agency and discriminate between human beings. Power and dominance as much as social institutions of caste, class, religion, and gender that limit human freedom and sanction oppression, she has argued, must be questioned and exposed to render reform. Her scholarship has consistently demanded the right of human freedom and dignity.

The effort to understand the oppressed human condition and free the restrictive limitations through research and analysis is an ethical project for Zelliot. To remain indifferent and fail to respond to the urgent human issues in South Asia, Zelliot believes, is the failure of the human spirit to recognize injustice and the pain of others. The point that she has repeatedly made is the responsibility of academics to account for and present the variety of human 'experiences' to generate ethical awareness for overcoming 'graded inequality' (2001).

Zelliot's passionate concern for the 'oppressed' has expanded her analysis to include the women's question. For her, a truly ethical approach to South Asian history and culture is a feminist humanist approach, and she urges radical transformation of the field of inquiry by using this lens. It is in this spirit of feminist humanism that I present my essay on 1971 focusing on the experiences of men and women in the violent moment of a postcolonial war for voicing the suppressed memories that are not included in the national retelling of history.[1]

1971 was a unique moment in the subcontinent. The three nation-states—India, Pakistan, and Bangladesh—came together, not in peace but in war and violence. The abstract concepts of nation and nationalism were transmuted into personal and communal identity to justify war; neighbours became enemies determined to destroy each other. The historical literature on 1971 has divided the memory of the war between the nation-states; Bangladesh calls it 'Liberation', India labels it an 'Indo-Pak war', and Pakistan has actively forgotten to give it a name, though some call it the 'betrayal of East Pakistan'.[2] The partitioning of memory allows for blame to be relegated to the 'other'; even thirty-six years after the event, the national memory of 'us' as the 'good self' that is different from 'them', the 'evil other', continues to frame the narratives of 1971.

Two types of national discourse, one highlighting military strategies and diplomacy (for example, Choudhury 1974; Qureshi 2003; Siddiq 1977) and the other glorifying the soldiers' personal experiences and memories (for example, Alam 2006; Niazi 1998; Islam 1995; Jacob 1997; Singh 1979), dominate the representation of 1971. But at the margins of these divided and celebratory national narratives are multiple stories of common people who tell about the pain of suffering, loss, death, and cruelty during the war and illuminate for us a shared human condition across and beyond the national borders. In this essay, I excavate the story of gender violence, the construction of Muslim and Hindu identities, and the process of nation-state formation in an effort to write a 'human biography' as an alternative way of rethinking 1971.

The graphic details of violence that I describe in this essay are not aimed at sensationalizing the horrors of inhumanity. I tell the stories of survivors, men and women I have met in Bangladesh, India, and Pakistan, in order to learn from their experiences not to live on the surface of history, but to observe the depths of horror in the subcontinent and to write from within it a history that can develop an 'ethical and political thinking' in our era of catastrophic global violence (Arendt 1953). As a South Asian, I understand the conflicting passions concerning 1971; on the one hand, there is a need to remember and, on the other hand, there is a desire to forget the episodes of violence. We are frightened to investigate because that would compel us to take a hard look at ourselves, at our communities, governments, leaders, and politics, and at the social and gender cultures in which we are both victims and perpetrators. Can we continue to live in a state of denial and exclusion, while we let our governments execute violence in the name of national and religious good?

THE BACKGROUND NARRATIVE

The general story of 1971 in circulation in India, Pakistan, and Bangladesh marks it as a time of two wars: a civil war between West and East Pakistan, and an international war between India and West Pakistan. In the two wars there were various groups of protagonists, but there is no consensus about whom to blame for the violence. From the fragmentary evidence available to us, it appears that during the period of the civil war, West Pakistani troops, along with their local supporters in East Pakistan, both Bengalis and Biharis (a group that had migrated from India in 1947), terrorized and massacred nationalist Bengalis, deemed 'Hindu turncoats' for justifying Muslim Pakistani violence against them (Mascarenes 1971; Sisson and Rose 1990). In turn, the nationalist Bengalis, with the assistance of the Indian Army, created a local militia called Mukti Bahini (Liberation Army) and wreaked havoc in communities deemed enemies of the Bengalis.[3] The Biharis, one such 'enemy' group, were transformed into 'stateless refugees' (Whitaker 1975), more than 250,000 of whom still live in refugee camps in Bangladesh.

The international war between India and Pakistan formed part of a long-drawn series of battles that had started soon after 1947. Twice, in 1948 and 1965, India and Pakistan went to war over Kashmir. In 1971, India fought on behalf of the Bengali secessionist movement in East Pakistan and partitioned Pakistan, settling scores for the 1947 partition of India. India was involved in the 1971 war at various levels and stages. In February 1971, India began providing logistical and financial support to the Bengali rebels to organize their resistance against the Pakistani army.[4] In April 1971, India gave permission for the first capital of the independent republic of Bangladesh to be established in Mujibnagar, bordering on West Bengal. Toward the end of November that year, the Indian Army marched into East Pakistan and conclusively ended the war by forcing the surrender of the Pakistani Armed Forces. Bangladesh came into being as an independent country on 16 December 1971.

While some may squabble over the finer details of the events and the roles of the different groups in the war, few can deny that state violence combined with ethnic and religious hatred to target the vulnerable, particularly women and children. Focusing on gender violence, this essay will explore the narratives of survivors to probe the mechanisms, motivations, and consequences of men's violence against women. The essay is divided into three sections. First, I outline women's experiences to provide a brief sketch of the framework of gender violence. Next, I probe the memories of perpetrators. The survivors of 1971, men and women, speak in a variety of voices, but repeatedly ask us to reflect on a few salient questions: What is meant by nation? What price does one pay for it? And, finally, what do we learn about ourselves and our nations from listening to the survivors' stories? Pursuing the last question, in the final section of the essay, I investigate the sources that inspired and justified violence in 1971. I evaluate the role of leaders in generating a politics of life and death and examine the postcolonial states' transformation into militarized polities. I aim to develop a critical understanding of the exercise of state and political power against citizens in contemporary South Asia.

MEN, WOMEN, AND VIOLENCE

The rape of women in 1971 is not unique, but a familiar though horrible feature of wars, including the more recent examples of Bosnia, Kosovo, Croatia, and Rwanda. In these and other wars, women have been targets of male violence but have been forced into silence thereafter due to limitations imposed by the state, militarized nationalism, patriarchal community culture, and religious and social norms. Silencing women, however, cannot erase the reality of masculine violence in war. In Bangladesh, women's silence has produced a powerful, unspoken narrative that complicates the representation of perpetrators. Perpetrators came in many forms and guises, the women tell us— Pakistani, Bengali, Bihari, and Indian. Indeed, women refuse to reduce men to 'good' (Bengalis) fighting 'evil' (Pakistanis). Women produce multiple images of perpetrators, all powerful men committing violence against powerless women.

In 1971, MB[5] was thirty-six years old, a wife and the mother of seven children. Her husband, a doctor, I was told, had helped many rape victims during the war. I went to MB to listen to their stories. What

I heard was not what I had expected. Between sobs, MB told me her own story:

I was the rape victim in this neighbourhood. No one knows it happened to me, not even my children. To this day I have not been able to talk about it to anyone. My husband was the only person who knew, but he kept my secret. The rape happened in my own home. We were a large family; my in-laws used to live with us. There were other relatives, too; there were thirty-two people in this house. At midnight I heard some voices outside our compound and I realized that Pakistani soldiers were knocking on our door and demanding that my husband come out. I also heard voices of people I recognized from our neighbourhood. They told the soldiers, 'We have shown you the house, now we are leaving. We cannot show our face to the doctor' .... I pleaded with the soldiers not to take my husband; I knew that they would kill him if they took him outside the compound. The soldiers argued with me and tried to intimidate me. I kept moving backwards as they kept coming forward toward me. Suddenly, I was pushed into a corner room and the door was bolted shut. A large Pakistani soldier pinned me down and ripped off my saree; I became unconsciousness. When I regained my senses I realized what had happened. The soldier had raped me. I was lying on the floor and my husband was looking down at me with tears in his eyes (2.17.2001).

In Bangladesh, women like MB are called *birangana*, female heroes—in other words, rape victims. Rape is an indelible stigma in South Asia. Hence, soon after the war, in order not to deal with the lasting scar of rape, the state of Bangladesh forced women to have mass abortions. I have interviewed several doctors who participated in the state abortion programme and can testify to the dehumanization of women in post-liberated Bangladesh. Fortunately for MB she did not have to go through the humiliation of an abortion in a public clinic, but she dealt privately with the consequences. Her experience in the war became private history, and she has borne the pain of her suffering in silence for thirty-six years. Listening to women's silence, however, is not fruitless. We begin to understand that gender violence had a purpose, an inhuman purpose, to terrorize vulnerable groups of non-combatant women and render them inarticulate by taking away their dignity, so that even at a further time they would never regain their voice. For women like MB history stopped in 1971, and no one even noticed.

In Bangladesh, I interviewed a variety of women who represented different religious, ethnic, linguistic, and socio-economic groups and collected more than fifty testimonials that I corroborated with nearly two hundred women. SB, a seventy-six-year-old Bihari refugee woman, summed it up for me: 'Men raped women. That is the truth. Why should it matter what the ethnic, religious, or linguistic background of the victims was? *Insan* (human beings) had become the enemy of insān. Is this something to talk about?' (2. 2001, Saidpur, Bangladesh).

Bangladeshi men today blame the Pakistanis for the brutality against women in the war. They assume the moral high ground of liberators and defenders of freedom. But when I asked a Bangladeshi veteran and decorated soldier if he had done anything to save even one woman from sexual violence, he replied, 'I did not join the army to save women. I joined the liberation war to save my country.' When I persisted that women were also part of his country and questioned why did he not do anything to save even one person from sexual atrocity, he rebuked me, saying, 'This is not a subject of history.' Further, he added, 'This talk about women and rape is okay to an extent. But the kind of history that should be written about the war is the glorious victory of the Bangladeshis against the Pakistanis. Rape happened in the war. But that is not something to tell the future generation' (11.22.2001, Dhaka, Bangladesh).

It is not just a matter of shame that restricts speech in Bangladesh. At the deepest level the stories of gender violence stir up disturbing memories of the breakdown of family and community; the self finds itself haunted by its own shadow. In the mirror of memories today, Bengalis, like Pakistanis, see a distorted image of both victim and perpetrator. Their speech is jarring, and silence hides the pain of the torturing realization. Gender violence has been neglected as non-narrativizable history.

To move beyond the silence that is imposed and actively encouraged by the state institutions, we have to turn to individual men who were part of the violence and hear their memories. The power to commit violence against women did not make these men heroes. Tormented by their horrific memories, the men, like their victims, live their lives repulsed, puzzled, and baffled by the shameful past. But national history has no space to accommodate the soldiers' experiences or the lessons learned from the violence.

MEN'S NARRATIVES

I interviewed more than thirty civil and military officers in Bangladesh; in India I met with more than two dozen army officers and civil administrators; and in Pakistan I interviewed 123 veterans of 1971. Barring a tiny minority, all of them refused to admit that sexual violence occurred in the war. I believe many of these men are innocent, but their refusal to talk about it cannot erase the fact that sexual violence happened. A few who dared to divulge the kind of violence they had indulged in in the war revealed their own degradation. I will present two narratives of perpetrators to describe men's brutal actions and their struggle with disturbing memories.

I met KM in Bangladesh in order to discuss the ethnic violence between the Biharis and Bengalis that had taken place in his neighbourhood. An hour-and-a-half into our conversation, KM suddenly stopped and asked me, 'Will you listen to my story?' Not knowing what to expect, I agreed to listen. This is what he told me:

In 1971, I was a higher-secondary student. My father was a government employee and the sole breadwinner in the family. Our grandparents lived with us. At home, my mother and my fifteen-year-old sister depended on me for protection. Because we lived alongside the Biharis, I worried about my family's safety and decided to get guerilla training. I was not a nationalist, but I thought it would be good to have some military training. After a few days, I returned home equipped with a gun. I felt very strong and powerful, and motivated some friends to join the unit. When we patrolled the neighbourhood everyone showed us a great deal of respect .... On 3 April, we heard that the Pakistan army had arrived in our area. The Biharis were emboldened. We saw them walking around the place without fear and it made us very angry. Five friends and I decided to punish them. We went to the house of one of our Bihari neighbours. I used to call him 'uncle' and his daughter was my sister's friend. She used to refer to me as 'brother'. But that day all human ties were broken. We forcibly entered the house ... grabbed the young girl, and stripped her naked in front of her parents. She was struck with fear and shame and bolted out of the house into the main street. We ran after her. The crowd pursuing her grew in size. I had only one thought in my mind: 'I want to rape and destroy this girl. I want to destroy the Biharis, they are our enemies....

CM, a Bengali man, saw us chasing the girl. I had never liked this man and considered him a coward because he did not approve of me joining the

Muktis. When he saw us chasing the girl down the street, he came out with a shawl, wrapped her with it and took her inside. He told the crowd, 'If you want to take this girl, take her over my dead body.' We all stood there. No one had the courage to enter his house and drag her out. At that moment I felt very sad. I told myself, 'I am a soldier of the Mukti Bahini; I am supposed to protect my country. But I have turned into a criminal. This gun that they have given me has made me think I am invincible. I have become cold like a snake. On the other hand, this ordinary, useless man who is not even involved in the freedom struggle has saved a helpless person. He is a real hero. What have I become? ... I was told I was a hero. Do you think I am a hero?' (11.16.2001).

When I heard this confession from a perpetrator of violence, I was dumbfounded. As I listened, confusing and contradictory thoughts and feelings clashed in my mind. I did, however, understand then, as I do now, that what I heard was the voice of a human damned by his memories and actions. His story has no place in a Bangladesh that revels in the victory of 1971. KM's testimony raised many new questions for me. I found myself asking: How was it possible for men to inflict violence on women with impunity? Did men who raped women relish the act and talk about it over a cup of tea? I raised these questions to MA in Lahore. His troubling confession revealed that duty and obedience were combined with masculinity and violence, the hallmarks of army training.

MA joined the army in 1968 at the age of sixteen, since his widowed mother could barely eke out a living. After a couple of months' training, he was posted to East Pakistan. For three years he lived there and did his normal duties. In 1971, when the war broke out, his unit was not well prepared; a recurring problem was the lack of food. So he, along with a few others, was given the responsibility of acquiring food for the mess. Since the Bengali merchants and shopkeepers refused to sell them food, they had to go to villages to acquire rations. He said, 'I did loot some shops and beat some Bengalis in the process, but I did not see it as violence. I was told to provide rations by my superior officer and I carried out his orders. In the army we are not allowed to question orders. We obey commands and do as we are told.' When I asked him if in the process of acquiring rations for his unit, he had also committed violence against women, he said, 'I did not beat or assault any woman. But I did not do anything to save a woman .... There was rape in East

Pakistan. I will not lie to you. In fact, some of my peers raped women and no one stopped them.' Did they talk about it? I probed.

Yes, some men would gather together and discuss the different villages they had been to and had raped in. Mostly, they talked about raping very young women; they did not rape married women or mothers. Some of the soldiers also brought back the women with them. But I think they married them in the camp and hence they were allowed weekly visits. Some even sent their Bengali wives to Pakistan. Since you ask, and I must tell you the truth, I will admit that there were occasions when my senior officers raped women. At times, I had to stand outside the house and guard it. I knew why they had gone inside the house; they went there to rape the women. But I could not stop them. I was a sepoy. It was not my place to question the commands of my officers. My duty was to stand guard and that is what I did (7.31.2004, Lahore, Pakistan).

MA's story of obeying commands, performing his duty without asking questions, his complete subordination to the orders of his superiors, troubled me immensely. I wanted to believe him, but I could not without asking why he did not rape. He took a long while to answer this question. Slowly, he said, 'my *zameer* (conscience) would not let me commit such a crime.' Later, when I met his old, invalid mother, I understood the pull of conscience that inhibited MA from sexually violating women. She told me,

MA used to write letters to me from East Pakistan and later from the POW camp in India. Since I could not read the letters I took them to the school teacher. The women would gather together to hear the stories MA recounted. Everyone was very proud of the battles that he participated in, but the violence also troubled them. The women blamed the East Pakistanis for the violence. But I would sit in a corner and think about the violence that my son was witnessing and my heart would cry, '*tauba, tauba*' (forgive our trespasses). I was very sorry that my son was part of such violence. But I knew he would not do bad things to women because he was raised by me, his mother. I prayed to God to save him from committing violence and to save the women and children of East Pakistan, because no women should suffer the loss of a child or be dishonoured in war. I know that MA still thinks about East Pakistan and what he witnessed there. The memory cannot be erased. He has taken refuge in religion to seek Allah's forgiveness. That is all we can do.

MA's mother's narrative made me hopeful that three decades after the war an understanding is possible if voices such as hers are allowed to emerge, so that people in Bangladesh today can hear and know that there were many in Pakistan who suffered along with them and understood the banality of evil (Arendt 1953). To grapple with and understand what happened in 1971, it is important for us, the listeners, to move beyond identifying specific groups as pathological criminals and to contextualize the condition of the war, the propaganda of hate, the manipulation of minds, the perverse exercise of power, and the breakdown of responsibility and leadership that transformed ordinary men into criminals. Many of the perpetrators cannot revisit the memory and help us make sense of it. For them dark things remain dark. In the course of my research I have encountered a variety of men in Pakistan, Bangladesh, and India who refuse to acknowledge that they committed crimes against humanity. Nonetheless, these men, though they may be in the majority, cannot stifle another voice that survives and emerges at the margin of the national story. KA, a retired brigadier in the Pakistan army, summed this up for me in these words:

I have now reached an age when I have to be honest about what I know and experienced. I can't keep on lying to my children and grandchildren. In the past, when my wife told stories to our children, about the Bengalis killing and brutalizing the Pakistani families in East Pakistan, I did not contradict her. But now when I hear her tell the same stories to our grandchildren, I tell her, 'There is no point in hiding the truth. The Bengalis did kill and brutalize many Pakistani men and women. They orphaned a lot of Pakistani children. But you and I know that the Pakistani Army retaliated against them with greater violence, which far exceeds what the Bengalis did to us .... There is no good or bad party in 1971. We all committed violence—Bengalis, Pakistanis, Biharis, and Indians. We were afraid of each other. The fear and learned hatred toward each other led us to violence. Don't take sides and distort the truth' (12.27.2004, Lahore, Pakistan).

If indeed, as KA expressly reminds his family, the truth resides in the people, should we not listen to what they say? In the testimonies of survivors we encounter the memory of people who refuse to mutely accept the rhetoric of the state. In turn, they create a luminous trail of a different history. Their memories are not pathos-laden stories of the disillusioned, but voices of speaking humans who claim and fill the empty space of violent history with an honest understanding to bear witness to the disgrace done to humanity in the subcontinent. I am not saying that we should absolve the rapists and killers. But listening to survivors' stories has made me realize that a hard line cannot be drawn between victims and perpetrators. Pakistani soldiers and their Bihari collaborators raped and killed to save a nation; Bengali men raped and killed in the hope of making a new nation. If people are cultivated to become perpetrators of violence, should we not examine the interdependence of all humans and expose the sites where the strategies that validate one human's killing, raping, and brutalizing another are conceived?

THE STATE, RHETORIC OF NATIONALISM, AND LEADERS

To explore the politics of violence in 1971 we have to begin with an understanding of the history of the postcolonial nation-state and its exercise of power to determine the life and death of citizens. The nation-states of India and Pakistan were created on the model of the British colonial state, in which the ruling class coerced subject groups into submission. To this was added religion as a political tool for dividing the subject communities. The politics of religion manifested itself in all-out violence during the foundational moment of India and Pakistan in 1947, and until recently has served the politics of hate between India and Pakistan. Along with militarization, the gendered representation of state power has also become more active. The war of 1971 has to be understood within this context.

Viewed as a disposable and killable group, women are sexualized and constructed as bodies for killing, raping, and brutalizing in order to anchor the sovereign power of the state. This ethos was enacted in 1971 when state and community actors unleashed their violence on women. Different communities of men targeted women to prove the legitimacy of nationalist ideology and masculine power. To understand this, we must examine the narratives produced by the nation-states and their leaders, who manipulated the discourse of duty and national good to further their own agendas. In this final section I will address in brief the rhetoric of nationalism that turned violent under the leadership of Yahya Khan, Zulfikar Ali Bhutto, Sheikh Mujibur Rahman, and Indira Gandhi.

Soon after taking power in March 1969, Yayha Khan, the new President of Pakistan, declared 'temporary' martial law. In consultation with his military generals and civilian cabinet, Yahya decided to hold elections on the basis of 'one man, one vote' for a single-chamber national assembly. But the results of the election were unexpected. Mujibur Rahman, the leader of the Awami League, won the majority vote in East Pakistan (160 of the 162 seats), while Zulfikar Ali Bhutto of the People's Party won only 81 of 138 seats in West Pakistan (Mamoon 2000; Khan 1998; Sisson and Rose 1990). Failing to generate an amicable solution for power-sharing between the two elected representatives, Yahya called upon 'his men' (soldiers) to display their spirit of Pakistani nationalism with violence. In a radio speech on 6 March 1971, he said, 'Let me make it absolutely clear that no matter what happens .... I will not allow a handful of people to destroy the homeland of millions of innocent Pakistanis. It is the duty of the Pakistan Armed Forces to ensure the integrity, solidarity and security of Pakistan, a duty in which they have never failed.' The public declaration of the possibility of organized state violence and its elevation to the level of national duty justified the grim actions that followed within a fortnight.

This speech established the vital point that West Pakistan was the centre of Pakistani nationhood. Yahya made a speech to his 'fellow countrymen', West Pakistanis, in a calm and official manner, explaining that military action 'over there' was necessary because of Mujib's 'obstinacy, obduracy, and absolute refusal to talk sense ... [which] lead but to one conclusion—the man and his party are enemies of Pakistan and they want East Pakistan to break away completely from the country' (Radio Pakistan broadcast). On 25 March the state declared war against the people of East Pakistan.

But Yahya was not alone in conceiving and executing state brutality against the citizens of East Pakistan. His actions were supported and endorsed by Zulfikar Ali Bhutto, the political leader in West Pakistan. On 1 December 1967, Bhutto and his supporters created the Pakistan People's Party (PPP) on a platform of progressive Islamic socialism. Although critics insisted that Islam and socialism were not compatible, many West Pakistanis saw in the PPP a hope for their economic future. Bhutto learned to speak Urdu, the official language of Pakistan, in a 'refreshingly pedestrian' manner (Syed 1992: 70). His fiery speeches 'insisting on democracy, for it is provided in Islam ... [and] socio-economic equality or *Musawat*' created a contagious dream (Wolpert 1993: 142). The general election of 1970, in which Bhutto's party won half as many seats as Mujib won in East Pakistan, made it obvious that Bhutto was not the sole spokesman for West Pakistan, but he managed to assert an image of power. He congratulated Mujib, 'We respect the majority', but simultaneously warned that 'Punjab and Sindh are the centres of power,' and 'if the PPP does not support it, no government will be able to work.'

When Bhutto realized that his dream of becoming the prime minister of Pakistan was slipping away, he became obsessed with reversing the course of history. In the process he polarized the Pakistani people into right and left, West Pakistanis and East Pakistanis, and demanded that Yahya 'crush Mujib through military action, if necessary' (Syed 1992: 98). To distract attention from the internal crisis that he had created, Bhutto used the 'Ganga incident', in which an Indian Airlines flight from Srinagar to Jammu was hijacked by two young Kashmiris and landed in Lahore, to claim that he was held 'double hostage' by Indian hostility and the Awami League's intransigence (Sisson and Rose 1990: 79). In the end, Bhutto's power-play worked. Yahya decided to put up a 'show of force to bring Mujib and his Bengalis to their senses' (Wolpert 1993: 153).

Mujibur Rahman, the leader of the Bengalis, was not an intellectual, nor was he a sophisticated politician, but he could connect to the masses and verbally express their desires and hopes. From the beginning he espoused a limited Bengali nationalism that made him popular. During the election campaign in 1970, Mujib made some emotional statements that scholars of Pakistan interpret as having incited the people of East Pakistan against the western wing. Mujib knew that to gain popularity he had to give more to his followers. But he had no magic formula for redressing the grievances of the Bengali people. So he introduced into the public domain a dangerous political rhetoric of regionalism and ethnicity. By claiming that East Pakistan's resources were the property of the Bengali-speaking people, he created a division between 'us' and 'them'. The 'us' from now on would be Bengali, and others in East Pakistan, such as the minority Biharis, were part of 'them', that is, West Pakistan, the enemy.

Mujib was able to nurture and fulfil his dream of an independent Bangladesh because of active support from the Indian prime minister Indira Gandhi, her cabinet, and a variety of politicians.[6] Beginning early in 1970, the Government of India became actively involved in the internal politics of East Pakistan and in alluring East Bengalis, particularly Hindu Bengalis, into leaving East Pakistan. Rumours of forcible occupation of Hindu properties, forcible conversion to Islam, disrespect of religious places, molestation of women, robberies, etc. were circulated, and the possibility of Bengali refugees getting land in West Bengal was used to entice landless cultivators to cross over (Prasad, unpublished: 90–1). Indira Gandhi made many public speeches in which she warned that India could not remain a silent spectator of the events in Bangladesh. Indira Gandhi's single-minded determination to unravel Pakistan, the ideological conflict of ethnic nationhood that she supported for the Bengalis (since she believed Pakistan was created on a dangerous, unworkable principle of religion), her unwavering support for military intervention, the long campaign that she and her government undertook for educating the world outside to support the Indian offensive strategy as a humanitarian response, and the support she provided to the Mukti Bahini—all these constitute crucial roles in the war.

Thus, each of the four state players played a destructive role. No one, however, took responsibility for the violence. They engineered the violence, but covered up their acts with rhetoric of national good and duty, manipulating ordinary people into executing violence on their behalf. To justify the cruel state policy of violence for power, the leaders helped their followers reduce their enemies to abstract demographic units categorized as 'us' and 'them': ethnic units of Pakistani, Bihari, and Bengali and religious communities of Hindus and Muslims, further subdivided as men and women. Bounded communities saw themselves as enemies of other bounded communities, but the vulnerable human, the victim, was not accounted for, and the lived experiences of real people were cancelled from the registers of national retellings. Our narrators, however, remind us to ask: Can we narrativize the war of 1971 as an act of glory and liberation, and neglect the pain and undying trauma that it unleashed on vulnerable groups?

Drawing upon Ernest Renan's lecture of 1882 and Eleanor Zelliot's scholarship on the question of the oppressed, I would like to suggest a possible space in which a people's history of 1971 can emerge and enable the communities of survivors to come to terms with the violent past. In his lecture, Renan tells us, 'to have suffered together is of greater value than identity of custom houses and frontiers ... for indeed common suffering unites more strongly than rejoicing. Among national memories, sorrows have greater value than victories, for they impose duties and demand common effort' (see Dahbour and Micheline 1999: 153). Awareness and recognition of suffering as a common human condition is conceived as 'transcendence'. In other words, the practices and institutions that mark differences and create human suffering, Renan envisions, can serve as the site for cohering and binding human beings within one society. In a similar vein, Zelliot understood the perplexing dualism inherent in the oppressive practices of caste, religion, and gender. On the one hand, these practices and institutions limit human freedom and mark one human as different from another human to continue oppression through social sanctions. Alternately, the oppressed through their experiences of suffering can become agents of change and provide the site for recognizing individual freedom and human dignity. Many politicians and ordinary men in South Asia may find the bitter effect of suffering in 1971 grounds for revenge rather than a site to develop a language of understanding to make a community of survivors and claim the history they have produced. Can we nonetheless make the ethos of common suffering in 1971 a language of empathy to bind survivors in Bangladesh, Pakistan, and India? Can we dare to look into the abyss of violence in 1971 and from within it write a history of the subcontinent that will enable us to overcome differences and claim the human dignity that is our due?

NOTES

1. This essay is part of a larger book project. Please accord the necessary courtesy for a project in progress and do not use the material without permission. Research for the project was completed with the support of the American Institute of Bangladesh Studies; American Institute of Pakistan Studies; Harry Frank Guggenheim Foundation; Vice Chancellor's office for Research and Economic Development, UNC-Chapel Hill; University Centre for International Studies, UNC-Chapel Hill; and University Research Council, UNC-Chapel Hill.

2. This is the title of Niazi's book (1998). Niazi was the head of the Eastern Command from July to 16 December 1971. In his tenure sexual violence became rampant.

3. These stories are detailed in the Urdu and English language newspapers in Pakistan. I have consulted the daily reports of the *Imroz* and *The Dawn*, March to December 1971.

4. A photo album documenting the clandestine activities of the Indian intelligence agents is available at the Centre for Armed Forces Historical Research, United Services Institution, New Delhi.

5. The names of the people I quote in this article here have been abbreviated in order to protect their identities.

6. See Parliamentary Debates, March 1971–3, vols VI–XX, Nehru Memorial Museum and Library, New Delhi.

REFERENCES

Alam, Habibul. 2006. *Brave of Heart*. Dhaka: Academic Press and Publishers Library.

Arendt, Hannah. 1953. 'On the Nature of Totalitarianism: An Essay in Understanding'. In Hannah Arendt. *Essays in Understanding*. Jerome Kohn (ed.). New York: Harcourt Brace, 1994, pp. 328–60.

Choudhury, G.W. 1974. *The Last Days of United Pakistan*. London: C. Hurst & Company.

Dahbour, Omar and Ishay Micheline. 1999. *The Nationalism Reader*. New York: Humanity Books.

Foucault, Michel. 1979. *The History of Sexuality, Vol. 1: An Introduction*. R. Hurley (trans.). London: Allen Lane.

Islam, Rafiqul. 1995. *A Tale of Millions*. Dhaka: Ananna.

Jacob, J.F.R. 1997. *Surrender at Dacca: Birth of a Nation*. New Delhi: Manohar.

Khan, F.A. 1998. *Spring 1971: A Center Stage Account of Bangladesh War of Liberation*. Dhaka: The University Press Limited.

Mamoon, Muntasir. 2000. *The Vanquished Generals and the Liberation War of Bangladesh*, Kushal Ibrahim (trans.). Dhaka: Somoy Prokashon.

Mascarenes, Anthony. 1971. *The Rape of Bangladesh*. New Delhi: Vikas.

Niazi, Amir Abdullah Khan. 1998. *The Betrayal of East Pakistan*. Karachi and New York: Oxford University Press.

Prasad, S.N. (ed.). 1992 (unpublished) 'History of Indo-Pak War, 1971', (5 vols). New Delhi: Ministry of Defence, Government of India.

Qureshi, H.A. 2003. *The 1971 Indo-Pak War: A Soldier's Narrative*. Oxford: Oxford University Press.

Siddiq, Salik. 1977. *Witness to Surrender*. Karachi: Oxford University Press.

Singh, Lachman Lehl. 1979. *Indian Sword Strikes in East Pakistan*. New Delhi: Vikas.

Sisson, R. and L.E. Rose. 1990. *War and Secession: Pakistan, India and the Creation of Bangladesh*. Berkeley: University of California Press.

Syed, A.H. 1992. *The Discourse and Politics of Zulfikar Ali Bhutto*. New York: St Martin's Press.

Trouillot, Michel. 1995. *Silencing the Past: Power and the Production of History*. New York: Beacon Press.

Whitakar, B. 1975. *The Biharis in Bangladesh*. London: Minority Rights.

Wolpert, Stanley. 1993. *Zulfi Bhutto of Pakistan: His Life and Times*. New York: Oxford University Press.

Zelliot, Eleanor. 2001. *From Untouchable to Dalit: Essays on the Ambedkar Movement*. New Delhi: Manohar.

9

CATARACTS OF SILENCE
Race on the Edge of Indian Thought

Vijay Prashad

In the warm summer of 1992, Ram Pyari sat with me on a grassy patch outside Indira Gandhi International Airport in New Delhi. A sanitation worker at the airport, Ram Pyari spoke to me of her predicament in tones familiar to working class people the world over. 'Poor people make rich people. Without poor people how would rich people become rich? Who makes them rich? We make them rich, and as they get rich and powerful, they suck our blood.'[1] Those who sat with us murmured their assent, and one spoke of how their supervisor was now building a new house with money earned from bossing the workers around.

But Ram Pyari is not just any worker. She is a Dalit, a member of a community oppressed for social, political, and economic reasons by communities that claim to be of a higher caste. One-sixth of India's population are Dalits. These 160 million people are divided into numerous communities with distinct customs and histories, bound together by a common history of grinding oppression. Dalit literally translates as 'broken people', with 'broken' often glossed as oppressed. Since the 1970s, radical Dalits have claimed the word for their communities and their liberation. Dominant castes used to call them 'untouchables' (*achhut*), Gandhian liberals call them Harijans ('children of god'), and the Indian Republic calls them Scheduled Castes (because they are on a government schedule that entitles them to certain protections and affirmative actions). Most Dalits are like Ram Pyari: poor folk who work in the fields, factories, streets, shops, and public buildings—wherever labour is in demand.

Unlike people of colour in the United States or blacks in South Africa, Dalits are not always physically distinguishable from other Indians. In some regions, occupation, surname, or dress can sometimes identify them, but Dalits are usually hard to pick out. The experience of Dalits shows that apartheid-like conditions can be imposed upon people who are marked by history, not appearance. India's powerful independence movement produced perhaps the world's most extensive system of affirmative action for oppressed peoples like the Dalits. Since the 1970s, Dalits like Ram Pyari have organized themselves to use these assets to overturn the caste system, organize for power, and fight for their rights. Yet Dalits still face an uphill struggle against starkly unequal conditions. The election slogan of the Bahujan Samaj Party (a Dalit-dominated, but largely opportunistic political group) in 1994 is still apt: 'Vote hamara, raj tumhara. Nahin chalega, nahin chalega' ('We vote, you govern. This won't go on, this won't go on').

When national level discussions for the United Nations World Conference Against Racism began in India in 2000, the problem of caste immediately stirred controversy. The Hindutva-Right-dominated government was chary to raise the issue of caste on the world stage, particularly at that juncture when it basked in US-sponsored praises for being the world's largest democracy (and wanted to secure India a much-coveted seat as a permanent member of the UN Security Council). The government sought to avoid anything that made India 'look bad' on the world stage. Apart from these international political reasons, the Hindutva-Right government had a commitment to the perpetuation of caste discrimination. Not only were its ranks filled with representatives of the dominant castes, but its public policy platforms frequently privileged those dominant, wealthy castes over oppressed castes and religious minorities. Furthermore, allied organizations of the Hindutva-Right have even convened conclaves devoted to a 'revival' of strict Brahmanical social organizations, such as the fourfold division of varnas (Brahmans, Kshatriyas, Vaishyas, and Shudras). On 7 February 2001, the External Affairs Minister Jaswant Singh noted that 'we must ensure that the Conference does not lose sight of its focus on racism'. In other words, the Hindutva-Right should be able not only to preserve itself as an anti-racist nationalist force, but also to occlude the discriminations and prejudices that structure the Indian polity.

Dalit rights activists have, naturally, been eager to raise the question of caste discrimination on the international stage. The Hindutva-Right government (1998–2004) was the first to block discussion of caste in international forums. Martin Macwan, national head of the National Campaign for Dalit Human Rights, reminds us that 'in earlier international forums, notably the Committee on Elimination of Discrimination Against Women, the Government of India had successfully taken up the issue of caste-based discrimination. Why is it insisting that caste is an "internal" matter?' (Kaur 2001: 95). The idea that caste is an 'internal' matter is specious, mainly because 'caste' as we know it today is decidedly fostered by a combination of Indian social relations, European-driven colonialism, and global capitalism. These three factors produce what we know as caste today, since the practice cannot claim to be an ahistorical reflection of what one reads in Sanskrit texts. Caste, then, is not 'internal', but a form of social discrimination that is in conversation with similar forms elsewhere. It is in this spirit that most Dalit rights activists (and the Communist parties, which supported the demand) wanted to hold the international discussion.

There are some, however, who want to reduce caste to a form of race, and therefore make a strong connection between anti-racist work and anti-caste work. Afrocentrics and Dalitocentrics are particularly notable here, especially with the claim that Dalits are 'negritos' and that they suffer oppression at the hands of their 'Aryan' oppressors, just as black around the world are held down by white folk. That the evidence for race as biology has been discredited does not seem to bother the indigenistas, many of whom deploy old racist texts to make their claims. One reason many indigenistas use the language of race in an unreconstructed manner is that they get ideological sustenance from a simple-minded US race politics, where the black-white dyad drives the political landscape. Indeed, in an interview with me, a leading US-based Afrocentric scholar who was instrumental in creating the Afro-Dalit thesis conceded, 'I feel bad about it. I think I oversimplified the situation of Dalits to make it palatable to a [US] Black constituency. I gave the impression that Dalits are Black people'. Nevertheless, he argued that 'large sections of Dalits would be seen as Black people if they lived anywhere else'.[2] One of the dangers of US imperialist hegemony is that the global anti-imperialist agenda may also end up being set in US anti-imperialist terms. That is, the anti-racist programme for organizations and activists from across the globe might replicate the terms of the US movement.[3] Race, then, as a central category for the struggle may be self-evident in the US context, but not as useful in other settings. The enthusiasm for epidermal determinism occurs despite the Dalitcentric editor V.T. Rajshekar's early warning that 'in India, it is no longer easy to distinguish a touchable from an Untouchable, especially for foreigners (unlike in the US where the difference between skin colours is more pronounced)' (Rajshekar 1978: 52). Whether it was ever possible to tell caste by skin colour is a debatable question, but such judgements are certainly impossible now.

After a brief overview of the history of the caste concept, allied as it has been since the modern period with its kin term of race, this essay will offer an analysis of the fight against caste in contemporary India. The problem of the Dalit struggle is posed front and centre in this article not to ignore other problems of caste, but to stress, with the Dalit leader B.R. Ambedkar, that 'the problem of Untouchability [and caste] is a problem of the class struggle' (quoted in Ahir 1990: 21).

APARTHEID BY ANY NAME

When the Portuguese first landed on the southwestern coast of India in 1498, they came upon a form of social organization to which they gave the name caste (from Latin, *castus*). What they referred to was not one system, but a series of social formations to which they gave one name. There was never just one simple caste hierarchy in India. Even today there are some 4,635 ethnic communities, many with distinct land bases and systems of hierarchy. What the Portuguese called caste was probably a social form called *jati* (community). The Europeans saw jati as rigid and oppressive, not unlike their own rigid feudal social order. Jati hierarchies emerged from the ancient world in various forms: occupations, marriage bonds, dietary habits, and religious customs. Indeed, no one principle explains 'the caste system'. Different jatis attained dominance in different parts of southern Asia, but all commanded the fealty and labour of others based on their monopoly over land and force. Over time, these others would come to be branded as 'Untouchables'. Suvira Jaiswal has written a wonderful account of the complex genesis of caste and the myriad genealogies that can be drawn for each caste.[4] There is no subcontinental-wide caste system, since each locality produced various forms of local oppression—where those who came to dominance, in and around the fight against Buddhism (and other *Sramanic* orders), adopted ideas of superiority. Many of these xenophobic and elitist ideas articulated with and drew from the Brahmanic texts of an earlier era, notably with the ancient system of four categories known as varna. Endogamy, ritual ranking, and class power are three of the most important forces that constitute, in varying degrees, the complex of social differentiation and power in South Asian pre-modernity. There was nothing polite about the way the dominant jatis made their demands. Dalits fought off routine violence from dominant jatis, who, in turn, tried to erect vicious mechanisms to control Dalits' will. As in the US South and South Africa, Dalits could touch all manner of dominant-jati things, if they needed to do so to provide labour. But when the Dalits worked for themselves, their touch was seen by the dominant jatis as a form of social pollution. Dalit women worked in the homes of the dominant jatis and fell prey to the sexual violence of elite men. However, these men disdained any other interactions with the women.

When Europeans began to conquer and administer South Asia in the eighteenth century, they began to pay careful attention to the social order that lay before them. Bernard Cohn has shown that the British impact on South Asian social life was decisive, mainly through the classification regime set in place by the colonial rulers (Cohn 1987). Certainly, work on two oppressed castes (Dalits) shows that the British intervention transformed their relations to production and power: the Balmikis, as Chuhras, and the Jatavs, as chamars, lived with control over land, as well as shares of the commons, until the British land officials decided, mainly in the late nineteenth century, that these Dalits should work only as drudge labour and not toil on land that was their own.[5] What was the reason for this British response and how was it put into place? The reason was the Haitian Revolution of 1791–2 (in the aftermath of the French Revolution) and the birth of raciology as a means to justify the brutal control over labour with dark skin.

In 1793, Jeremy Bentham, otherwise quite clear about the importance of the 'rights of man', asked, 'Would the declaration of rights translate into *Sanscrit*? Would *Bramin*, *Chetree*, *Bice*, *Sooder*, and *Hallochore* meet on equal ground?' Being culturally relativist *avant la lettre*, and justifying the rule of joint-stock multinational corporations like the English East India Company, Bentham noted, 'if it is to be determined that they must have masters, you will then look out for the least bad ones that could take them: and after all that we have heard I question whether you would find any less bad than our English company' (Majeed 1992: 125). In 1807 Hegel, after the Thermidor in Paris and in Port au Prince, checked his enthusiasm for freedom with the caveat that 'universal freedom can produce no positive work or deed, only *negative action* remains to it; it is the *fury of destruction*' (Taylor 1975: 416). Like Bentham earlier, Hegel wrote that 'the English, or rather the East India Company, are the lords of the land [India]; for it is the necessary fate of Asiatic Empires to be subjected to Europeans', and to be ruled without even qualified freedom for the darker skins.

The East India Company (EIC) disregarded, indeed squelched, the dynamic for freedom within South Asia, as they produced knowledge about India that was, in many ways, the template for their land revenue and other public policies. Europeans liked the stereotypical order of the 'caste system' and they did all they could to bolster the Brahmanical order (in cahoots with their monarchial allies, many of whom retained their nominal rank, but lost their real power).[6] An early text was *Hindu Manners, Customs and Ceremonies* (1906) by the Abbé Dubois, who had fled the French Revolution with the Missions Étrangères in 1792. 'I believe caste division to be in many respects the *chef-d'oeuvre*, the happiest effort of Hindu legislation,' he wrote in this book which was very influential for the EIC officialdom (the manuscript was purchased from Dubois by Major Wilkins, the Resident of Mysore, published by the EIC and distributed to its officials). 'I am persuaded that it is simply and solely due to the distribution of the people into castes that India did not lapse into a state of barbarism, and that she preserved and perfected the arts and sciences of civilization whilst most other nations of the earth remained in a state of barbarism' (Dubois 1906: 28). The point is taken further in his discussion of the Pariahs, the Parayars of the Tamil-speaking regions: 'I am persuaded that a nation of Pariahs left to themselves would speedily become worse than the hordes of cannibals who wander in the vast waste of Africa and would soon take to devouring each other.' If Africans can be ordered by the brutality of chattel slavery (in the Americas) and by a reconstructed tribalism (in the continent of Africa itself), then the dark skins of South Asia can be ordered and managed by the reconstruction of caste along imperial lines. The discourses of race and caste (as well as tribe), then, emerged simultaneously, as both terms enabled the Europeans to justify the expropriation of values from certain parts of the world to what was to become the centre of the world economy: Europe. In the aftermath of the French Revolution, European conservatives justified their ill-gotten gains on the basis of race/caste, now rendered in terms of biology, and they continued relying upon military force on the basis of their imputed racial superiority. Caste-Tribe became the words used to index the lesser forms of social organization in India-Africa, social forms used by racial inferiors. This had labour effects: as the labour power of the European worker was commodified, the labour power of the darker skins was animalized, treated as something that required physical coercion to extract the maximum effort. The notion of race, then, was at the foundation of the reconstruction of caste in modern times.

In an act of bad faith, the European powers blamed the oppressed for their own oppression and exculpated themselves from manufacturing biological ideas of inferiority. Take Dubois again: 'The idea that the [Dalit] was born to be in subjection to the other castes is so ingrained in his mind that it never occurs to the Pariah to think that his fate is anything but irrevocable. Nothing will ever persuade him that men are all made of the same clay, or that he has the right to insist on better treatment than that which is meted out to him' (Dubois 1906: 29). But if Dubois and the early EIC officials asked the Parayars what they thought of their subjection, they would have got a different answer: when the colonial ethnographer, Edgar Thurston, did just this in 1909, the Parayars of the Tamil-speaking region told him that they suffered the social indignity because of an ancient betrayal due to a linguistic error. Two poor brothers went to pray to the divinity, but they found a dead cow on the road. God instructed them to remove it. The elder brother said, *een thambi pappaan*, or 'my younger brother will do it.' The divinity misheard him: *een thambi paappaan*, or 'my younger brother is a Brahman' (Thurston 1909: 84). The elder became a Parayar, the younger a Brahman. But Dubois did not care for this self-awareness. The Balmikis tell a similar story, but end with one of the young men declaring, 'I wish to make a nation of my own' (Prashad 2000b: 28). The political economy does not allow this resolution to their oppression.

In the transition to capitalism, Karl Marx argued, labour is freed in a 'double sense, free from the relations of clientage, bondage and servitude, and secondly free of all belongings and possessions, and of every objective, material form of being, *free of all property*, dependent on the sale of its labour capacity or on begging, vagabondage and robbery as its only source of income' (Marx 1973: 507). The means of production are wrenched from the workers at the same time as they are free to sell their labour-power as a commodity on the market. At the periphery of capital, labour is made free only to be damned to unfreedom through the Brahmano-colonial mythology of an ancient division of labour known as the caste system. Caste, as a form of social relations, certainly predates colonial rule. However, caste as we know it today was radically transformed during the colonial period. Colonial sociology and policy worked together to expropriate Dalits from the soil (many then turn to cities to be hired into specific occupations, Balmikis as sweepers and Chamars as leather-workers). In Punjab, for instance, the land laws in the late nineteenth and early twentieth centuries noted that Dalits, as drudge labour, should not be allowed to own land, a marked departure from the facts of land holding at that time: these Dalits lost control over their resources and fell prey to the direct, brutal exploitation of new landed classes and of the wiles of capitalism's economic cycles. Modern employment was segregated along a stereotyped version of 'native tradition' despite the fact that these 'traditional' modes had not previously existed (except perhaps in ancient Brahmanical texts). This process demonstrates how labour is freed in the Indian colonies—freed, that is, into caste.

In 1999, Human Rights Watch (New York) published a report entitled *Broken People: Caste Violence Against India's 'Untouchables'* (Human Rights Watch 1999). HRW called the Dalits' situation 'hidden apartheid'. There is nothing *hidden* about the violence against Dalits; it moved M.K. Gandhi (1869–1948) in the 1930s to bring their struggles to the centre of the Indian national movement. His was a liberal gesture, far from the radicalism of the political Dalit movement led by B.R. Ambedkar (1891–1956). Ambedkar felt that 'it is wrong to say that the problem of Untouchables is a social problem', a reference to Gandhi's attempt at social reform. Rather, Ambedkar argued, 'the problem of the Untouchables is fundamentally a political problem (of minority versus majority groups).' It is also, as we have seen, an economic problem, one of land rights and control over capital. Rather than becoming the 'mere recipients of charity', Ambedkar called upon Dalits to 'educate, organize and agitate' for 'the reclamation of human respectability' (Prashad 2000b: 128).

DALITS AS CITIZENS

In 1947, the Indian national movement ejected British colonialism and inaugurated a period of national construction. These were heady days, as anti-colonial movements from Indonesia to Ghana used State power to make freedom something tangible for the masses. The first Indian Prime Minister, Jawaharlal Nehru (1889–1964), was impatient to rework the oppressive present, so in the 1950s the State took a few bold steps toward emancipating Dalits. Ambedkar is known as the architect of the Indian Constitution. Recruited by Nehru, and well known for his outspoken views on the need for a wide sense of democracy, Ambedkar pushed through many enlightened articles in the Constitution, and, as India's first Law Minister, helped create a progressive legal regime to ensure protections for Dalits. With no Dalit political movement to back up Ambedkar, the judiciary provided that cover: a Supreme Court justice argued that 'advantages secured due to historical reasons cannot be considered a fundamental right guaranteed by the Constitution' (Prashad 2000b: 143). When Martin Luther King, Jr, travelled to India in 1959 he was stunned by the State's monetary and legal commitment to Dalit emancipation. Asked if this discriminated against other jatis, Nehru replied that 'well it may be, but this is our way of atoning for the centuries of injustices we have inflicted upon these people' (King 1986: 24).

While Article 14 of the 1950 Indian Constitution guaranteed equality before the Law, the Courts refused to interpret this as absolute and unequivocal equality, and thus prevented the notion of equality from suppressing active governmental intervention on behalf of certain groups. In order to produce social and economic equality, the Courts allowed the State to intervene on behalf of oppressed and exploited groups, to use equality as the means to freedom.[7] The Courts identified women and backward classes as the two major groups towards whom the State was enjoined to act in a compensatory manner.[8] In 1964, Justice Subba Rao argued the logic of compensation forthrightly:

centuries of calculated oppression and habitual submission reduced a considerable section of our community to a life of serfdom. It would be well nigh impossible to raise their standards if the doctrine of equal opportunity was strictly enforced in their case. They would not have any chance if they were made to enter the open field competition without adventitious aids till such time they could stand on their own legs.[9]

The institutions that the Indian State created were a means to politicize 'equality' in order to produce a free and moral future community. Rather than bear the full implications of this courageous policy, the Indian administration settled for a 'reservations' policy that enabled a few Dalits to join what was once called the 'Harijan elite' (Sachchidananda 1976). The benefits were not evenly distributed among the Dalits: certain caste groups benefited more than others and only a few individuals and families were able to capitalize on State policy. The vast mass of Dalits remained outside the purview of the 'reservations'. Balmikis, for instance, could take advantage of the reservations scheme only in their monopoly over Class IV employment in the municipalities, typically with the sanitation departments. Most reservations are in low-skilled, low-paying jobs that do little to move Dalits up the economic ladder. Since compensatory discrimination is restricted to government jobs, the much larger private sector remains free to discriminate against Dalits.[10] Reservations are thus a far cry from the enlightened State policy envisaged by the Indian Judiciary.

By the mid-1960s, the limited compensation schemes began to suffer from the economic and political crisis that followed the Sino-Indian war of 1962, the Indo-Pakistan war of 1965, and the monsoon failures of 1965 and 1967. A serious crisis of political hegemony followed, developing into the ruling clique taking extraordinary powers into its own hands through centralization—most notably, the Emergency in 1975. Dalits raised serious doubts about the State's commitment and ability to provide the conditions for equality. In 1969, L. Elayaperumal's report for the Department of Social Welfare 'found that untouchability was still being practised in virulent form all over India' (Government of India 1969: 15). In 1970, the Minister of State for Home, R.N. Mirdha, announced that between 1967 and 1969, 1,117 Dalits had been reported murdered. Of these, 63 cases were in Maharashtra, 332 in Uttar Pradesh, and 76 in Punjab (Murugkar 1991: 41). The 'Harijan Atrocity' of the 1970s was not part of any ancient story of the caste system, but imbedded in the caste struggle that intensified after Dalits felt emboldened by their constitutional protections. When Chief Minister Kapoori Thakur's regime in Bihar (1977–80) opened space for Dalit advancement, the dominant castes, the Kurmis, massacred some of Pipra village's Chamars. Pipra was in line with a host of such massacres whose aetiology may be the revanchist attempt by dominant castes to hold onto power that seemed to be on the wane.

In response to India's failure to resolve the contradictions of political democracy, young Dalits in the late 1960s took inspiration from world-wide student movements, the Black Panther movement in the US, and the resurgence of militant left-wing activity within India to escalate their own struggle for freedom. In June 1972, the Dalit Panthers emerged as the major political formation of this new militancy. They declared themselves in favour of 'a complete revolution' as opposed to 'partial change'. After independence, they argued, the 'government did nothing to eradicate [untouchability] except passing some laws against it.' The Panthers' eighteen-point programme called for land redistribution, increased wages, free education, censorship of offensive literature, an end to economic corruption, and, most radically, 'all means of production must belong to the Dalits'. Calling for 'people's democracy', the Panthers argued against the contradictions of the liberal state and used the slogan, 'in our struggle we will become free.'[11]

The Panthers alert us to the Indian State's attempt to resolve the contradictions of 'equality'. The Untouchability Offences Act of 1955 and the Commission of Scheduled Castes understood untouchability as the social and cultural oppression of the Dalits by caste-Hindus and Muslims. Compensating for the lack of access to public buildings (including restaurants, temples, etc.) and the lack of expression (whether in choice of clothing or of speech) was central to the state's anti-untouchability campaign. Most of the early recorded complaints by Dalits to the Commission were along these lines. By the late 1970s, however, most complaints concerned issues such as land rights, housing, and education. Harassment remained an important issue, but not the major one.[12] For the Panthers, untouchability had to be seen as both status and class inequality. The Panthers dramatized the structural critique of untouchability: caste is not only a political-cultural-ritual system, but also a form of socio-economic exploitation.

The Panthers were unable to craft wide-enough solidarities to make a mark on the national political scene; further, infighting among the leaders and the cadres about whom to ally with ended any hope of building political opposition to the State's limited policy towards untouchability. In recent years, the most effective, but largely opportunistic, Dalit political bloc to emerge on the national scene has been the Bahujan Samaj Party (BSP). The BSP has its roots in the All-India Backward Scheduled Caste, Scheduled Tribe and Minority Communities Employees Federation (BAMCEF) founded in December

1978 by Kanshi Ram to organize the Dalit elite to fight for social change. In 1987, Ram told the media that the Dalits 'nurse a feeling that the government in spite of its best efforts has not been able to remove poverty. This is truly unfortunate. The bureaucracy, which we inherited from the British, is caste-ridden and officers have yet to rise above caste. I have seen how they work half-heartedly towards implementing the government's programmes for the backward communities.'[13]

The BSP is not the only organization to lay claim to the social democratic tradition of Ambedkar. It is joined in its commitment to Dalit politics by the older Dalit parties, the Scheduled Castes Federation (founded by Ambedkar in 1942) and the Republican Party of India (founded shortly after Ambedkar's death in October 1957) and by various socialist parties which draw from Rammanohar Lohia and from Jayaprakash Narayan. These parties share a commitment to protecting the Dalits from the harshness of capitalism: as Barbara Joshi put it, 'Political power could generate more paved streets in Scheduled Caste neighbourhoods, more education and jobs for the neighbourhood's young men, as well as protection from what the businessmen saw as the discriminatory harassment of government bureaucrats and the encroachment of higher caste business competitors' (Joshi 1982: 125). The recurrent alliance between the BSP and militant Hindutva since 1995 has demonstrated the impoverishment of this defensive agenda that has been cultivated by the social democratic parties which draw inspiration from Ambedkar (Gatade 2005). However, the BSP's recent political outflanking of Hindutva in the electoral arena of Uttar Pradesh is yet to provide sufficient ground to demonstrate what this new dispensation will mean for the grievances and hopes of Dalits (Kumar 2007; Padavala 2007).

The contradictions of equality reappeared on the national political agenda in the 1980s through the second Backward Classes Commission, appointed on 1 January 1979 under the chairmanship of B.P. Mandal. The Commission offered its report on 31 December 1980. On the issue of equality, the Commission was remarkable:

In fact, what we call merit in an elitist society is an amalgam of native endowments and environmental privileges .... The conscience of a civilized society and the dictates of social justice demand that 'merit' and 'equality' are not turned into a fetish and the element of privilege is duly recognized and discounted ... when 'unequals' are made to run the same race .... On the face of it the principle of equality appears very just and fair, but it has a serious catch. It is a well-known dictum of social justice that there is equality only amongst equals. To treat unequals as equals is to perpetuate inequality (Government of India 1980: 21–2).

The Mandal Commission warned in 1980 of the very contradiction identified by Ambedkar in 1949: that between the principle of equality before the law and social and economic inequality. Unwilling to grapple with the contradictions at the foundation of Indian society, many Indians were reluctant even to consider the project of producing equality. The attacks on the 'protections' to 'minorities' (communalism) and to the 'public sector' (liberalization) have made the struggle for freedom hard and yet imperative. The State is pledged to interpret untouchability as harassment and the anti-untouchability movement as a struggle for civil rights; once the struggle is seen as one for human rights and the question of structural disenfranchisement is raised, the dominant classes and castes enjoin the state to undercut those political gestures. 'Mandal' has hampered the dialogue about equality: the privileged have used it as a means to mock the project of compensation, the State has used it as a means to roll back on the project, and the Dalits and the Left are once again forced to praise policies that do not truly get at the heart of exploitation. For the Balmikis, compensation means that a few of them succeed and that they are allowed to control the sanitation departments in municipalities; from the Balmikis' point of view there is little to defend in the system. Nevertheless, many do defend it, saying much the same thing as a Dalit socialist said to Joshi about the Dalit Congress leader Jagjivan Ram (1908–86): 'I don't know his caste and I don't like his politics, but I do know he is "achut" like me, and when I see him at the top of the government, I laugh at the Brahman landlord who used to be afraid I would "pollute" his well. I am no more afraid of any Brahman. For us, democracy works' (Joshi 1982: 68). Democracy works in that Dalits now have the possibility to effect change; that they have not been able to gain power is a mark of the strength of the dominant classes and castes in India.

Dalits still fight forms of apartheid. The State failed the Dalits because it did not truly dismantle the 'advantages secured due to historical reasons', such as land relations and control over capital. Attempts by the State to extend favour to Dalits (such as in the 1980 Mandal Commission Report) draw enormous resistance from the dominant jatis. As a result,

Dalit literacy is barely 22 per cent, only 16 per cent of Dalits live in cities, about 50 per cent are agricultural labourers, and only 4 per cent are part of the industrial workforce. The extent of their poverty is about 50 per cent (as against 30 per cent for the population as a whole). Of those who work in the fields, 71 per cent are marginal farmers who must sell their labour at low rates to dominant jatis. The poverty of Dalits is matched by their lack of political power. Since the 1970s, militant Dalit groups emerged to fight landlords and to use the franchise. The exertions of these Dalits have, by all accounts, increased anti-Dalit violence. In this cauldron of struggle, many Dalit organizations, such as the Dalit Panthers, the Republican Party of India, and the BSP, have foundered on the rocks of either opportunism or extreme caste chauvinism. In recent years, liberal Dalit groups have made linkages with non-governmental organizations to create such platforms as the National Campaign on Dalit Human Rights. Their exertions, Smita Narula of HRW says, drew the attention of the organization to the atrocities against Dalits. The National Campaign has produced a series of 'Black Papers' with a stark subhead: 'Broken Promises and Dalits Betrayed'.[14]

The lack of focus on land relations is what differentiates the fight for anti-racist justice in the advanced industrial North with the relatively rural South. The Indian government's compensatory discrimination scheme concentrates on public jobs (of which a seventh are 'reserved' for Dalits and Tribes), but only 16 per cent of the total Dalit population live in urban India. Most of the rest are marginal farmers, sharecroppers, or landless labourers (despite the various prescribed occupations of certain Dalit communities). For these Dalits, land ownership is the cornerstone of liberation. The recent reports by P. Sainath confirm the centrality of land, as do news reports of anti-Dalit violence in rural Bihar and Haryana (for example, Sainath 1999 and Sainath in process). Indeed, the failure to underscore the importance of the land question underscores the centrality of the Left to Dalit liberation. When Dalit landless workers forcibly occupied the land of the ex-Raja of Benaras in Uttar Pradesh, the BSP Chief Minister Mayawati sent in the police to arrest them. Her actions once more subordinated the Dalits to poverty. The centrality of land to the Left, on the other hand, is made clear by the 20 December 1998 All India Democratic Women's Association Convention in support of Dalit women's rights against untouchability and oppression. The first demand of the convention reads as follows: 'Land reforms—land distribution, joint *pattas*, special priority to Dalits and in particular to Dalit female headed households. Return of land to Dalits which are in illegal occupation and arrest of the guilty. Access to all community land and use for fuel and fodder collection.'

Meanwhile, change is afoot. In 1996, the Dalits of Melavalavu (Tamil Nadu) won control of the local governmental body. As they tried to take office, local goons killed six of the leaders, beheading the one elected to lead the body—a 'brutal reminder', Brinda Karat of the Communist Party of India (Marxist) notes, 'that, for the non-Dalits, Dalits are meant to serve, not rule'. Karat points to the data from West Bengal, where the Left has been in power since 1977. Only there, she says, have Dalits benefited from land reforms and from the devolution of political power. West Bengal has only 3.58 per cent of the cultivable land in the Indian Republic and yet has contributed over 20 per cent of the total surplus land that falls under the land ceiling laws. Of the 4.8 million acres distributed in the country as a whole, West Bengal contributed 920,000 acres. Further, of the two million landless cultivators who received land, 56 per cent came from socially oppressed communities (37 per cent Dalits and 19 per cent Scheduled Tribes). Apart from land reform, in 1978 the Left Front initiated Operation Barga, which registered 1.4 million tenant farmers and provided them with legal instruments to stave off eviction and to struggle for shares of the harvest. These land reforms are 'the backbone of Dalit self-respect and dignity in the state' (Karat 1999).

In 1949, Ambedkar told the political leaders of India that their hesitant approach to land reform (and wealth redistribution) did not bode well for democracy: 'How long shall we continue to deny equality in our social and economic life? If we continue to deny it for long, we will do so only by putting our political democracy in peril.' Caste, as constructed in colonial times and lived in the contemporary moment, is not identical to race, even though both emerge simultaneously as methods to exert imperial control and to justify white supremacy. Where caste and race share much is in the way they relate to the economic domain: both are about denying the means of production to certain people. Nevertheless, the agenda for social justice is not identical, since the social contexts of the fights are separate: where the human rights agenda of civic justice is more important in one context, the fight for land rights is central in the other. To collapse the contexts of social justice in the service of internationalism and solidarity is to harm all our struggles (Teltumbde 2005).

The Left and liberal Dalit groups have taken it upon themselves to be the guardians of political democracy by fighting for social and economic democracy. One hopes that their struggles will make India *truly* the world's largest democracy in the fullest sense of the word.

NOTES

This paper was originally presented at a United Nations Research Institute for Social Development session in Durban, South Africa, 2001.

1. The discussion with Ram Pyari took place during fieldwork for Prashad 2000b.
2. Interview with Runoko Rashidi, 22 December 1999. See also Prashad 2000a.
3. For a polemical analysis on these lines (but for Brazilian sociology), see Bourdieu and Wacquant 1999, including responses to it in the same issue and in Volume 17 of the journal.
4. Jaiswal 1998. For a useful overview of the sociological literature, see Deliege 1999.
5. Prashad 2000b for the Balmikis, and Rawat 2003.
6. For the latter point, see Dirks 1987.
7. *Chiranjit Lal Chaudhury v. The Union of India* (1950).
8. For women, see *Anjali Roy v. The State of West Bengal* (1952); *The University of Madras v. Shanta Bai* (1954); for backward classes, see for example *The State of Madras v. Champakam Doirajan* (1951).
9. *Devadasan vs The Union of India* (AIR 1964, Supreme Court 179).
10. For details, see Mendelsohn and Vicziany 1998: Chapter 4.
11. The manifesto is reproduced in Murugkar 1991: 232–9; Chapter 5 offers a fine analysis of the political fights over the contents of the manifesto.
12. In 1977–8, land, agriculture, etc. accounted for 54.71 per cent of the complaints, and harassment for 45.29 per cent; by 1978–9, 58.88 per cent was for the former and 41.11 per cent for the latter. Mujahid 1989: 31.
13. *Illustrated Weekly of India*, 8–14 March 1987.
14. National Campaign on Dalit Human Rights 1999 and interview with Smita Naruja, 1999.

REFERENCES

Ahir, D. C. 1990. *Buddhism in Modern India*. Delhi: Sri Satguru Publications.
Bourdieu, Pierre and Loic Wacquant. 1999. 'On the Cunning of Imperialist Reason'. *Theory, Culture, Society*. vol. 16, no. 1, pp. 41–58.

Cohn, Bernard S. 1987. *An Anthropologist Among the Historians*. New Delhi: Oxford University Press.

Deliege, Robert. 1999. *The Untouchables of India*. Oxford: Berg.

Dirks, N. 1987. *The Hollow Crown*. Cambridge: Cambridge University Press.

Dubois, Abbé J. A. 1906. *Hindu Manners, Customs and Ceremonies*. Oxford: Clarendon Press.

Gatade, Subhash. 2005. 'Subverting the *Shudra-Ati-Shudra* Revolution': The Uttar Pradesh Way'. In Anand Teltumbde (ed.). *Hindutva and Dalits: Perspectives for Understanding Communal Praxis*. Kolkata: Samya, pp. 187–207.

Government of India. 1969. *Committee on Untouchability, Economic and Educational Development of the Scheduled Castes*. Delhi: Government of India.

———. 1980. *Report of the Backward Classes Commission*. First Part. vols I and II. Delhi: Government of India.

Human Rights Watch. 1999. *Broken People: Caste Violence Against India's 'Untouchables'*. New York: Human Rights Watch.

Jaiswal, Suvira. 1998. *Caste: Origin, Function and Dimensions of Change*. New Delhi: Manohar.

Joshi, Barbara. 1982. *Democracy in Search of Equality: Untouchable Politics and Indian Social Change*. New Delhi: Hindustan.

Karat, Brinda. 1999. 'Remembering the Melavalavu Six'. *The Hindu*, 30 June.

Kaur, Naunidhi. 2001. 'Caste and Race'. *Frontline*, 6 July.

King, Martin Luther, Jr. 1986. 'My Trip to the Land of Gandhi'. In James M. Washington (ed.). *A Testament of Hope*. New York: Harper (originally *Ebony*, July 1959), pp. 23–30.

Kumar, Vivek. 2007. 'Behind the BSP Victory'. *Economic and Political Weekly*. vol. 42, no. 24, 16–22 June, pp. 2237–9.

Majeed, James. 1992. *Ungoverned Imaginings*. Oxford: Oxford University Press.

Marx, Karl. 1973. *Grundrisse*. New York: Vintage.

Mendelsohn, Oliver and Marika Vicziany. 1998. *The Untouchables: Subordination, Poverty and the State in Modern India*. Cambridge: Cambridge University Press.

Mujahid, Abdul Malik. 1989. *Conversion to Islam: Untouchables Strategy for Protest in India*. Chambersburg, PA: Anima.

Murugkar, Lata. 1991. *Dalit Panther Movement in Maharashtra*. Bombay: Popular Books.

National Campaign on Dalit Human Rights. 1999. *Broken Promises and Dalits Betrayed*. New Delhi: National Campaign on Dalit Human Rights.

Padavala, Chittababu. 2007. 'On Judging Mayawati'. *Economic and Political Weekly*. vol. 42, no. 33 (18–24 August), pp. 3430–1.

Prashad, Vijay. 2000a. 'Badge of Colour: An Afro-Dalit Story'. *The Toronto Review*, Summer.

———. 2000b. *Untouchable Freedom: A Social History of a Dalit Community*. New Delhi: Oxford University Press.

Rajshekar, V. T. 1978. *Dalit Movement in Karnataka*. Bangalore: Dalit Sahitya Akademy.

Rawat, Ram. 2003. 'Making Claims for Power: A New Agenda in Dalit Politics of Uttar Pradesh, 1946–48'. *Modern Asian Studies*. vol. 37, no. 3, pp. 585–612.

Sachchidananda. 1976. *The Harijan Elite*. Faridabad: Thomson Press.

Sainath, P. 1999. 'The Borderlines of Caste'. *The Hindu*, 7 April.

———. Forthcoming. *The Glass Struggle*.

Taylor, Charles. 1975. *Hegel*. Cambridge: Cambridge University Press.

Teltumbde, Anand. 2005. *Anti-Imperialism and Annihilation of Castes*. Dombivali: Ramai Prakashan.

Thurston, Edgar. 1909. *Castes and Tribes of Southern India*. vol. VI. Madras: Government Press.

10

MAINSTREAMING MARGINALIZED VOICES
The Dalit Lekhak Sangh and the Negotiations over Hindi Dalit Literature[1]

Laura R. Brueck

Since its origin as a modern form of social resistance literature among the Dalit Panthers in Maharashtra in the 1970s, Dalit literature has been principally concerned with community identity formation. In recent decades this has proved an increasingly complicated goal, as political and economic changes among many segments of the Dalit population contribute to an expanding definition of the 'Dalit experience', and as Dalit literature itself expands into all of India's major literary languages. But in the face of this diversity Dalit literature continues to press for a distinctly Dalit identity; for this reason the boundaries of the genre are zealously guarded and debated, and the direction of its development is carefully constructed by its most dominant purveyors. As the literary movement continues to grow, however, and as new authors continue to add their individual voices to the collective cry of resistance, it is inevitable that Dalit literature will also diversify, and that challenges to these changes will inevitably emerge within the literary community itself.

This essay is concerned with the issues and debates that are emerging in the contemporary community of Dalit writers working in Hindi as they negotiate the changing boundaries of their literary genre, its growing popularity, and the changing reality of the Dalit experience. The issues that emerge, both in Hindi Dalit literary texts and in public discussions among writers, address broadly both Dalit literature's relationship with 'mainstream' Indian literary and social spheres and the question of representing 'authentic' Dalit perspectives. These issues will be explored here through the lens of one prominent north Indian Dalit literary organization, the Dalit Lekhak Sangh, or Dalit Writers Forum, based in Delhi. This comprises a group of writers and critics who are at the forefront of determining the aesthetic and thematic character of modern Hindi Dalit literature. A look at the activities of the organization and a close textual analysis of the short fiction of one of its members show clearly that Dalit literature has evolved from the initial outcry of a silenced majority on the margins. It has become a carefully mediated body of texts that are increasingly forcing their way into mainstream Indian literary and social consciousness. And yet, the increased interaction between Dalit literature and non-Dalit media, literary institutions, and individual editors, authors, and critics remains a terrain fraught with anxiety for many Dalit writers.

Dalit literature in Hindi traces its contemporary proliferation back only as far as the early 1980s. Besides the texts of a handful of early pioneers of Dalit literature in Hindi, including Hira Dom[2] and Bihari Lal Harit,[3] Dalit literature was not established as a generic body of texts that shared similar authorial, thematic, or structural traits until formal literary organizations were formed, and regional and national-level literary conferences and meetings convened, in the last quarter of the twentieth century. In the mid-1980s eminent authors Omprakash Valmiki, Mohandas Naimishray, and Jaiprakash Kardam began publishing careers that continue to define Hindi Dalit literature for many critics and scholars. The 1990s saw an explosion of Dalit literature, including many of the texts—autobiographies, short story and poetry collections, and novels—that are considered to be hallmarks of the Hindi Dalit genre.[4] The most striking development in recent years has been the enormous growth of Dalit literary criticism and the introduction of a discourse of Dalit aesthetics.[5]

The institutional heart of the Hindi Dalit literary sphere is largely based in Delhi, with smaller corollary regional and local participants scattered in cities and towns across north India, and is made up of several different literary and activist groups and individuals who participate in the creation, dissemination, and reception (analysis, criticism) of Hindi Dalit literature. These include organizations such as the populist Bharatiya Dalit Sahitya Akademi (Indian Dalit Literary

Academy), whose inexpensive publications and frequent rallies and conferences focus on reaching as massive a Dalit audience as possible; CADAM (Center for Alternative Dalit Media), whose efforts are more globally focused on creating associations with international social activist organizations; and the Dalit Lekhak Sangh, a collective of authors and intellectuals that serves as the focus of this essay.

These networks of writers and critics are working to carve out a space for the Dalit voice in Indian and international literary contexts.[6] Their debates and discussions of Dalit literature in meetings, magazine interviews, and books are formulating the future of Dalit literature, establishing the guidelines and standards by which an increasingly large body of Dalit writing is received, judged, and celebrated. These individuals are actively involved in defining contemporary Dalit literature, from analysing its 'traditional' origins to conceiving its 'modern' innovations. A new generation of writers is transforming Dalit literature from a broadly communal narrative of suffering to include such issues as feminism, literary self-consciousness, and individual introspection, while increasingly wrestling with the question of how mainstream this literature may become without losing its authentic Dalit identity. The following pages will trace some of the sites where this deliberation is taking place, both in the literary activities of groups like the Dalit Lekhak Sangh and in the pages of contemporary works of Dalit literature.

THE DALIT LEKHAK SANGH

The Dalit Lekhak Sangh (DLS), founded in Delhi in the late 1990s by a small group of writers, is the infrastructural centre of the contemporary production of and debate over Dalit literature in north India. According to General Secretary Sudesh Tanwar, the original aim of this group was to increase awareness of Dalit literature across north India, to create 'jan-chetna' (mass consciousness), and to deliver Dalit literature into every home in every village.[7] Over the years, the group has evolved into a sophisticated community of activist-writers and intellectuals who have created a forum in which Dalit literature is being read, analysed, criticized, and debated, ostensibly in an effort to develop the genre further. According to President Vimal Thorat, 'the Dalit Lekhak Sangh is trying to fulfil the responsibility of deciding what direction Dalit writing is taking, and developing that consciousness across India.'[8]

It is debatable whether the current activities of the DLS are helping to bring an awareness of Dalit literature to the masses, or whether the group is more aptly described as creating an elite forum for Dalit intellectuals to debate issues of representation, identity, and aesthetics. The literary conversations and debates that Thorat refers to as the negotiations over the direction and consciousness of Dalit literature take place largely within insular groups of Delhi-based authors and intellectuals. DLS regularly holds meetings and sponsors conferences for the promotion of Dalit literature in the elite institutions of the urban Hindi intelligentsia, including the offices and conference rooms of the Sahitya Akademi and the Indian Social Institute in Delhi. A recent event was a conference on 22 August 2004 to celebrate the 75th birthday of Rajendra Yadav, an acclaimed Hindi fiction writer of the Nayi Kahani school and, since 1986, editor of the Hindi literary monthly *Hans*. Yadav has been an important supporter of Dalit literature in Hindi, publishing Dalit stories and poems regularly in his magazine, and even releasing an entire special issue dedicated to Dalit literature and interviews with Dalit writers and critics.[9] He explains that when he began publishing *Hans*, he was focused on progressive, left-oriented literature, and gradually came to realize that the most radical and powerful literature was coming from women and Dalits.[10]

At the conference in Yadav's honour, organized and sponsored by the DLS, several writers, both Dalit and non-Dalit, spoke about the power of *Hans* as a literary vehicle in the fight against literary elitism and Brahmanical exclusivism. These writers cited *Hans'* access to more mainstream Hindi literary audiences and Yadav's own special willingness to emphasize Dalit voices among his readership. Thorat even claimed that the work of *Hans* and the DLS both lay along the same continuum: while *Hans* laid the groundwork for challenging the limits of 'traditional' literature, the DLS is continuing that project by creating and promoting work that privileges the Dalit perspective. Indeed, Yadav's own celebrated status as a popular Hindi writer, translator, and editor provides the DLS with both the credibility and the popular forum needed to intervene in mainstream literary spheres, an intervention that becomes possible only through a vehicle of the very literary dominance the Dalit writers wish to challenge.

Other activities of the DLS include monthly '*kahani-paths*' (story-readings) that feature two different authors who read their stories aloud to a small audience followed by commentary from a panel of other

Dalit writers, activists, and critics. The stories are usually distributed ahead of time by mail, so participants can read them in advance, and the literary debate is both critical and constructive, centring largely on the faithfulness of the stories to 'Ambedkarite philosophy', the most widely heralded benchmark of quality in Dalit literature, as well as on the clarity of the language and the use of innovative metaphors or literary images. According to Ajay Navariya, media representative for the DLS, the group's discussions about literature focus largely on issues of style, content, and authentic representation of the Dalit experience. These elements combine in the ideal of 'Dalit consciousness' (*chetna*), the fundamental component of an emerging Dalit aesthetics (*saundaryashastra*). Dalit consciousness then is more than just an understanding and expression of Dalit life based on experience or sympathy. It is a 'realistic' portrayal of the exploitation and oppression of Dalits coupled with a 'revolutionary mentality connected with struggle'—to quote Dalit literary critic Sharankumar Limbale (2004: 32). Dalit consciousness ascribes a seal of 'authenticity' to writers of Dalit literature whose literary perspective is shaped both by the experience of caste inequality and by devotion to Ambedkar's secular and modernist ideology.[11]

Much of the literary discussion about Dalit consciousness centres on whether or not texts speak to 'the masses', and how closely they adhere to 'reality'. In late July 2004, an interesting debate emerged at one of these readings over the story 'Badbu' ('Stench') by the popular author Surajpal Chauhan.[12] The story centres on a family of Bhangis, or sweepers, living in a small town outside Delhi. The simple narrative follows a young woman, educated through ninth class, who is married into this family. Soon after her wedding she finds herself accompanying her mother-in-law on daily excursions to clean the outdoor latrines of a residential neighbourhood, carrying human waste in a basket on top of her head. The story depicts how a bright young girl, at first horrified by the prospect of taking part in this work, is slowly conditioned to accept it through fatalistic resignation to her caste duties. Chauhan's aim in writing this story, he explained before he read it aloud, was to show the world that this kind of work still happens, and to demonstrate the depths to which a bright young mind can sink when the rhetoric of social backwardness and inequality is deeply imagined.

What seemed to be a very straightforward, moving depiction of people who are forced to carry out inhuman work drew significant

criticism from several other members of the group. The most
controversial point in the story occurs when an upper-caste housewife
notices the new girl cleaning her latrine. When she discovers that the
girl has had some education, the upper-caste woman admonishes the
girl's mother-in-law for dragging her new daughter-in-law into this filthy
work, and suggests that the girl might have some other opportunities in
life. The mother-in-law replies simply that this is her family's work
and the girl is expected to lend a hand now that she has married their
son. This drew fire from some other writers, who suggested that it was
not realistic to portray Brahmans who employ sweepers as more
progressive than the Dalit characters, indeed that it was 'against Dalit
consciousness' and harmful to the broader movement for social reform
to suggest that Brahmans want to change casteist society and Dalits
do not. More specifically, another Dalit writer criticized Chauhan for
misrepresenting this Bhangi community, explaining that she was
familiar with this particular Bhangi neighbourhood and that, while once
this kind of work was prevalent among them, the community has since
refused to transport human excreta. She charged that it was deeply
harmful not to ground the story clearly in historical time, thus suggesting
that this was still happening, and thereby to rob a community of its
hard-fought social progress and political consciousness. Others wanted
Chauhan to somehow remind his readers that the opposite of this story
is also often true, that Dalit families sometimes make great sacrifices so
that their children, including their daughters, can get education and
pursue legitimate jobs.

The frame of this debate underscores the importance and specificity
of the idea of representing reality in Dalit literature. Limbale (2004: 19)
explains that the basic premise of the Dalit literary aesthetic is that it is
'life-affirming' as well as realistic. This was made clear in the charges
from some members of the audience that Chauhan's story propagated a
negative image of the Bhangi community and suggested progressivism
in a Brahman character but obstinacy in the mind of the Dalit. The
nature of this debate also demonstrates how in some cases Dalit literature
has evolved from descriptive testimonies that elaborate on the material
hardships of an exploited existence, to politically charged social narratives
with characters drawn starkly as symbols of a Dalit political awakening.

The responses to Chauhan's story also reveal some anxiety about
mainstream attitudes toward Dalit society and mainstream reception
of Dalit literature, as well as the fundamental distrust many Dalit

writers often bear toward non-Dalit sympathizers to the Dalit cause. Such scepticism is visible in the condemnation of the Brahman character's concern for the young Dalit girl as 'unrealistic'. Such misgivings are also often evident in the reception of literature penned by non-Dalits that incorporates Dalit characters. Chauhan himself, the author of a full-length autobiography and several collections of poetry and short stories, argues in his introduction to an anthology of the first published stories of several new Dalit writers that while a few non-Dalit Hindi texts are widely regarded as sympathetic toward Dalits, most notably the celebrated fiction of Premchand, these are just belittling representations of Dalits as victims of their own suffering and not authentic portrayals of a revolutionary Dalit perspective (Chauhan 2004: 1).

LITERATURE OF ALIENATION

This kind of anxiety over how far a fundamentally caste-conscious mainstream India will ever allow Dalits to emerge from the margins of society, and indeed, how fully Dalits themselves are able to relinquish their own sense of estrangement from the mainstream, is largely the subject of Ajay Navariya's short fiction. Navariya, cited above, is a protégé of Yadav, who publishes his work regularly in *Hans*. But Navariya's work often garners criticism from other sections of the Hindi Dalit literary sphere, largely for straying too far from the approved themes of community struggle and Ambedkarite political philosophy, as well as for writing prose that is too 'difficult' for an uneducated Dalit audience. There are also many moments in his narratives where he takes experimental steps, plays with time and space and liminal transitions, and subtly challenges many of the prescribed aesthetic and thematic norms of Dalit literature.

Navariya's characters are true individuals, rather than archetypal stand-ins for an entire community, and they often undergo psychological transformations in the course of the narrative. Navariya's stories largely address the crisis of identity that befalls middle-class Dalits who have achieved a relatively high professional and material level in the modern Indian city. His characters are educated and politicized, speak comfortably in the modern vernacular of urban India, steep themselves in Ambedkarite religious and social theory, and patronize institutions of capitalist modernization such as fast-food restaurants and mobile phone dealers. Navariya's stories can be read as narratives of alienation, accounts of complex negotiations with the modern, and meditations on the widening gap between urban and rural spaces in the Indian subcontinent and their attendant social and political ideologies. His authorial voice makes it clear that the journey of many newly urbanized Dalits from village to city, from feudal caste hierarchies to the pseudo-equality of a secular modernity, is fraught with difficulty and conflict. The conflict is domestic and personal and it is manifested in a pervasive sense of alienation from oneself, one's community, and one's physical environment.

The conflicts or contradictions, of the educated middle-class Dalit body in an urban space are especially compelling in Navariya's short story '*Upmahadvi*' ('Subcontinent') (Navariya 2004). The characters in this story have benefited from such avenues of social advancement as reserved seats in education and government, and yet retain a subjectivity that ultimately falls short of the promise of full citizenship. A closer look at the thematic and aesthetic strategies employed in the story will illustrate this point more clearly.

The story moves fluidly and often between past and present. The bulk of the narrative consists of two major flashback episodes which are actually independent narratives woven within the main story. The narrative frame that brings it all together is the voice of Siddharth, a young professional Dalit living in Delhi, a government bureaucrat married to a college lecturer, and the father of a girl. The story is set in their fourth-floor Delhi flat, in the late evening when the sun is going down and the narrator is just waking from a nap. The liminal qualities of the time of day, and his own mind, mired in a kind of half-sleep, allow for the narrative's fluid transitions across time and space. In the two flashbacks Siddharth remembers his childhood, and then his adolescence. Both the stories are set in his ancestral village.

The first flashback takes place when Siddharth was a small boy. He is walking with his father and grandmother from their village to a neighbouring one, to visit his aunt, his father's sister. His father has recently found work in the city, and the trio are wearing new clothes bought in the city with his wages. It is a beautiful day and they are in high spirits. But when the flashback narrative begins, they have already been attacked by a group of upper-caste men from Siddharth's village. These thugs, one in a worn-out police uniform, have taken offense at Siddharth's family's new clothes and the influence the family appears to have come under in the city, a burgeoning awareness of their rights. As their attackers explain to the village pandit,

'The old man is right, Panditji, you can't trust whores or bulls. They'll fuck anything. And this bastard is trying to be so brave. The *bhenchod* was threatening to go to court! Now we'll see if you wear nice clothes around here a second time. Will you dare show off in the village again?' The boy who was cursing Father was the same one who had beat Amma with his shoes. He said all this staring at Father who was lying face-down on the ground, half-dead.

'The fucker got a big head goin' to the city! We'll show the know-it-all,' one said as he was rolling up his sleeve.

'He forgot the village rules. This ain't no city motherfucker. It's the village ... the *gaon*! Here you live by the rules. Only we make the rules. Break 'em and we'll break something of yours.' (Navariya 2004: 174)

The infraction of the Dalit characters is evident: in their association with an urban space and the new kinds of socio-economic opportunities that entails, they have transgressed their prescribed socio-economic roles dictated by village caste hierarchy, and for this they are punished bodily. Siddharth's father is beaten unconscious, his body bloodied and the pockets of his *kurta* emptied of rupees. The boy is hit hard across the mouth, and stands mute, watching his family being beaten. His grandmother is humiliated, made to writhe in the dust at the feet of her attackers, begging for mercy; she is called a whore and kicked repeatedly. The men and the pandit saunter back into the village, leaving the small family on the ground to put themselves back together.

Siddharth's reverie is broken by a cup of chai falling to the floor and smashing in the present time, in his urban apartment, and he is given to thinking about how different his life has become since he moved from the village to the city. He thinks about how there is no place for Dalits in the village, except as exploited subjects of the upper castes. He explains, 'Over there is our village, our roots, our land. Where there is indignity, abuse. Helplessness and weakness. Every moment the fear of dishonour .... The land was not ours, only the labour. The harvest was theirs, the fields were theirs, the houses were theirs, the earth was theirs and for us there was one hut' (Navariya 2004: 177). Siddharth continues with the contrasts of his new life, and that of his wife and daughter, in the city. It is a life of modernity, one made possible by an urban anonymity. They have a house, a car, and a driver. His daughter takes singing lessons and attends a private convent school. They eat at Pizza Hut and talk on cellphones. But the narrator is still haunted by his caste; he and other Dalit workers in his office are believed to have achieved their positions only because of the quota system, and for this they are regularly taunted. This is not at all comparable to the beatings and humiliation suffered in the village, but it is not absolute equality, nor is it a true fulfilment of the supposed unmarked citizenship of the 'modern' man. Rather it is a life still bounded by caste, fettered by prejudice and 'tradition'.

Descriptive language throughout the story offers insight into the pervasiveness of the alienation felt by the characters, principally the protagonist, of 'Subcontinent'. In his half-awake, half-asleep state, haunted by dreams of a traumatic past that Navariya describes in realistic and straightforward prose, Siddharth's own apartment and wife look and feel strange to him, as though he is viewing his life from the perspective of a confused outsider. Navariya strings sentence fragments together to highlight the protagonist's state of disarray: 'Thinking too much wouldn't let me sleep. Squandered sleep, ravaged wakefulness. Just a little light, the tiniest brightness. Light in ruins. Consciousness in ashes ....' This string of unfinished, abject thoughts, punctuated by staccato repetitions of adjectives, is broken by Siddharth's wife's query about whether or not he will drink some tea. This is a familiar pattern in the story, Siddharth repeatedly slipping into reverie, a transitional dream-speak that leads him to his overwhelming reality: the village, the past. He is suddenly snapped back to the present by her voice, or the sound of a teacup smashing to the ground, or a shrill scream as a rat runs across the floor. He is almost an unwilling participant in the present, or perhaps unable to fully be in the present, in the city, until the atrocities of his rural past are resolved.

The natural world too is hemmed in by the structures of the city— for example, the evening light when Siddharth awakes from his reverie: 'My eyes opened and I saw a broken piece of sky, agitated, caught in the square of the window. A big, inky black cloud had grabbed the feeble sun and squeezed, as though it had broken the sun's legs' (Navariya 2004: 173). And later, when the daylight becomes faint enough to turn on the lights inside, 'Like a tuberculosis patient, the old tube light coughed seven or eight times then filled the room with a lacklustre light the yellowy shade of mucous .... With the light inside, the darkness outside seemed even more inky, more scary' (ibid.).

These descriptions of both the feebleness of the daylight, trapped by the walls of buildings and overwhelmed by looming clouds, and the menacing nature of the night, which the electric light of the urban apartment does little to diffuse, creates a sense of unease in the narrative. This is a conscious construction of liminal space and time to match the fogginess of Siddharth's mind. These narrative descriptions create a mood of disquiet and apprehension, a mood that eventually becomes focused on obvious markers of modernity such as the advertising of foreign products and a collection of academic books whose titles are in English:

There was a small boy on the back of her white t-shirt clutching a bottle of some foreign brand of soda, and sticking up his thumb. I watched him until she turned into the kitchen. He was climbing my wife's back, in the skin of some charming sheep? Thinking about this made me uneasy.

My glance fell on the English titles at the head of the bed, 'Riddles in Hinduism', and 'Art and Social Life'. Delhi ... was this our home? (Navariya 2004: 175)

Everything in Siddharth's line of sight is off-putting; it either threatens him or perplexes him. Though he must look at the books at the head of the bed every day, they still appear foreign and cause him to question the authenticity of his own presence in this urban apartment setting.

The pervasiveness of Siddharth's unease, and the disquieting descriptions of the threatening darkness of an agitated, angry sky outside the window, barely held at bay by the weak electric tube light, contribute to the narrative construction of alienation, well before Siddharth tells his tale of himself and other Dalits feeling isolated and reviled in his government job; coming near the end of the story, this is the example that most clearly spells out Siddharth's sense of displacement in the 'caste-blind', secular city. This narrative of anxiety reveals Siddharth's deep-seated awareness that his 'elite' status hangs by a delicate thread of 'enforced' equality, while in the chasm of people's hearts there yet lurks the same malicious discrimination and prejudice, the same human cruelty and its religious justification that remain untouched in villages not yet transformed by the social interventions of modernity. What alienates Siddharth from all the elements of his modern life, what makes him uneasy, is the knowledge of the proximity of this lurking malevolence:

Here in front of us there are only smiles, no one would dare laugh at us. Here there are police. Here there is an expensive lawyer whose only concern is our happiness in this nameless world .... This anonymity continuously fills our rainbow dreams with colour.

But here in the known world there are snakes. Here is their hissing, their poisonous, subdued smiles. Our 'quota is decided', I have achieved all of this only because of the quota .... that's it. Otherwise ... otherwise maybe I would still be dirty, still be beneath them (ibid.).

The pervasiveness of the alienation Navariya describes is, as Fredric Jameson suggests a common feature of the 'late capitalist culture critique ... the expression of a pathos inherent in the traditional romantic diatribe against "modernity" and its ills' (Jameson 2002: 130). The presence of such a critique in Navariya's fiction is quite remarkable in the context of the literature of contemporary Dalits, for whom the promise of modernity has traditionally meant, as Gopal Guru (2001: 123) explains, 'the language of rights to equality, freedom and dignity, self-respect and recognition'. Modernity for Dalits in the colonial period heralded new opportunities for advancement through increased access to education as well as professional development in the British army. For recent generations, institutionalized systems of reservations and affirmative action have allowed a minority of Dalits to establish a middle-class population in Indian cities, with increased political participation and a wider dissemination of the rhetoric of self-awareness and community liberation. Phule and Ambedkar embraced modernity almost without qualification as the route to emancipation for Dalits, and the post-Ambedkar generation of Dalit writers and politicians has tended to hold to such pro-modernity ideology, citing education, secularization, and political participation as the most promising avenues for Dalit advancement. Navariya's questioning of the efficacy of modern life for urban, middle-class Dalits, his asking whether modernity has truly delivered on its promise of freedom from the oppressive caste hierarchies, is an important innovation in Dalit literary discourse. In Navariya's stories, the narrative subject's entry into the modern leads him to alienation from himself and from the extended bodies of his family and community.

Navariya's stories address both the limits of modern social and political institutions, as well as the silencing of Dalit identity that is intrinsic to the theoretical construction of the modern subject. Navariya's fiction participates in a contemporary critique of modernity, but in a deeper sense than merely by publication of his stories as a means to insert his own 'Dalit voice' into public discourse. Rather, the crises of identity and alienation of Navariya's characters point to a recognition of the impossibility of universal subjecthood—no 'secular society' is truly secular—but also to an acknowledgement of the personal and collective losses of self and community that are inevitable when Dalits strive for a total identification with 'the mainstream'.

CONCLUSION

Dalit literary spheres across Indian linguistic regions are striving to make a significant intervention into a literary culture that has traditionally been reserved for the elite. Like the others, the Hindi Dalit literary sphere is an extremely diverse collection of people, institutions, publications, and texts. However, at the heart of this sphere is a commitment to changing the very nature of what is considered 'literature' in the Hindi-speaking, and -reading, world. Many Dalit authors claim that they write only for a Dalit audience and that whatever impact their texts may have in the non-Dalit world is merely secondary. And yet the texts that I consider within the rubric of Dalit literature are not merely attempts to recover a Dalit voice, but rather to *incorporate* it into the Hindi literary canon. This essay has considered the nature of this incorporation, from debates within the Hindi Dalit literary sphere about questions of identity and authenticity to analyses of contemporary Dalit fictional texts.

The DLS utilizes certain organs of the dominant Hindi public sphere—the institutional authority of the national, government-sponsored Sahitya Akademi and the platform of the long-standing popular literary magazine *Hans*—to claim its separate space as a (counter) public sphere and to assert its distinct social and literary identity. The DLS also makes use of these organs in order to indicate its willingness to operate as an integrated, enriching *addition* to the rhetorical space of the dominant social and literary public rather than as a discordant entity opposed to its norms. The DLS is aware of its subaltern character in the face of the dominant Hindi discursive sphere, and is committed to erasing the hierarchical distinction not by an aggressive counter-campaign, but by working to assert and insert into this established sphere a new recognition and respect for alternative Dalit discourse.

In its simultaneous attempts to engage mainstream Hindi readership and maintain a distinct alternative Dalit perspective, the DLS is tackling—in its oral and written, public and private discursive spaces—important social and aesthetic issues that continue to face

Dalit literature in changing material and socio-political contexts. While it would be far from the truth to suggest that the need for a revolutionary Dalit public identity is losing its relevance in contemporary India—indeed, in many rural areas atrocities against Dalits continue to rise, and much Dalit literature continues to battle the prevalence of exploitative stereotyping—it is also true that there is a new class of Dalits: an employed, urban, educated, financially secure Dalit elite that is beginning to create new kinds of narrative that reflect its own diverse realities.

NOTES

1. All translations of fiction, poetry, and interviews in this essay are by the author from the original Hindi.
2. Hira Dom's famous poem '*Acchut ki Shikayat*' ('An Untouchable's Complaint') was published in Mahavir Prasad Dvivedi's magazine *Saraswati* in 1914.
3. Bihari Lal Harit (1913–99) was a poet, essayist, and activist from Agra whose writing career spanned more than fifty years and earned him the title of *Jankavi*, or people's poet. He published his first poetry collection, *Bhimayan*, in 1942 and continued, until his death, to write literary works that have recently begun to be celebrated as the first north Indian Dalit literature dedicated to the Ambedkarite political and ideological path.
4. Though the material in this article comes from a body of *self-consciously* literary texts, ones that aspire to a formal, generic status, it is important to note that the definition of 'Dalit literature' can also be extended to include a large body of informal publications, brief and inexpensive booklets distributed at political gatherings and from person to person, simply-written treatises that reconsider history, philosophy, politics, and religion from a Dalit perspective. The production of these booklets in north India grew along with Dalit political parties such as the Bahujan Samaj Party and the Republican Party in the latter decades of the twentieth century, and spiked in the late 1980s and early 1990s when Dalit political activism coalesced around the Mandal reforms. See Narayan and Misra 2004.
5. See for example Singh 2000, Valmiki 2001, and Naimishray (forthcoming).
6. The internationalization of Dalit literature is taking place in the translations of Dalit literary texts, in the establishment of international networks of Dalits through organizations such as *www.ambedkar.org*, in activities such as the International Dalit Conference in Vancouver, Canada in 2003, and through the contingent of Dalits who attended the International Conference on Race in Durban, South Africa in 2002.
7. Interview with Sudesh Tanwar, General Secretary of the DLS, 24 August 2004.

8. Interview in *Hans*, August 2004: 228.

9. See the August 2004 edition of the annual *Hans* special issue, entitled *Satta-Vimarsh aur Dalit* ('Dalits and the Struggle for Power') and guest-edited by Shyoraj Singh Bechain and Ajay Navariya, both current members of the DLS.

10. Interview held in the offices of *Hans*, in Daryaganj, Delhi, on 3 September 2004.

11. For a discussion of the ways in which the concept of Dalit consciousness is applied as a theoretical frame in which Dalit critics consider literary representations of Dalits by major non-Dalit authors such as Premchand and Nirala, see Brueck 2006.

12. Published originally under the name 'Ahalya' in *Hans*, December 2002: pp. 32–5.

REFERENCES

Brueck, Laura. 2006. 'Dalit Chetna and the Emerging Dalit Literary Critical Perspective'. *Seminar*. vol. 558, February, pp. 51–5.

Chauhan, Surajpal. 2002. 'Ahalya' (Badbu). *Hans*. December, pp. 32–5.

_____. (ed.). 2004. *Hindi ke Dalit Kathakaron ki Peheli Kahani*. Delhi: Anubhav Prakashan.

Guru, Gopal. 2001. 'The Interface between Ambedkar and the Dalit Cultural Movement in Maharashtra'. In Ghanshyam Shah (ed.). *Dalit Identity and Politics*. New Delhi: Sage, pp. 97–107.

Jameson, Fredric. 2002. *A Singular Modernity: Essays on the Ontology of the Present*. London and New York: Verso.

Limbale, Sharankumar. 2004. *Towards an Aesthetics of Dalit Literature*. Alok Mukherjee (trans.). Hyderabad: Orient Longman.

Naimishray, Mohandas. (Forthcoming). *Hindi Dalit Sahitya* ('Hindi Dalit Literature').

Narayan, Badri and A.R. Misra (eds). 2004. *Multiple Marginalities: An Anthology of Identified Dalit Writings*. New Delhi: Manohar.

Navariya, Ajay. 2004. '*Upmahadvip*' ('Subcontinent'). *Hans*. vol. 19, no. 1 (August), pp. 173–8.

Nigam, A. 2000. 'Secularism, Modernity, Nation: Epistemology of the Dalit Critique'. *Economic and Political Weekly*. vol. 35, no. 48 (25 November), pp. 4256–68.

Singh, Tej. 2000. *Aj ka Dalit Sahitya* ('Dalit Literature Today'). Delhi: Atish Prakashan.

Valmiki, Omprakash. 2001. *Dalit Sahitya ka Saundaryshastra* ('Aesthetics of Dalit Literature'). Delhi: Radhakrishna Prakashan.

11

REPRESENTATIONS OF DALIT WOMEN
Translating Urmila Pawar's Short Stories

Veena Deo

Urmila Pawar's is a serious, emergent voice in Marathi short fiction that marks an unusual space of intersections of gender, caste, and class in the modern, urban Maharashtrian environment. Born on 7 May 1945, two years before India gained independence from colonial rule, Pawar was an eleven-year-old schoolgirl when Ambedkar led four million Indians (most of them from the Mahar caste) into Buddhism in a mass conversion ceremony in Nagpur in 1956. She grew up to be an adult woman at the time when Dalit families who had converted to Buddhism were negotiating their new cultural identity and instituting new cultural practices in independent India. Her experiences as a young Dalit woman in rural as well as urban communities; her familiarity with a variety of uses of the Marathi language and its regional variants; her insider/outsider perspective on Dalit women's lives; and her active participation in Dalit women's literary and social organizations provide her storytelling with an edge that throws into relief the many ironies and contradictions in the lives of Dalit women. Her agenda, like that of any other Dalit writer, is to write for social change; to critique Hindu caste divisions, traditions, and superstitions; to motivate activism; and to encourage a rational, critical perspective among readers committed to human rights. Having recently translated some of Urmila Pawar's short stories, I reflect here on her representations of Marathi Dalit women as well as on my representation in translation of her works.[1]

Both Mahatma Phule (1828–90) and Babasaheb Ambedkar (1891–1956) involved women closely in their struggle for individual rights and social reform. Urmila Pawar and Meenakshi Moon have recorded these women's many contributions in their history of women in the Ambedkar movement, *Amhihi Itihas Ghadavala* ('We Too Made History', 1989).[2] Growing educational opportunities for women in independent India have had an impact in the concerted efforts made by individual women and women's organizations to define their roles and issues. Dalit women writers' voices have emerged late in the written literary traditions.

Asha Mundale (1987) explains this late coming of Dalit women to the world of letters and argues that a written tradition is not a good yardstick to measure Dalit women's cultural contributions. A Dalit woman's personality is shaped by her environment. She is exploited sexually by upper-caste men and has rarely been able to complain about that. This has made her relationship with her husband sometimes ambivalent, making her vulnerable to his abuse and/or frustrations. Her children revere her and have compassion for her because they always see her working hard to keep the family fed. Mundale recounts Dalit women's social history to explain what she sees as their unique expressive contributions. She explains that a Dalit woman is not afraid to express herself; she can be sharp and quick-witted with her words. She is often open about her sexuality, as expressed in the *lavani* and *tamasha* forms.[3] Her silence is not always quite like the silence of middle-class or upper-caste women. She is articulate and forceful, even though written literary expression is a relatively new avenue for her.

Urmila Pawar's recently published autobiography (2003) provides an excellent example of Mundale's assertion about Dalit women's use of language. Pawar tells a story about her sister, who was so influenced by the language of upper-caste women that she decided to emulate it after she was married. This emulation meant never calling her husband by his first name or speaking to him directly as an equal. Pawar explains that this language shift created a hierarchy between them and a distance that most Dalit women would never accept. Educational opportunities where the middle-class and upper-caste values and cultural ethos are uncritically presented as normative create a need for critical understanding of the limits of formal education for Dalit girls and boys. Pawar's stories often address the gaps that Dalit children experience as they negotiate integration into middle-class society.

Urmila Pawar was the youngest of four children of Lakshmi Arjun Pawar and her husband, Arjun Chimaji Pawar. Urmila grew up in modest circumstances in a household managed by her mother, where hunger and poverty were very familiar. Urmila's father, a school teacher, died when she was in the third grade. She was nine years old then. Her mother raised the family on her income from basket-weaving and from a couple of rooms she rented out. Both parents encouraged their children's educational aspirations. Pawar's autobiography, entitled *Aaydaan* ('Baskets', 2003), wonderfully parallels her mother's basket-weaving to her own writing. '*Aaydaan*' can also be translated as 'a mother's gift'; as such it becomes a rich metaphor for the multiple connections Pawar finds between her mother's life and experiences and her own. Urmila lost her eldest son, Mandar, when he was only twenty-one years old, just as her mother lost her eldest son early in her life and never recovered from the shock. Urmila married her husband, Harishchandra Pawar, at a very young age and against the wishes of her family, but continued her education and writing after her marriage. Her autobiography candidly provides insight into the tensions her literary aspirations and social involvements brought to the family, but it also shows that her husband supported her endeavours. Her stories were published in smaller magazines and subsequently collected into volumes. The first collection, *Sahav Bot* ('Sixth Finger'), was published in 1988; the historical study mentioned above, *Amhihi Itihas Ghadavala*, co-authored with Meenakshi Moon, was published in 1989; Pawar's second volume of stories, *Chauthi Bhint* ('Fourth Wall'), in 1990; her travelogue *Mauritius: Ek Pravas* ('Mauritius: One Journey'), in 1994; and two one-act plays in 1996. Her autobiography is her most recent publication (2003). In a conversation with Pawar in 2005, I learned that she is now trying her hand at a novel and hopes to publish a third volume of short stories.

As a child of parents inspired by the ideas of Babasaheb Ambedkar, Urmila Pawar grew up in a family that emphasized education and accorded equal treatment to her brother and to her and her sister. She speaks of first-hand knowledge and experience of the practices of untouchability as she was growing up in Ratnagiri—not being allowed to sit with the caste-Hindu children in school, not being allowed to enter a caste-Hindu's home or to touch anyone's hand when delivering cane baskets woven by her mother or other women of the community, receiving money for the baskets only from a distance, and so on—all this seemed perfectly ordinary and correct behaviour to her. Belonging to a low caste seemed like a god-given verdict never to be questioned. So she insists that there is a difference between awareness of discrimination, which she always had, and a sense of outrage at the discrimination, which was fostered deliberately in her community as a result of Ambedkar's teachings and the later mass conversion to Buddhism.

Pawar lives in Mumbai and is now widowed and retired from her job as a draftsperson in the Public Works Department of the city government. Her two daughters, Malavika and Manini, are professional women. Urmila always speaks of writing as a hobby rather than a profession, even though, now that she is living alone, she sees it as a necessary occupation. She wanted to work on a PhD dissertation on Ambedkar, but was discouraged by advisors who pointed out disciplinary constraints–her Master's degree is in Marathi and the dissertation on Ambedkar she wished to write would only have been considered in Sociology. Pawar is critical of the tokenism accorded to her when she is asked to join delegations of Marathi literary people for various events at home and abroad, but is seldom offered the podium to speak. Writing then becomes an avenue for recording, protesting, and expressing personal as well as group experience.

By bringing narratives of Dalit women of rural Maharashtra and/or older generations and more educated Dalit working women together with narratives of other, middle-class urban women who may or may not be identified as Dalit, Pawar inscribes the narrative of 'woman' in its multiplicity and variety. Her short story entitled 'Baichi Jaat' ('Woman's Caste') from *Chauthi Bhint* speaks to this identification of the gendered reality that all women experience. This group shares issues across class and caste, and Pawar often imagines friendships and connections among its members, but also keeps boundaries visible that enable women to retreat into caste and class privilege whenever convenient. Pawar makes these subtle negotiations and nuanced differences available to her readers without polemic, but also without compromise.

I have translated a total of twelve of Pawar's short stories over the years. Nine of them are from her published volumes of short stories, *Sahav Bot* and *Chauthi Bhint*, and three others were published in

Diwali magazines, a kind of magazine that is read widely in middle-
class Maharashtrian homes and circulating libraries sometimes deliver
from door-to-door for a small monthly fee. 'Dhamma Chakra' ('The
Cycle of Dhamma') was published in *Akshar* in 1994, 'Vartool' ('Circle')
in *Jwala* in 1992, and 'Dhind' ('Public Disgrace') in *Bayja* in 1992.

The stories I have selected for translation offer a wide
representation of experiences of Dalit women in rural as well as urban
settings, focusing on their experiences in terms of generation, class,
and caste. These stories are also examples of Pawar's varying tones,
ranging from ironic to serious and from comic to didactic, so that
readers of the translations can see the broad scope of her interests in
storytelling. While Pawar's Marathi audience comprises Maharashtrian
readers in general, readers of my translations are likely to be American
academics, feminists, and others interested in multiculturalism, world
literatures, or area studies. The feminism that informs Pawar's
storytelling is directed toward Dalit women's concerns, which are very
different from issues feminists address in the United States. It is
important for the reader to understand these differences in order to
be prepared for a cross-cultural reading experience. Short stories never
have footnotes, but my translations do. I try to recreate the linguistic
environment of Pawar's storytelling, and regional dialect variations
cannot be captured effectively in standard English. To that extent the
translations are approximations of the stories' texts, and readers must
understand the retelling implicit in the translations. Even with these
limitations in mind, I believe, it is important to provide Pawar's storytelling
to a larger audience.[4]

Pawar's use of language is quite remarkable, as she moves effortlessly
between rural and urban dialects and standard Marathi. She uses a
variety of dialects (the Konkani of her native Ratnagiri, her husband's
native Malvani, and standard Marathi) based on differing contexts of
her stories, and captures local speech patterns effectively. It is impossible
to convey all those nuances of language in translation. I have tried to
be faithful to the text of her stories while also being aware of the readers
of the translations. I have, therefore, not always translated literally,
but in a manner that allows Pawar's text to exist while being remade
in a new language for a new audience.

Some of Pawar's stories are closely fashioned after her own life
experiences. For instance, 'Aaye' ('Mother') tells the story of a mother
who wishes to stay in the city to raise her children, but after her husband

dies his family tries to move the mother and children back to the village so that the homestead can be sold for a profit. The basic outline of this story, Pawar records in her autobiography, is her mother's own experience. Many other stories in which women interact with family members or each other in the marketplace, and a story about the name of a place that caused much harassment to women, are based on real experiences that she heard about from her sister or the older women of the community and reworked into effective written stories.

Pawar's storytelling depends a great deal on dialogue and interactions. She has always had considerable interest in theatre and as a young woman often acted in school and community theatrical productions. She still speaks fondly of her experiences, and even in an ordinary conversation will recall dialogues from plays to illustrate her point. Her emphasis on dialogue and short, staccato conversations is an interesting feature of her storytelling. The objective in her stories is always to focus on human interactions rather than spending time on descriptive or ornamental prose. Indulgence in the beauty of the prose for itself is meaningless for this Dalit writer, whose social agenda is clearly at the centre of her storytelling. In her stories the theatrical and performance mode is often used to illustrate the communal aspect of life in Maharashtra, where ideas of privacy and individual space are minimal; many characters in her stories use community members and communal space to attain what they want.

The stories I have translated offer an insight into themes that are important to Dalit women in Maharashtra—the redefinition of women's roles in general and Dalit women's roles in particular in post-Independence India; the effects of conversion to Buddhism; the memories of 'untouchability' as well as its continued practice in differing forms in rural and urban areas; Dalit women's relationships with other women, with Dalit men, with family, and with children; their concerns about work and workplace issues; their leadership roles in the struggle to define their own autonomy; concerns about finding progressive marriage partners; community support and activism; and many other issues. The concerns of Dalit women represented through the selection of Pawar's stories also reflect her ideas about women's issues and women's rights. None of the stories suggest a radical rejection of social structures or institutions, but they do suggest that women have a role to play in revising and reshaping unjust social practices that affect their everyday realities.

One of the stories I have translated, 'Mukti' ('Freedom'), is unusual in that it is a retelling of one of the old narratives of Buddhist women exemplars. Pawar mentioned to me in a phone interview in June 2004 that she had read a number of these Buddhist narratives translated from Pali into Hindi. Of the many exemplars, she chose the story of Kundalkesha to rework for modern Buddhist women because it explores the theme of physical punishment and suffering as restriction to self-realization. Pawar's concern here seems to be to explore what freedom means for a woman physically and metaphysically, as well as to probe Buddhist teachings for insights into her present cultural context.

My interest in Pawar's work is related to her articulation of a subject position that can be understood as the 'odd one within'. The voice that occupies this position is at once that of an outsider looking in and an insider looking out. Its multiple inflections are captured in several stories on different registers. Although Pawar identifies herself as a Dalit writer, the boundaries of that identification are as large as life itself. She extends and enriches Marathi literary language to incorporate women's narratives that the modern short story form has not always acknowledged. In the final section of this essay, I take a closer look at some of the stories I have translated to show Pawar's deft use of the insider/outsider perspective in her storytelling.

'Shalya' ('Pain') from *Sahav Bot* is a story about a woman, Jyoti, whose awful secret cannot be given public voice. She talks a sympathetic midwife in a hospital into exchanging her girl-baby with the boy-baby of another young woman who is yet unmarried and, therefore, indifferent to her own maternal experience and her baby. This exchange is plotted because Jyoti has five other daughters and the birth of a sixth girl would reduce her in the eyes of her family, whom she has no courage to face. After the exchange, the midwife goes on leave, and Jyoti is torn by the manner in which her daughter is ignored by the new mother in the other bed while the boy-child gains immense prestige amidst Jyoti's family. She suffers for the fate of her daughter and even argues with the mother in the next bed for being so inhuman. Jyoti is praised for being nurturing and compassionate, as a woman who is affected by the fate of the girl in the next crib despite the fact that she has five daughters of her own. The new mother across from her is depressed because she will not be able to convince anyone to adopt the girl child with whom she is now saddled. Jyoti is completely compressed in a place where she prefers to remain silent at the expense of her girl baby and a new unwed mother rather than risk unveiling her own false public image.

Pawar's narrative voice is dubiously sympathetic with Jyoti. The middle-class expectations, internalized values of gender superiority, and wide gap between Jyoti's impassioned words of appeal to the next-door new mother's humanity and her incapacity to act according to her own words indict Jyoti in indirect ways. As a result, the last sentence of the story, which exclaims, 'Who was she going to show her wounded heart to!' rings hollow with ironic sympathy (Pawar 1988: 9). The story that indicts Jyoti is also the story of a devalued female child whose voice will be stifled unless Jyoti can say what she knows true humanity demands. Agency has to be earned with courage, and often in Pawar's stories it is women who use street-wise common sense in rural places and backwoods small towns, or Dalit women in urban settings, who demonstrate this courage, rather than urban, educated women from middle-class (and probably upper-caste) households. The narrative voice expresses appropriate sorrow for the fate of a girl-child as well as an ironic sympathy for the woman who has failed her own humanity.

While Jyoti's story is probably that of an upper-caste or Dalit upper-class woman, 'Vegli' ('The Odd One'), also from *Sahav Bot*, is a story of an educated, working Dalit woman named Nalini. Nalini's determined struggle for a better future for herself and her child helps her to leave her manipulating in-laws, whom she considers hopelessly backward, as well as her husband, whom she sees as easily manipulated and tied to his mother's apron strings. Pawar carefully constructs Nalini's environment for her readers. Nalini finds an apartment in a housing complex because she applies for it as a Dalit woman, and at the same time she continuously listens to her co-workers (identified as '*maitrini*', (friends) complaining about how reservation and quota systems benefit 'these people' while creating unfair situations for all the others. Nalini's happiness at her success is, therefore, mediated by constant reminders that she does not really deserve what she has gotten. Her in-laws at home continue to live as if they were in a slum and are suspicious of her status as a working woman who brings money and wields unusual power over their son. Nalini finds herself somewhat alone amidst all the noise, and quietly assesses her situation as her husband first tries to convince his parents to go to the new apartment and later gives in to their manipulations when his mother fakes a fit.

Throughout the story, Nalini does not say much at all—all the noise and clutter of various positions is outside of her. To an extent, her ability to keep the noise out is itself an indication of her determined move at the end of the story: she picks up her baby and leaves her in-laws' home while her husband pleads with his mother, who briefly opens a shocked eye at her daughter-in-law's determination. Pawar's language here has a superb power of shifting between various forms of speech, from educated upper-caste speech to uneducated Dalit speech, and the fast-paced narrative makes the clutter and noise around Nalini more foreboding. The noise created by educated and uneducated, upper-caste and lower-caste communities around her emphasizes a need for a subject position that consistently moves between worlds; the woman in that position has to centre herself through inner resources that are not necessarily voiced or articulated.

Dalit writers often emphasize their investment in modernity, progress, rationality, scientific thinking, and enlightenment (all ideas under attack from postcolonial critiques of nationalism). Buddhism as a way of life is reinvented in the modern contemporary world. Community enrichment programmes of the 'Viharas' are clearly contrasted with rituals of Hindu temples. Social advancement of upper-caste women is seen as a progression encouraged by society, while women of lower-caste and outcaste communities remain oppressed. Such rhetoric signifies that the value attached to development includes some envy of upper-caste lifestyle and opportunities that could also become uneasy models for social and cultural development.

Pawar carefully negotiates this trap. Her story 'Kavach' ('Armour') illustrates beautifully the double edge of social development. A young Dalit boy, Gaurya, is inhumanly beaten by his mother, Indira, because she wants to take mangoes to the market to sell and Gaurya insists she should not go there to sell them. His father lies in bed in a drunken stupor and obviously shows that he is not a dependable wage earner for the family. As the story unfolds, we find out that in school Gaurya has heard his female teacher protest loudly against her male colleagues' use of certain words with double meanings. The village where Gaurya lives is called 'Choli', or blouse, and the male teachers make a remark about 'Choliche ambe' (mangoes in the blouse) that the female teacher insists is insulting and deliberately provocative. The men of course refuse to understand. Gaurya remembers the way customers talk to his mother and is ashamed of her and for her. The sexual exploitation of Dalit women is highlighted here in a market system where the woman as sole wage earner is left with little recourse to justice.

The rest of the story is about Gaurya's keen observations about his mother's poorly clad body, the vile customers, his attempts to detach himself from her so he can deny any kinship with her. He wishes she was more like his upright schoolteacher. However, when two drunken men haggle about 'show us your mangoes', Indira strikes back very pointedly, but calmly: 'Yes, yes they are mangoes from the choli, but your mother's choli. Go buy those and make sure they are firm' (Pawar 1990: 102). Gaurya is surprised to see the two men retreat mumbling obscenities. His seemingly uneducated, unrefined mother takes the edge out of those words without much drama. Pawar's focus on *double entendres*, and the ability of speakers to appropriate language and distort meanings in order to dehumanize, harass, and oppress those who are considered powerless, raises the stakes a little higher for what kind of language use ought to be valued. What the young boy considers desirable behaviour illustrated by his teacher is ultimately seen as much less effective, although a necessary action on the teacher's part. This possibility of interpretation, critical perception, and evaluation is accorded a narrative voice only because it is both inside and outside of Dalit experience. In her 1998 interview, Pawar says that Dalits have been exploited and oppressed for so long that they have not had a chance at self-improvement, and that domestic violence and abuse of women and children in Dalit homes are 'bad habits' that have become a way of life. Her fiction doesn't say that this improvement is going to happen from educational facilities provided by government programmes, but rather that these resources are within Dalit communities and they need an opportunity to understand and define their own humanity and strength; this will lead to self-respect.

It is significant that this story of Pawar's became a target of controversy in Mumbai in terms of language use and its appropriateness for young students. The charge of 'vulgarity' levelled against the story clearly indicates the fear of those who control language when they are challenged to rethink their language use and their actions. After much deliberation, the story is now part of the curriculum at an all-women's school (SNDT College).

Challenges to language use may also be afforded by discourses offered by Buddhism. Pawar has translated Buddha's sayings (from Jagdish Kashyap's Hindi translation) in *Udaan* (1989), and her study and research in Buddhist literature continue. With the story 'Mukti' ('Freedom') in *Chauthi Bhint,* Pawar's fiction takes another turn for Dalit writing. The story is in the form of an allegory, written in the highly literary Marathi appropriate to the time after Gautam Buddha. It is the story of a Jain woman scholar, Kundalkesha, who grows up as a very rich, bright, wilful girl who always gets her way. She marries a man who is about to be executed as a dangerous thief and who has escaped the hands of the law multiple times. She prevails on her father to enable a backdoor release of this famed robber, so she can marry him. After their marriage, the robber is free, but he is out of his element since he has nothing to do. Hence, he devises a plan of escape. It is a rude shock for her when one day, on an excursion alone with him at the top of a cliff, he is transformed into a man who wants his freedom from her at all costs. She realizes that her role as his saviour does not hold him to her. In danger of losing her own life, she pushes him off the cliff and survives. She is then transformed from Subhadra to Kundalkesha, a Jain nun of great reputation and austerity.

As Kundalkesha she roams through the land, challenging scholars to defeat her in the art of argumentation. She reigns supreme until she encounters a Buddhist mendicant and scholar, Sariputra. He is able to demonstrate to her that by changing her name and avocation she has not changed herself. Her wilful desire for supremacy and control has continued, while her pride in herself is enormous. His discourse disarms her and she gains true transformation. This allegorical piece, which focuses on transformations and self-improvement, suggests the power of Buddhist teachings and discourse. This transformation is more than simply a matter of education and self-control; it implies self-criticism, insight, and self-knowledge that can lead to transformation, increased humanity, and inner peace. Although this allegory provides Buddhist discourse its power, the gendered relationship of a male Buddhist scholar as teacher and a woman in the role of a learner is kept intact. Whether gender difference is elided here is a question Pawar might have to struggle with. However, her story opens up a space in modern Marathi literature for Buddhist forms of representation and storytelling—an important point of departure for Dalit writing as a whole.

'Cheed' ('Anger') from *Chauthi Bhint* is a story about the friendship of two working women in Mumbai—Shanta and Neema. Shanta believes that their friendship is based entirely on shared goals for life and their similarity in tastes and age. She cherishes her friendship enough to let Neema see every frustration with her adolescent children and their problems. Neema has no children, but her relationship with her husband is very close and seems ideal. In a series of conversations about her worries for her daughter, Shanta comes to terms with the fact that Neema shares every detail of their conversations with her husband and is continuously influenced by his opinions. Neema does not seem like a trusted autonomous friend any more, but a persona always shifting from herself to her husband's borrowed self. Shanta is distraught at this possibility and her story raises the question about the importance of autonomous, independent identity for women versus the middle-class, romantic ideal of lovers as two entities in one. The story indirectly proposes a different basis for male/female relationships as well as female friendships—a realization that Shanta comes to very late, although both she and Neema are involved with feminist movements, attend lectures together, and so on. The male/female relationship, which was a focus of envy and desire, and perhaps emulation, becomes for Shanta more invasive and problematic. The female/female relationship, on the other hand, which is always considered much less significant, provides an important insight into the need to fashion female autonomous selves.

Pawar's writing, then, provides a very nuanced and sophisticated articulation of an emergent voice that moves through a variety of discourses and enriches Marathi literature as a whole. This voice is involved in redefining realities and roles for contemporary Maharashtrian women. It is a voice that needs to be heard.

NOTES

1. Urmila Pawar was first introduced to me by Eleanor Zelliot and I am most grateful to her for that. Eleanor not only introduced me but also encouraged me to translate Dalit poetry and prose. I had always been interested in Dalit writing but my area of formal study is African-American Studies. Eleanor's encouragement, her help with books from her personal library, and her inclusion of me on panels in professional conferences about Dalit writing have all been fundamental in my persistence in this area.

2. Throughout this essay, translations of titles of books, short stories, quotations from texts etc. in parentheses are my own.

3. *Tamasha* is one of the best-known forms of folk theatre in Maharashtra.
    It includes song, dance, and interludes of comedy. *Lavani*s are song-and-
    dance numbers within a tamasha. Lavanis are typically characterized by
    dancing that is both highly energetic and erotic.
4. The translation of 'Dhamma Chakra' has been published in a literary
    journal, *Northeast*, in 2005. Other translations are to appear in a volume
    that is being prepared for publication.

REFERENCES

Mundale, Asha. 1987. '*Dalit Streecha va Tichya Baddalcha Bhashavyavahar*'.
    In Shobha Bhagwat (ed.). *Dalit Purushanchya Atmacharitratil Stree
    Pratima*. Pune: Streevani Prakashan, 1987, pp. 61–74.
Pawar, Urmila. 1988. *Sahav Bot*. Mumbai: Sambodhi Prakashan.
———. 1989. *Udaan* (translated from Hindi). Pune: Sugawa Prakashan.
———. 1990. *Chauthi Bhint*. Mumbai: Sambodhi Prakashan.
———. 1992a. 'Vartool' ('Circle'). *Jwala*, Diwali issue, pp. 71–5.
———. 1992b. 'Dhind' ('Public Disgrace'). *Bayja*, Diwali issue, pp. 3, 4, 54–60.
———. 1994. 'Dhamma Chakra' ('The Cycle of Dhamma'). *Akshar*, Diwali issue,
    pp. 157–61.
———. 2003. *Aaydaan*. Mumbai: Granthali Prakashan.
——— and Meenakshi Moon. 1989. *Amhihi Itihas Ghadavala*. Mumbai: Stree
    Uvach Prakashan.

12

NAMDEO DHASAL*
The Maverick Dalit Poet who Changed Marathi Poetry

Dilip Chitre

He is, arguably, one of the major world poets of the twentieth century, alive and kicking. Namdeo Dhasal is not important just because he happens to be a Dalit, nor because he is a Marathi poet. His poetry is as striking as it is intriguingly complex. It withstands translation, however, even as it defies it. When he presented his poetry at the First Internationales Literaturfestival in Berlin in 2001, with simultaneous translations provided in German and English, he made a sensation. He was in very select company of one—thirty writers representing five continents and many different languages.

In his home country, India, he is yet to be discovered outside of his native Maharashtra, though by now a few of his poems have been translated into Hindi, Bengali, and English. In *India: A Million Mutinies Now*, V.S. Naipaul devotes a whole chapter to his meeting with Namdeo, but fails to comprehend its significance, as his communication with Namdeo relied on an interpreter. Dom Moraes, too, has described his encounter with Namdeo, and, being more perceptive than Naipaul, Dom not only did his homework on Namdeo but also got some of Namdeo's poems translated in order to understand him better.

There is something exotic and fascinating about a Dalit poet who is also a militant political activist and who claims to have grown up in Mumbai's infamous red-light district, who has rubbed shoulders with notorious gangsters as well as the top political leadership of Maharashtra, has been awarded a Padma Shri, and is rated highly among contemporary Marathi writers. Namdeo makes good copy for journalists, but unless they are fluent in Marathi—the only language Namdeo speaks—they won't even know what they are missing. Very few people outside Maharashtra know that Namdeo is not only an outstanding poet but also the author of two impressive novellas, a brilliant book of essays compiled from his journalistic columns— *Andhale Shatak* ('The Blind Century')—and his amazing memoirs, *Those Magical Days of the Dalit Panthers*, published in a Diwali special number of the magazine ABaKaDaEe.

Namdeo describes himself as a member of the lowest of the low class, scum of the earth, or 'lumpen', as well as Dalit, which means 'oppressed' or 'downtrodden'. People who have seen him only a few years ago driving a sports car or being chauffer-driven in an imported sedan may say that he is a political opportunist who has sold the Dalit movement down the river like most other Dalit leaders, whose political alliances and alignments cover all 360 degrees of our vicious circle of electoral politics. But Namdeo himself will patiently explain to you precisely why he is with the Shiv Sena today as he was earlier with the Lohiate Socialists, the Communist Party of India, the Congress, and the failed 'united' Republican Party of India.

In an interview with the Munich-based film-maker Henning Stegmüller and me for a film we made on the city of Mumbai in the late 1990s, Namdeo said that India's entire system was criminal and corrupt and paid only lip-service to Constitutional morality—which left few options to the poorest of the poor fighting for survival in a grossly uneven world. Therefore, he asserted, the 'compromises' of the *lumpen* seemed crude and criminal to those who lived off more atrocious though extremely sophisticated crime. Be that as it may, I am not Namdeo Dhasal's political apologist or ally. I am only an unabashed admirer of his literary genius and achievement, and the human values his uncompromising art asserts.

Though I knew Namdeo's poetry a little earlier than him, we met in the mid-1960s when he was a young taxi driver who wrote strikingly original poems and spoke with brash conviction. We met again later, in 1972, just before his first collection of poems, *Golpitha*, was published by Narayan Athavle, a journalist, with an introduction by Vijay Tendulkar; both of them were my colleagues then in the Indian Express group of newspapers in Mumbai.

Golpitha is a landmark in the history of not only Marathi but the whole of South Asian literature. In this slim book of poems we find for the first time the voice of 'the scum of the earth' rising high above the sophisticated murmur of 'literary' poetry without compromising its artistic authenticity and intensity. Namdeo is a big poet in the sense that Whitman, Mayakovsky, and Neruda are big. His poetry contains, unlike theirs, large chunks of a real and dirty world peopled by the have-nots and speaking their many slangs. Henry Miller once said, 'I am not creating values; I defecate and nourish.' Namdeo did precisely this for Marathi poetry. He restored its soil-cycle by feeding it the very excrement and garbage that could fertilize it for the future.

Today, most serious literary critics agree that Namdeo is one of the major Marathi poets of the twentieth century and is in a class of his own. No other Dalit or non-Dalit poet or writer of the period will produce that kind of consensus. On the other hand, Namdeo's political career remains nothing but controversial. But even so, it cannot tarnish his singular literary achievement. He is a pioneer, an innovator, and a true maverick.

Born in a small hamlet called Pur-Kanersar in the Khed Taluk of Pune District in Maharashtra in 1949, Namdeo could be described as almost one of Midnight's Children. His father was a small-time Mahar farmer who, along with his fellow Untouchables, lived off land granted to the Mahars just outside the village limits. Namdeo was his only surviving child. Unable to feed his family and forever cash-strapped, Namdeo's father went to Mumbai to work as a Muslim butcher's assistant, bringing home daily wages plus discarded portions of beef. Namdeo and his mother joined his father when Namdeo was about six or seven. He recalls his sense of wonder and awe as he stepped out of the Victoria Terminus station, his eyes immediately arrested by a huge hoarding of the film 'Mother India' then showing at the Capitol cinema.

Namdeo grew up in Dhor Chawl in the Arab Galli near Golpitha— the 'black hole' of central Mumbai's traditional red-light district—among small-time smugglers, drug-traffickers, hired killers, burglars, thieves, loan-sharks' henchmen, and goons living on protection-money. A brilliant student at school, he was an avid reader and a prodigiously talented writer at a precocious age. Still in his early teens, he fell in love with a caste-Hindu girl and eloped with her to Pune, nearly causing a communal riot where he lived in Mumbai. The 'couple' were eventually separated and the issue was hushed up. His schooling ended, Namdeo read Ambedkar and also came under the influence of Ram Manohar Lohia. Later he read Marx, and when he married Mallika, daughter of the Communist folk-singer and poet 'Shahir' Amar Shaikh (a Muslim by birth), the Communist leader S.A. Dange took him under his wing for a while.

Disillusioned with Lohiate Socialists, Communists, Naxalites, and the Congress party, as all of them seemed limited by their bourgeois and caste-Hindu leadership one way or another, Namdeo became a co-founder of the militant activist movement Dalit Panthers in 1972. This movement had some parallels with the Black Panthers in the United States, and of its four founders only Namdeo had the kind of charisma that Malcolm X or Stokely Carmichael possessed. Namdeo was able to galvanize Dalit youth and turn them into extremely effective urban guerrillas with their own social, political, and cultural agenda. They became such an irritant to the powers that be that the Mumbai and Maharashtra police were instructed to hound them and snuff their movement out. Then, during the Emergency—when there were over three hundred 'cases' filed against him and his Panthers—Namdeo got an audience with Indira Gandhi in Delhi, and she was so impressed by him that she asked the government of Maharashtra to drop all charges against the Dalit Panthers and stop harassing them.

Namdeo's critics still refer to this to make the case that Namdeo is an opportunist and a mercenary, and they point out that today he is an ally of Bal Thackeray and the Shiv Sena, once his sworn enemies. But then, what Dalit leader in India cannot be similarly charged? The Dalits are wooed as a vote-bank at election time, but they are politically the most fragmented of the country's caste groups. Political parties flush with black money and other sources of funding, with higher stakes in power, have turned our entire system into a corrupt enterprise and a mockery of our Constitution's republican promises and democratic aspirations. Even an Ambedkar would have found it difficult to deal with our current political situation.

Namdeo Dhasal, the poet, has been remarkably consistent in his world view and its fullest artistic expression in his unique voice. His politics may be errant, his judgement of friends and allies flawed, but nobody can say that he stashed up money, made personal property, or created wealth for his kin. Though Namdeo's lifestyle is flamboyant, larger-than-life, his young followers find him transparent and direct, human and honest, warm and caring. Plagued for years by myasthenia gravis, an incurable condition that compels him to take steroids daily in order to prevent a sudden collapse of muscle tone and other serious crises, Namdeo somehow summons the energy to lead young Dalits across Maharashtra, and his appeal has survived.

But the true strength of his personality lies in his instinct to survive, the tenacious spirit of the marginalized and the oppressed who have discovered an inextinguishable source of life in uncompromising self-belief. This is what makes Namdeo Dhasal a poet of survival whose voice can represent the anguish of all those marginalized micro-minorities of South Asia oppressed by the macro-realities of inequity and the monstrous machinery of states driven by religious fanaticism, racism, populist politics, economic greed, corruption, and crime.

'The Tree of Violence', from Namdeo's collection *Moorkha Mhataryane Dongar Halavile* ('The Crazy Old Man Moved Mountains'), is a poem about violence in Indian society, where the power of the state itself becomes the primary source of violence against human dignity. The poem was written in 1975, the year that the Indian Republic completed twenty-five years of existence, the year in which the government proclaimed a national emergency, suspending civil liberties. The poet's point of view is that of a lumpenized Dalit, and the poem raises the spectre of mass lumpenization spreading throughout the Republic. Dhasal's vision in this poem extends far beyond the Dalits who are denied civil rights by the still-operating, oppressive caste system, and points to the Dalitization of huge sections of the population that are being uprooted from their habitat, deprived of life supports, and driven to the teeming cities.

THE TREE OF VIOLENCE

It was destined. Like a Tulsi Vrindavan they planted violence in front of their door. Every day they watered it with blood and with great devotion. They fed it flesh as well to fertilize it. The Sun appeared in the morning on the Earth like a bridegroom with impotence written all over his face. He died every evening a chronic death. Solar systems and galaxies played their daily game of hide and seek. The tree of violence continued to grow. Each of its cells aimed at the sky. The climate of the city of smugglers suited the tree of violence.

'Here comes Krishna, O friend,
To shower *gulal* on me!'
The tree danced. The tree sang.
The tree fought as it danced and sang.
Then, one day, a miracle happened:

A saint steeped in the culture of the Parliament passed by the tree. The blinding light of the tree struck him like the blow of a hammer and he fell to the ground. One of his arteries burst.

He blacked out.
He fell to the ground.
A crowd gathered.
They took him to a hospital.
He remained in a coma for several days.

Specialist physicians toiled day and night to bring him back out of his coma. Newsmen from around the world prayed to their beloved Almighty God that the flame of the saint's soul would not be extinguished. His serious condition

Cast its dark shadow on the Union government.
Every other minute, the Prime Minister called the Dean of the hospital,
'Has His Holiness recovered?'
'His Holiness is recovering, isn't he?'
And the Dean kept answering, 'No! No! No!'
And the Prime Minister's face instantly darkened.
Newspapers delivered pictures of the holy man like milk every day.
Finally, it was the nation's good fortune that the holy man came to.
International correspondents accompanied by television crews and cameras
Surrounded him
And played around his body.
He solemnly warned the reporters about the fierce propensities of the awesome tree.
The next day the tree was besieged by headlines.
Column after newspaper column was filled by the story of the fearsome tree.

Terrorized by the tree, the whole city bent under the burden of its story.
Ministers and their cronies wanting to chop down the tree went berserk.
From little lanes to the nation's capital
There was panic everywhere.
Hundreds of thousands of skilled woodcutters were summoned to chop up the tree.
In the kitchens of State Assemblies and of the Parliament itself
A menu to cut down the tree was given shape.
Foreign experts, always eager to help, were given a desperate call.
A campaign was launched to cut down the tree.
All sorts of weapons and instruments were tried on the tree.

The tree couldn't be broken.
The tree couldn't be sawed off.
Not even a chip of its bark would come off.
Why doesn't the tree break?

Someone said, 'This is a tree of steel.'
Someone said, 'This is an iron tree.'

Global experts in botany were invited to take a look.
They began investigating the tree.
The tree wouldn't fit their measuring instruments.
The tree defied all analysis.
All the experts unanimously endorsed the opinion:
'This tree is the product of a unique chemical process.
Only a nuclear bomb
Can destroy it.'

To launch the campaign to break down the tree, all the locked up State Assemblies and the Lower House of Parliament were opened again.
The ruling party—with the cooperation of all the opposition parties—initiated a debate to discuss the means to destroy the tree.
They resorted to a voice-vote to determine whether to drop an atom bomb to destroy the tree.
The entire Honourable House was in a state of jitters.
The response was: 'If a nuclear bomb is used to destroy this tree, it will finish us and not the tree.'

Someone said, 'The nuclear bomb is just a paper tiger.'
Some else said, 'This is a passive government.'
'This is a lifeless government.'
'This is a frozen government.'
The government does not speak, the government does not move.
The government's brain cannot function.
The plan to drop a nuclear bomb on the tree was scrapped.

The entire country was worn out by the anxiety about the tree.
Ministers lost their appetite.
Ministers lost their sleep.
Ministers stopped eating.
Ministers stopped drinking water.
Ministers couldn't shit.
Their condition was like Hamlet's.
They dreamt of the unstoppable tangled growth of the tree's roots.

Armed commando units were dispatched, like hungry packs of wolves, to search and destroy the tree's roots.
They searched for those roots in farms, they searched forests, they searched factories.
Every nook and corner of the country was searched.
The boots of the commandos trampled and crushed little children, adolescents, youngsters,
Mothers, fathers, whole neighbourhoods,
Tender seedlings and shoots in fields.

The government went on a rampage more violent than the tree's.
Its echoes resounded in the Parliament.
A new Bhagat Singh was born.
The smoke of a Molotov cocktail melted in the refined air of the Parliament.
The Parliament began to float in the molten lava that the explosion spread.

'*Garibi Hatao!*'—eradicate poverty
'Nationalize!'
The Maintenance of Internal Security Act—a black draconian law.
The freezing of wages.
The palanquin-bearers of democracy running for their lives.

The soldiers for power to the people who bragged,
'Prison walls are
Hollow walls.
Our rib-cage is made of steel.
It will not crack,'
Found their torture-chambers afloat in the rising lava.
From every direction came salvos of slogans in fussilades
'*Inquilab Zindabad!*'—'Long Live the Revolution!'
The wounds of the tree began to heal.
The tree started dancing in ecstasy in its haven.

Every city, every village that was covered by the tree was dug up for its roots.
The whole nation was bulldozed.
Finally they found the roots of the tree
In the palatial villas of the Zamindar landowners and in their *Mehfil*s.
Finally the roots of the tree were found
In the safety vaults of capitalists and monopolists.
Finally the roots of the tree were found
Under the throne of the Empress.
In the end for cutting down the tree
In accordance with the international policy
In collusion with the social imperialists
Hit-men already on red alert were summoned.
The tree was cut down.
A prolonged siren was sounded.
The danger had been averted.
The tree was broken.
At the very moment
The tree was born
It sprouted and took root, it turned into many trees.
Those who nurtured the tree
Sacrificed their own homes.
They smiled their way to the gallows.
For they knew for sure that
As long as the circumstances that gave birth to the tree are not rooted out
The tree will not die.
Really, the tree will not die
But it will multiply by hundreds, by thousands, by millions, by billions.

Trees after trees after trees will spring and grow everywhere
To be sure that tree cannot be killed.
A government that does not root out the circumstances that created it will
fall apart.
People will kill such a government in broad daylight.
The Parliament will flow out and fill paddy fields
In the ghettoes of the Dalits—the Mangs, the Mehetars,
The Mahars, the Chambhars, in farms and in factories,
Garlands and pennants will be woven to be put on the gate of a new nation.
And the tree of violence shall turn
Into the the tree of wish-fulfilment.
Truly it shall.

13

THE PARADOXES OF DALIT CULTURAL POLITICS

Bali Sahota

INTRODUCTION: THE UNANTICIPATED

Disappointment, disorientation and, perhaps, even disillusionment—such must be the present state of those who have witnessed the course that anti-caste politics and Dalit insurgency have taken in recent years. Eleanor Zelliot's generation could not help but see in Ambedkarism and the activities of the Dalit Panthers the blossoming of liberal humanism through the imminent overturning of Brahmanical hegemony. Such political programmes and activities were to have resulted, at most, in the establishment of a new revolutionary order, or, at the very least, in the upsurge of an egalitarian civilizational undertow. Yet, this vision of the future has had to contend recently with more than it could have predicted. Now low-caste parties ally themselves with reactionary governments, the old Panthers become the ardent voices of Fascist forces, and Harijan brothers and sisters institutionalize what looks like another version of caste discrimination wherever they come into power. These days only the most crassly conservative or rapaciously instrumentalizing would be inclined to identify with such forms of subalternity.

What happened? Could it be that in trying to untie this knot one becomes subject to that proverbial Wittgensteinian 'mental cramp'? Is the problem of the Dalit today the category of 'the Dalit', and does the 'cramp' consist in attempting to maintain as the solution what itself might be the problem? The paradoxes are boundless: a political identity that remains attached to its own victimhood and thus fettered to the very thing that it seeks to destroy; the attempt to reform the hegemonic culture that in turn threatens always to assimilate the critique to its own culturalist rhetoric; the trickling down of civilizational solutions in the age of dissolving boundaries; the securing of particularistic privileges within the nation-state form as the latter wanes under neoliberal policies on a global scale. The list could go on. All the problems seem to derive from a culturalist framework. It is about time then to attempt to spell out exactly why the turn toward culture became necessary, what was productive about it, and what possibilities tend to get elided once all the solutions are to be derived from the cultural sphere alone. Perhaps the problem could simply be one of location. Once an issue of national proportions, are the caste system and its discontents in the throes of a new system for which a particularly located, national or civilizational political critique has little purchase? If so, the transmogrifications of low-caste politics over the last couple of decades may express various deep conflicts, bringing into relief certain limitations and apparently irresolvable dilemmas of the neoliberal state.

THE CULTURAL TURN

The cultural turn attains its clearest expression through the romantic vision in the writings of D.R. Nagaraj on the history of caste politics. In his provocative discussion of the Dalit movement, D.R. Nagaraj traces contemporary anti-caste politics to a whole range of indigenous yogis and *sadhu*s of pre-colonial and colonial history. For these Indian figures 'colonialism hardly mattered either as a transitory phase or as a source of confrontation', and they 'did not see their society as a part of the nation-state'. As 'the task of fighting the caste system had been one of the spiritual requirements of their tradition', the field of action and manoeuvre in this fight was immediate, situated in local orders of caste domination (Nagaraj 1993: 4). The interconnections of such institutions as biradaris (clan orders) and the deferential relations of the *jajmani* (patron-client) system were the most concrete manifestations of caste in the traditional Indian political order. The subsidiary or subsumptive nature of this political order made the state a distant, even irrelevant, agent for the transformation of caste relations. The leaders and participants of these indigenous movements understood that an anti-caste ethos needed to be embodied first and foremost in everyday practice and actualized through distinct collective institutions and discourses (Zelliot 1992: 3–50; Mendelsohn and Vicziany 1998). In this context, a politics centred on the state was meaningless.

Considering the nature of this political landscape, the tradition's broad ecumenical cultural politics was, Nagaraj suggests, more effective. Through poetic and figurative language a distinctly unorthodox transcendental realm of existence was evoked in the works of the poets Nagaraj valorizes. Such a vision of the transcendental, as it became embedded in practice, served as a crucible for the transformation of actual social life. '[T]he liberation of the self from the phenomenal world was the spiritual goal, and both the arrogance and humiliation of the caste system were major obstacles in the path of moksha or nirvana' (Nagaraj 1993: 4). In examining this history around issues of untouchability, Nagaraj prescribes a new kind of politics in the post-colonial context: a vernacular politics disjunct from the political institutions of the state. Dalit poetic play, an ensemble of words and actions, projects new possibilities in civil society. This politics draws its energy from a poetics distinct from that of hegemonic religious forms and seeks incommensurability with respect to the bureaucratic logic of the liberal secular state.

As democratically oriented politics over the colonial and postcolonial periods have politicized everyday degradation and domination on the basis of caste hierarchy, the caste system has been upset, producing an unstable, if not critical, situation practically everywhere in India. As creating a democratic and egalitarian nation-state was one of the guiding rationales of the mainstream independence movement, the politicization of caste became all the more acute after British rule came to an end. Thus, Article 46 of the 1950 Constitution of India declared: 'The State shall promote with special care the educational and economic interests of the weaker sections of the people, and, in particular, of the Scheduled Castes and the Scheduled Tribes, and shall protect them from social injustice and all forms of exploitation' (Hay 1988: 337). Later, the Untouchability (Offenses) Act of 1955 outlawed the most egregious practices of caste discrimination, such as exclusion of Untouchables from wells, schools, eating houses, and other public places.

But at the same time the postcolonial state was perpetuating the archaic inequalities and sub-species distinctions of caste by incorporating them into its developmental schemes. Partha Chatterjee writes, 'That concrete structures of existent communities were by no means homogeneous or egalitarian [as prescribed by the liberal secular constitution] but were in fact built around precapitalist forms of social power was not so much ignored or forgotten as tacitly acknowledged [by state development planners]' (Chatterjee 1993: 213). Formally against caste but substantially dependent on caste inequality for its economic foundation, the state was forced at times to deal with the politicization of the very relations that buttressed its own development schemes. The postcolonial Indian state can thus be seen to encompass social contradictions that have the potential of bringing into crisis the state's founding liberal secular principles and undermining its image as a universal sovereign or neutral arbiter in the political arena. This problem has surfaced during both secular and anti-secular governments, affecting many domains of social life over the last five decades. The studies of Marc Galanter (1984), Rajni Kothari (1997), Zoya Hasan (2000), and Oliver Mendelsohn and Marica Vicziany (1998) have considered the import of such contradictions in the socio-political fabric of the state, and the plight of bonded labourers and other such constituencies has made it clear that state agencies cannot respond in any adequate fashion to their demands. State agencies may often abet rather than ameliorate the lower order's difficult conditions. In sum, the state may at times prove unaccountable to its own laws.

This crisis in the politics of the state provided the lessons and the most general context for the shift in Dalit political energy toward culture and civil society as a more fertile plane for social and political transformation. Essays such as Gangadhar Pantawane's 'Evolving a New Identity: The Development of a Dalit Culture' (Pantawane 1986) and Nilam Gupta's 'Qanunon aur karyakramon ke bavajud' ('In Spite of Governmental Programmes and Laws)' (Gupta 1994) are, alongside Nagaraj's own account, instances of this very turn to culture. The immediate context of everyday experience and intimate social relations seemed to demand a political strategy of its own. As Omvedt acutely observes, 'Hunger and unemployment were hard realities, but caste discrimination was not simply a "social" or "cultural" issue but rather the framework for [untouchables'] experience of hunger and unemployment' (Omvedt 1993: 49). Because economic oppression was seen to be embedded in conventions of discrimination, the valorization of culture as the domain of effective political activity promised to reconstitute the total organization of society and eventually the state. Yet, in providing a pre-modern precedent for such an emphasis on culture as the proper domain of Dalit political activity, Nagaraj may have overlooked the limits and proscriptions of the modern state. Does an anarchistic politics of aesthetic inspiration—a romantic attempt to reconstitute the everyday life-world as if the modern state's governing categories had dissolved—have any realistic potential for transforming the contemporary political order? Could the kind of culturalism that Nagaraj valorizes be ensnared by the logic of the state itself?

THE BODY POETIC

In order to see what the new Dalit aesthetic practice is up against, let us begin with what is most traditionally alive and generative in Nagaraj's analysis. This is the capacity for the newly constituted lower orders to project a distinctly new sensibility through aesthetic practice and have it reach beyond their own socially circumscribed domains. A distinct ethos and way of life are certainly crucial for any political movement, and aesthetic creation is certainly an important means for imagining a future polity and personhood. What kinds of pressures do these place on the current political order in India? And what sorts of obstacles has the postcolonial state erected that make it impervious to such aesthetic and cultural strategies? Do the pre-modern traditions of anti-casteism provide prescriptions for a politics that is irrelevant for current Dalit configurations? Such questions reveal the discrepancy between Nagaraj's pre-modern visions of an anarchistic sublime and the current subjection to the modern state.

Let us begin by examining the potentials of the new democratic order of the postcolonial state. The conditions set by a democratic political system, new educational opportunities for non-elite citizens, and the expansion of media have apparently unleashed all kinds of possibilities for a specifically Dalit reconfiguration of self and community. Old constraints of caste, the source of so much internal fragmentation within the untouchable population for so long, have come under threat from attempts at establishing greater horizontal solidarity. Caste distinctions certainly remain, but at the lower levels traditional caste categories seem more often than not like so many exoskeletons that internal dynamics have outgrown. As these distinctions cannot be cast aside or adopted at will, a particular internally distinguished consciousness has taken expression: there are now imminent ambivalences and differences. By the early 1990s, once the old system of vote banks and party patronage had dissolved across the north, uncertainty and volatility marked the lower levels of the political order.

Emerging hand in hand with this political situation has been an innovative poetics and ever-widening dissemination of aesthetic production from the margins of the urban centres. Such creations generally exacerbate the potential for political crisis by opposing the numbers game of ordinary *Realpolitik* and proffering a sense of the impossible. This kind of politics—seeking to reconstitute the world through new ways of representing things—is, as Nagaraj says, an elaboration of the precolonial traditions, especially the organic anti-caste movements.

The most promising of the new Dalit poetic creations operate within a trans-subjective expressivist aesthetics of this longstanding Indian tradition. Far from remaining corporeally abstracted or socially distanced, this aesthetics addresses an interrelated sphere of the body, emotions and everyday sociality. The aesthetic sensibility of contemporary Dalit writers conjures up old poets such as Kabir, Tukaram, and Chokhamela, who ecstatically conflated their own selves with, and laid claim to, the entire collectivity. The terms of this tradition were uncompromising, negating actual conditions and evoking the promise of the counterfactual. Aesthetics and poetic expression were integral to making the audience feel the promise of a different order: the messages of this poetic tradition could not subsist apart from their figurative embodiment, and their figurative expression was not to be cognized so much as embodied. The emphasis is on producing a transformative affect. The force of what is expressed in any poem of this tradition is embedded in its form, its sounds, and its extra-referential discourse, and the meaning produced is to be experienced initially as potentially transformative bodily sensation. Authentic aesthetic work, in this tradition, demands something extraordinary of the medium of communication and pushes at the limits of staid conceptions of selfhood and society.

The underlying notions of this old Indian tradition are brought to light in the modern Dalit Dharmaraj Nimsarkar's poem 'Experiment'. It is this aesthetic theory that Nimsarkar thematizes and turns into an experiment (Nimsarkar 1992: 35):

Such experiments are bound to recur
Time and again, of picking suns
From the dead blackness of blood
And painting days
On the Canvass of darkness
I'm available always, all the time
My protests are wordless
And complaints have no voice—
Darkness of the night
Knows no direction
The seeds of moss sown in my flesh
Never bloom At times
The skin grows thorns
Which prick me.
Darkness of the eyes
Breaks into flowers of flame
And I alone am reduced to ashes.
What a journey this which shifts
My crematorium from day to day.
There is no room for my dwelling
Claims of love resound all around
And hands weary of acclaim shall rest
Only when my bowels are plucked out
And spread
I should be all set
For such an experiment.

Sensing the skin that 'grows thorns/which prick me', or the vacillation of elated hope and distanced despair—states embodied as if the seed of moss were 'sown in my flesh', as if 'I am reduced to ashes'—depends upon the transduction that our senses must perform for these words to take aesthetic effect. The excess in '[d]arkness of the eyes/[b]reaks into flowers of flame' would most appropriately be apprehended within the body as an actual physical state. The words place too great a burden on the intelligibility of language, straining a world where there 'is no room for my dwelling'.

Yet, being entertaining, thought-provoking, or pleasing is not the aim; social transformation is. Like pre-modern low-caste poets, new Dalit writers glimpsed the necessity of socio-political change as the objective correlate of aesthetic affect. The theory underlying both the old aesthetic and that of modern Dalit writers at their best envisions true art as working against a decrepit conservative order and as being conducive to much more than simply vague other-worldly consolations. Nagaraj saw the source of this urge in the radical Indian tradition in the capacity of figurative language to free up hidden potential and indeterminacy in reality—in outright defiance of ordinary language's foreclosure of that very potential and indeterminacy.

The tendency towards actual social existence explains the focus on language—perhaps the most social of all things—as a theme in its own right in modern Dalit works. Not only is language a medium through which aesthetic effects are produced; it is also, as in Arun Kamble's poem 'Which Language should I speak?' a metaphor for a radically altered social order (Kamble 1992: 54):

Chewing trotters in the badlands
My grandpa,
The permanent resident of my body,
The household of tradition heaped on his back,
Hollers at me,
'You whore-son, talk like we do.
Talk I tell you!'

Picking through the Vedas
His top-knot well-oiled with ghee,
My Brahman teacher tells me,
'You idiot, use the language correctly!'
Now I ask you,
Which language should I speak?

The inadequacy of any existing language to reference the desired form of sociality and the impossibility of expressing one's thoughts with the tools of the old can only be remedied by the figuration of language itself as the society to come. Experimentation with the existing language becomes the best way to prefigure the language that one ought to speak if less dire conditions obtained. Moreover, a question on language not only draws attention to its own expression, but highlights the distinction between what is demanded of the existing language and the burden of tradition slowing its emergence. The existing order suffers the brunt of the critique all the more powerfully for its indirect nature.

Such poems, aesthetic ideologies, and realms of affect constituted the strategic bases for the cultural politics that Nagaraj and others advocated and in which they partook. There is much to be commended in these experiments, especially the new, even inchoate, configurations of self and collectivity produced by bringing commonsensical language into peril. The figurative embodiment of language in Dalit discourse and the correlation of the figurative aspect with embodied states make it possible to imagine a selfhood and social collectivity that could further destabilize the traditional political order. In bringing together an individual poet's emotion through an elaborated linguistic technique and an audience that may make the poetic sentiment its own, Dalit poetics could, it is believed, lead to translating the sentiment into ethical or political practice. Such a strategy, if successful, would overcome the governing categories of the modern state. In their stead, the 'imaginary totality' of Dalit poetics would erase distinctions based on caste affiliation, nation (Pandian 1998), religion, gender, and so forth: a new kind of cosmopolitan liberalism from below was always in the offing in these early Dalit expressions. As in pre-modern anti-caste movements, the interrelated spheres of the body, emotions, imagination, and everyday practice become the ensemble of ethical substances for a utopian poetics to work social and political transformations, adumbrating an as-yet-unimaginable collective subjectivity.

So far, this has only been the greatest, most utopian, promise of Dalit participation in the more radical strains of the Indian literary tradition. In its era, social blockages prevented that old tradition from translating or actualizing its ethical critique of subjectivity in the objective realm. Now, though, at issue is how the radical picture presented in the modern strands of this tradition can produce political conflict or bring it into focus. In a manner exactly opposite to the pre-modern situation, has contemporary Dalit subjectivity become increasingly circumscribed in its imagination of collectivity? Has it become swayed by the very state operations to which it was supposed to offer resistance? That is, despite the unbounded imagination of some Dalit works, do governmentally informed or civilizationally ordained subjectivities prevent the particular objective possibilities from becoming absorbed in contemporary politics? To look into this would mean to doubt some of Nagaraj's assumptions. These subjectively concretized resistances—reflecting the particularizing identitarian logic of the state—cannot be wished away as easily as Nagaraj seems to have imagined. Perhaps literary creation under the category 'Dalit' may only further reify them. The question becomes simply: is it possible that such particularistic resistances are not simply the blind spots but the concomitants of a culturalist strategy in the first place? Before attempting an examination of that question, we must see how the problem first comes into being: through an ambivalence of belonging.

THE AMBIVALENCE OF BELONGING

Dalit literary expression in the late twentieth century brought into focus an ethics marked by a mixture of distance from and proximity to the hegemonic social form. A sense of ambivalence characterizes the relationship between high Hinduism and the subordinated Dalit communities. A variety of groups associated with untouchability have deeply mixed feelings about the romantic reinvention of the ideal-typical order of *varnadharma* under Hindutva. Exponents of Hindutva characterize caste relations in a way that disavows their coercive and demeaning qualities. Undeniably, contemporary articulations of selfhood and collectivity in Dalit discourse have taken shape through the catalyst of colonial and postcolonial institutions. But at the same time, these articulations draw into relevance the nature of India's pre-modern socio-political order and phenomena that remained autonomous with respect to colonial governance. Precolonial currents, colonial knowledge, recent anthropological inquiry, and the divergent political tendencies captured under names like Gandhi and Ambedkar have gotten into the mix of tensions constituting Dalit subjectivity today. In defining Dalit selfhood and the politics proper to it, what usually seems to be at stake is the character and potential of traditional Indian society itself.

That traditional Indian society becomes so charged with significance is understandable considering the ambiguities about this order and the untouchables' relationship to it in modern times. In the late nineteenth century, as part of an effort to map all of India socially and politically, British census officers were interested in uncovering the units and interconnections that made up the social order, especially relations between untouchables and upper-caste communities. The effective reality the census officers produced was equivocal, allowing for divergent historical trajectories. Mendelsohn and Vicziany explain: 'in 1871–2 the Chamars ... were in the province of Bengal lumped into a category called "Semi-Hinduized Aborigines". In other provinces Untouchable castes including the Mahars and Pariahs were placed with Buddhists and Jains ... into a category called "Outcastes or Not Recognizing Caste"' (Mendelsohn and Vicziany 1998: 27). Early on in the census project, British officers complained of high-caste-Hindus' reluctance to bring low castes under the rubric of 'Hindoo'. Yet, by the beginning of the next century, champions of a Hindu society responded to the new numbers game of colonial politics by seeking to bring all untouchable castes under the saffron fold. The field of anthropological studies is similarly disorderly. Perspectives have vacillated between Dumont's securing of the untouchable's consciousness squarely within the brahmanical representation of society, on the one hand, and ethnographic reports demonstrating the discrepant and even contradictory attitudes of untouchables toward dominant religious doxa, on the other (Dumont 1986; Kolenda 1997; Freeman 1979). Nothing, though, has heightened the tensions of belonging to a vague Hinduism more than Ambedkar's 1935 announcement, 'I was born a Hindu, but I will not die a Hindu' (Hay 1988: 326). Dalit poetics takes its cue from Ambedkar's critique and manifests an ethics of selfhood and collectivity that is ambivalent about belonging within the larger civilizational or national order (Jaffrelot 2000: 17–25, 213–40).

What has resulted from this ambivalence? The question of belonging has placed on the Dalit subject the burden of working out a political identity that can go in diametrically opposed ways. Dalit subjects are left trying to conjure up an entirely different framework for thinking politically when a language for that way of thinking has yet to come into prominence across the new global scene. The question of belonging can thus either allow Dalits to be reabsorbed into the fabric of a Hindu political imaginary or engender a widespread ambivalence in the larger public sphere that could tear apart the culturalist patchwork, making it imperative to rethink the social totality through altogether different principles.

The source of this ethical ambivalence regarding the larger collectivity is the body of the Dalit writer. What becomes most manifest is the struggle to relinquish the untouchable body for something more ethereal and less particularly marked. And yet this struggle makes the body all the more acutely felt. In Dalit poetics, a body deemed polluted and thus inassimilable to a larger ruling society becomes an object of ironic negation. In the modern order, the embodiment of such negativity can be tolerated only grudgingly, but it cannot be magically shed. For even with education and political power, residues of a low-caste past remain embedded in accents, manners, and experiences of discrimination. Thus the poetics shifts back and forth between the embodiment of particularity and the imagining of universality superseding the current hegemony.

Waman Nimbalkar's poem 'Caste' configures this paradox simultaneously as an abstraction and as a brutally concrete experience (Nimbalkar 1992: 123):

When I knew nothing, I knew
My caste was low.
The Patil had kicked my father,
Cursed my mother.
They did not even raise their heads.
But I felt the 'caste' in my heart.
When I climbed the steps to school
Then too I knew my caste was low.
I used to sit outside, the others inside.
My skin would suddenly shiver with little thorns,
My eyes could not hold back the tears.

Our lips must smile when they cursed.
I don't understand anything—
I heard this, I learned that,
I became a man like a man.
Even now I don't know—

How is caste? Where is it?
It isn't seen so does it live inside the body?
All the questions float like smoke,
And the wick of thought is sputtering.
But when I knew nothing, then I knew
My caste was low.

In words as bare as the naked oppression that they describe, this poem uses interrogatives to disfigure the metaphysics of caste relations. Instead of taking caste for granted, the poem testifies to a knowledge that is embodied, a pre-conceptual attunement to one's place in the world, an inheritance of practices that constitute a tradition of the oppressed. Caste is baffling for having no manifestation in untouchable experience except in force. It has no separate existence from the feeling of 'little thorns' on the skin, or tears in the eyes. Caste can be concretely experienced only as an embodied state, and in the case of the untouchable it makes a disembodied subjectivity difficult, though desirable, to imagine. Such a desire is certainly behind the figurative reversal central to the poem's narrative. The parents of the speaker thought of their situation before the Patil as the effect of an eternal cause, for 'they did not even raise their heads'. Now caste is something that can erode away, an underdetermined effect of everyday practice. The speaker's ambivalence arises from the tension between the unbearable embodiment of caste and the impossibility of fully ejecting it from one's own self-conception. Even despite ironic negation—'Our lips must smile when they cursed'—the thought of caste's disappearance goes against the formative memories and sense of one's own person. Exactly where to locate oneself in ethical and political terms—within the order that produces the pain, or at some imaginary distance from it— becomes the speaker's dilemma.

Namdeo Dhasal's influential poem 'Song of the Republic and the Dog' (Dhasal 1986: 106–9) gives voice to this ambivalence in the broader context of the postcolonial public sphere. Dhasal's aim is to deliver a message powerful and direct enough to move Dalit politics well beyond the constraints of Hindu orthodoxy and the stigmatizing resolutions of a liberal democratic order. The play of distance and proximity with respect to one's own embodiment of negativity characterizes Dhasal's discourse. The ironic gesture comes across in the depiction of the Dalit self as a lowly animal: 'Dog, leashed dog, / He howls and barks from time to time. / This is his constitutional right.' The promise of a liberal democratic order is false; it occludes an abject reality:

> In the crowded streets
> the drums of bunkus freedom are played.
> Friends, I ask an uncircumcized boy
> the meaning of democracy,
> 'do you have any inkling of it?'
> I ask the mother with the wornout old patched sari
> the worth of breast milk.
> I ask the man who works like an ox
> about fulfillment, prosperity, deprivation.
> These riddles have turned my mind helter-skelter

The reifying effect of the governing categories on the Dalit subject is one of the essential problems of the current order of things:

> He whose heart has become stone
> and his skin a rhinoceros hide
> and he is hanging stuffed with sawdust in a museum
> now only can his head remain
> cool, cool, expansive, and peaceful.

Later the return from metaphor to more direct and vehement speech hammers home the vast gulf separating the reigning liberal categories of the new polity and their underlying reality:

> We are not even allowed to weep.
> Liberty, equality, fraternity, the banyan tree of private property—
> everything is equal before the law.
>   'Eat, drink and be merry,
>   Go to hell'
> O how strange is this age, this dark age.

At the centre of the poem, in accordance with Dhasal's poetic strategy, the utopian image breaks against the actually existing order. Notions of transcending the marked body and of collective re-fashioning work against the liberal individualism and other divisions of the postcolonial state:

We live to drink tea in hotels.
We touch cup to cup, saucer to saucer.
We search the railway timetable for a two hour journey.
We try to fill up the Kumbhamela of our existence
with many colours and many fashions.
After excessive tension we gather in public gardens.
We play the rhythmic flute of our breaths.
The two children of poverty,
One white, one black.
Sea-saws are played on in sovereign gardens.
Dry tombs are impressed on the screen of the mind.

Here everyday discriminatory practices are overcome in the reconstitution of civil society. The dream-vision takes shape through a re-conceptualization of the past as a general human one, the '[d]ry tombs ... impressed on the screen of the mind'. A humanist notion provides the basis for the collective body in which one could 'live to drink tea in hotels', 'touch cup to cup, saucer to saucer', and so on. Yet, despite this urge toward a trans-historical conception of human being, a Hindu trope surfaces that cannot go ignored: the Kumbhamela. Would it be off the mark to suggest that the universalistic conception of human being as the cornerstone of the utopian impulse is matched by a particularistic pull toward the civilizational ethos that gave rise to untouchability in the first place? Is there ambivalence in the very utopian image of this poem? Do the abuses suffered by the Dalit body demand redress and redemption by the order that produced the pain in the first place?

My reading, of course, is informed by the recent turn of events relating to the author of this poem. In 1997, long after the Shiv Sena had adopted a Hindutva programme and entered into alliance with the Bharatiya Janata Party (BJP), Dhasal turned away from his Dalit Panther past and the party founded by Ambedkar, the Republican Party of India, to join forces with the Shiv Sena. The fact that a prominent Dalit literary figure who has been most uncompromising in articulating a utopia incommensurate with the liberal democratic order can make the shift from one extreme to another on the political spectrum only reinforces the point about the ambivalence of belonging. Moreover, the fact that the Bahujan Samaj Party (BSP) under the leadership of Mayawati, the first Dalit to hold the highest office in any state in India, can enter into alliance with the country's most reactionary forces may indicate a larger structural stoppage and not just a case of politics making for strange bed partners. Does such a tendency toward right-wing particularism result inevitably from the focus on culture as a site of political activity? Or is there another political tendency, diametrically opposed to this one, to which the aesthetic productions intimating a radically alternative collective subjectivity could give rise if the proper conditions obtained? Or do these two tendencies have more in common than initially meets the eye?

CONCLUSION: BEYOND THE CONTRADICTIONS

The turns that Dalit politics has taken in the postcolonial period have been perplexing, especially in recent years. How is it that the most radical element of the political scene could break away so easily and become embedded in the politics of reaction? And not just that. Dalit political leaders have themselves implemented practices and policies that resemble the hierarchical distinctions of brahmanical Hinduism. The aim of this essay has been to bring to light the transformations within Dalit political and aesthetic ideologies and to understand them within the larger institutional, social, and political shifts that mark modernity. The problems within the Dalit world are large. They can only be understood, I believe, by investigating broad, sweeping trends and tendencies over long stretches of time. Only then is one able to grasp the several paradoxes of cultural and identitarian politics as such. Confining socio-political problems into culturalist frameworks can be seen as a primary source for some of these paradoxes. To the degree that culture becomes the exclusive realm for deriving the solutions to social and political problems, Dalit politics can become subject to the dominant social and political institutions that reproduce untouchability and the hierarchies of the social order. Placing the greatest emphasis on culture as a distinct repository of inherited wisdom establishes a political orientation that can easily be assimilated into the broad contours of reaction, which are themselves culturalist in their ideological orientation.

Yet, whatever the particular line of politics for the Dalit subject, that politics, when fully articulated, seems to be at odds with the typical liberal secular order. Whether of the Left or the Right, this politics seems never to be easily assimilated to liberal secular norms. On the one hand, the Communist Party of India (M-L) works to incorporate the lower caste orders within its critique of the neoliberal state. On the other hand, high-caste anti-secular Right coalitions have included lower-caste political agendas. The situation suggests a vast dissatisfaction with liberalism and undermines the homogeneous, universal society that is supposed to characterize the end of History and the underlying conditions of the Last Man (Fukuyama 2002). This is obviously the case with parties like the Shiv Sena, the BJP, and other, smaller factions of the Right. But it applies equally well to Ambedkar's thinking and to the contemporary parties that claim to be his legatees. Dalit material demands exceed liberalism's compromise of granting equality only at a juridical level. The Dalit imagination of community often violates liberal notions of a homogeneous mass.

It is impossible to tell how these countervailing strands of anti-liberalism will play out in the current context of neoliberalism. We can only ascertain the conditions in which the political struggles will unfold. The chaotic aspects of the political scene in the Dalit sphere could simply be indications of the virtual hollowing out, reconstitution, and subsumption by capital of the civilizational form in its entirety. What is most needed for resolving the internal problems of the nation in these conditions is an internationalist framework. But this is exactly what seems only faintly available and fragmentarily translatable into the current local conjunctures, especially when these are consumed by a culturalist rhetoric that forecloses political and social contacts beyond the cultural frame of reference. Nevertheless, this ultimate horizon of the international framework is what the most uncompromising utopian image of Dalit aesthetics, inherited through the centuries, always refers to as its proper material domain of possibility.

Articulating a new internationalism through this old aesthetic may be key in obviating Dalit politics' self-imprisoning logics. The image of utopia in Dalit aesthetics captures a fractured intimation of an as-yet-emergent collective subjectivity. In this context, it may be possible to rework the category of 'Dalit' for more imaginative, empowering ends, to envision it against the backdrop of ever larger and richer human life-worlds. Such social, political, and cultural ends are more easily longed for than articulated clearly, let alone programmatically. Nevertheless, the seeds of new political configurations are perhaps being sown in the Left and Right Dalit politics' dissatisfaction with the neoliberal dispensation. The struggles of the two tendencies against each other create imaginative friction for dealing with the new global system. The struggle itself, played out at various levels, will indicate the course of the history to come.

REFERENCES

Chatterjee, Partha. 1993. *The Nation and Its Fragments: Colonial and Postcolonial Histories*. Princeton: Princeton University Press.

Dhasal, Namdeo. 1986. 'Song of the Republic and the Dog'. Translated by Vidya Dixit, Gail Omvedt, Jayant Karve, Eleanor Zelliot, and Bharat Patankar. In R. Barbara Joshi (ed.). *Untouchable! Voices of the Dalit Liberation Movement*. Atlantic Heights, NJ: Zed Books, pp. 106–9.

Dumont, Louis. 1986. *A South Indian Subcaste: Social Organization and Religion of the Pramalai Kallar*. Translated by M. Moffat and L. and A. Morton. New Delhi: Oxford University Press.

Freeman, James. 1979. *Untouchable: An Indian Life History*. Stanford: Stanford University Press.

Fukuyama, Francis. 2002. *The End of History and the Last Man*. New York: Perennial.

Galanter, Marc. 1984. *Competing Inequalities: Law and the Backward Classes in India*. Berkeley: The University of California Press.

Gupta, Nilam. 1994. '*Qanunon aur Karyakramon ke Bavajud*' ('In Spite of Governmental Programmes and Laws'). In Rajkishor (ed.). *Harijan se Dalit*. Nayi Dilli: Vani Prakashan, pp. 42–53.

Hasan, Zoya. 2000. 'Representation and Redistribution: The New Lower Caste Politics of North India'. In Francine R. Frankel, Zoya Hasan, Rajeev Bhargava, and Balveer Arora (eds). *Transforming India: Social and Political Dynamics of Democracy*. New Delhi: Oxford University Press, pp. 146–75.

Hay, Stephen (ed.). 1988. *Sources of Indian Tradition*. vol. 2: *Modern India and Pakistan*. Second edn. New York: Columbia University Press.

Jaffrelot, Christophe. 2000. *Dr Ambedkar: Leader intouchable et pére de la constitution indienne*. Paris: Presses de Science Politique.

Kamble, Arun. 1992. 'Which Language Should I Speak?' Translated by Priya Adarkar. In Arjun Dangle (ed.). *Poisoned Bread: Translations from Modern Marathi Dalit Literature*. Hyderabad: Orient Longman, p. 54.

Kolenda Pauline. 1997. 'Purity and Pollution'. In T.N. Madan (ed.). *Religion in India*. New Delhi: Oxford University Press, pp. 78–94.

Kothari, Rajni. 1997. 'Rise of the Dalits and the Renewed Debate on Caste'. In Partha Chatterjee (ed.). *State and Politics in India*. New Delhi: Oxford University Press, pp. 439–58.

Mendelsohn, Oliver and Marika Vicziany. 1998. *The Untouchables: Subordination, Poverty and the State in Modern India*. Cambridge: Cambridge University Press.

Nagaraj, D.R. 1993. *The Flaming Feet: A Study of the Dalit Movement*. Bangalore: South Forum Press.

Nimbalkar, Waman. 1992. 'Caste', translated by Graham Smith. In Mulk Raj Anand and Eleanor Zelliot (eds). *An Anthology of Dalit Literature (Poems)*. New Delhi: Gyan Publishing House, p. 123.

Nimsarkar, Dharmaraj. 1992. 'Experiment', translated by Charudatta Bhagwat. In Arjun Dangle (ed.). *Poisoned Bread: Translations from Modern Marathi Dalit Literature*. Hyderabad: Orient Longman, 1992, p. 35.

Omvedt, Gail. 1993. *Reinventing Revolution: New Social Movements and the Socialist Tradition in India*. New York: M.E. Sharpe.

Pandian, M.S.S. 1998. 'Stepping Outside History? New Dalit Writings from Tamil Nadu'. In Partha Chatterjee (ed.). *Wages Of Freedom: Fifty Years of the Indian Nation State*. New Delhi: Oxford University Press, pp. 292–309.

Pantawane, Gangadhar. 1986. 'Evolving a New Identity: The Development of a Dalit Culture'. In Joshi (ed.). *Untouchable!* London: Zed Books, pp. 79–87.

Zelliot, Eleanor. 1992. *From Untouchable to Dalit: Essays on the Ambedkar Movement*. New Delhi: Manohar.

14
ART OF PARIAHS*

Meena Alexander

Back against the kitchen stove
Draupadi sings:

In my head Beirut still burns

The Queen of Nubia, of God's Upper Kingdom
the Rani of Jhansi, transfigured, raising her sword
are players too. They have entered with me
into North America and share these walls.

We make up an art of pariahs:

Two black children spray painted white
their eyes burning,
a white child raped in a car
for her pale skin's sake,
an Indian child stoned by a bus shelter,
they thought her white in twilight.

*Meena Alexander, 'Art of Pariahs' © Meena Alexander, 2005, 2006, *River and Bridge*. New Delhi: Rupa and Co., 1995. Published by permission of the author.

Someone is knocking and knocking
but Draupadi will not let him in.
She squats by the stove and sings:

The Rani shall not sheathe her sword
nor Nubia's queen restrain her elephants
till tongues of fire wrap a tender blue,
a second skin, a solace to our children

Come walk with me towards a broken wall
—Beirut still burns—carved into its face.
Outcastes all let's conjure honey scraped from stones,
an underground railroad stacked with rainbow skin,
Manhattan's mixed rivers rising.

APPENDIX
Published Writing of Eleanor Zelliot
[as of May 2008]

'Buddhism and Politics in Maharashtra'. In Donald E. Smith (ed.). *South Asian Politics and Religion*. Princeton: Princeton University Press, 1966. Paperback edition, 1969.

'Background of the Mahar Buddhist Conversion'. In Robert Sakai (ed.). *Studies on Asia, 1966*. Lincoln: University of Nebraska, 1966.

'The Revival of Buddhism in India'. *Asia*. vol. 10, 1968.

'Gujarat'. *Encyclopedia Americana*. International edition, 1975.

'Learning the Use of Political Means: The Mahars of Maharashtra'. In Rajni Kothari (ed.). *Caste in Indian Politics*. New Delhi: Allied Publishers, 1970. Reprinted 1973, 1985, 1991 (Orient Longman).

'The Nineteenth Century Background of Mahar and Non-Brahman Movements in Maharashtra'. *Indian Economic and Social History Review*. vol. 7, no. 3, 1970.

'Literary Images of the Indian City'. In Richard G. Fox (ed.). *Urban India: Society, Space and Image*. Durham: Duke University Press, 1971.

'Gandhi and Ambedkar: A Study in Leadership' and 'Bibliography on Untouchability'. In J. Michael Mahar (ed.). *The Untouchables in Contemporary India*. Tucson: University of Arizona Press, 1972. Reprinted as a pamphlet by Triratna Grantha Mala, Pune, 1983.

'Dr Ambedkar and the Mahars'. *Illustrated Weekly*. vol. 92, no. 14, 2 April 1972.

'The Medieval Bhakti Movement in History: An Essay on the Literature in English'. In Bardwell L. Smith (ed.). *Hinduism: New Essays in the History of Religions*. Leiden: E.J. Brill, 1976 (Numen Series). Reprinted in 1982.

'Dalit Sahitya: The Historical Background' together with a translation (with Vidyut Bhagwat) of Baburao Bagul, *Maran Swast Hot Ahe* ('Death is Getting Cheaper'), from Marathi. *Vagartha*. vol. 12, 1976.

'The Psychological Dimension of the Buddhist Movement in India'. In G.A. Oddie (ed.). *Religion in South Asia: Religious Conversion and Revival Movements in Medieval and Modern Times*. Second edition. New Delhi: Manohar, 1991 (first edition, 1977).

'The Leadership of Babasaheb Ambedkar'. In B.N. Pandey (ed.). *Leadership in South Asia* (University of London symposium). New Delhi: Vikas, 1977. Translated into Marathi as 'Dr Ambedkarance Netrutva' by Vasant Moon. Pune: Sugawa Prakashan, 1986.

'The American Experience of Dr B.R. Ambedkar'. In R.D. Suman (ed.). *Dr Ambedkar: Pioneer of Human Rights*. New Delhi: Bodhisattva Publications, Ambedkar Institute of Buddhist Studies, 1977.

'Dalit: New Cultural Context of an Old Marathi Word'. In Clarence Maloney (ed.). *Language and Civilization Change in South Asia. (Contributions to Asian Studies*. vol. 11). Leiden: E.J. Brill, 1978. Reprinted in *Contemporary India* (Professor Sirsikar Felicitation Volume). Pune: Continental Prakashan, 1982.

'Introduction to Dalit Poems' (with Gail Omvedt). *Bulletin of Concerned Asian Scholars*. vol. 10, no. 3, 1978.

Maps and texts for the following plates in Joseph E. Schwartzberg (ed.). *A Historical Atlas of South Asia*. Chicago: University of Chicago Press, 1978: Revolt of 1857, Political Events of the Nationalist Period, the Indian National Congress, the Muslim League and other Political Parties, Fiction depicting South Asian Life, the Daily Press, Religious Revival and Reform, the Growth of Lahore and Calcutta.

'Religion and Legitimization in the Mahar Movement'. In Bardwell L. Smith (ed.). *Religion and Legitimization in South Asia*. Leiden: E.J. Brill, 1978.

'The Indian Rediscovery of Buddhism, 1855–1956'. In A.K. Narain (ed.). *Studies in Pali and Buddhism* (Jagdish Kashyap Memorial Volume). New Delhi: D.K. Publishers, 1978, 2006.

'Journals of Indian History for the Scholar, the Student and the Limited Library'. *South Asia Library Notes and Queries* (December 1978).

'Dalit Poetry'. *Illustrated Weekly*. vol. 100, no. 33, 1979.

'Tradition and Innovation in the Contemporary Buddhist Movement in India' (with Joanna Macy). In A.K. Narain (ed.). *Studies in the History of Buddhism*. Delhi: B.R. Publication Corporation, 1980.

'British Nostalgia: The Long Look Back at Empire' (annotated bibliography). *South Asia Library Notes and Queries* (March 1980).

'Chokhamela and Eknath: Two Bhakti Modes of Legitimacy for Modern Change'. *Journal of Asian and African Studies*. vol. 15, 1980. Reprinted in Jayant Lele (ed.). *Tradition and Modernity in Bhakti Movements*. Leiden: E.J. Brill, 1981. Reprinted in Aloka Parasher-Sen (ed.). *Subordinate and Marginal Groups in Early India*. New Delhi: Oxford University Press, 2004.

'An Historical View of the Maharashtrian Intellectual and Social Change'. In Yogendra K. Malik (ed.). *South Asian Intellectuals and Social Change: A Study of the Role of Vernacular-Speaking Intellectuals*. Columbia, Mo.: South Asia Books/New Delhi: Heritage Publishers, 1982.

'A Marathi Sampler: Varied Voices in Contemporary Marathi Short Stories and Poetry'. Eleanor Zelliot and Philip Engblom (eds). *Journal of South Asian Literature*. vol. 17, no.1, 1982.

'A Medieval Encounter between Hindu and Muslim: Eknath's Drama-poem *Hindu-turk samvad*'. In Fred Clothey (ed.). *Images of Man: Religion and Historical Process in South Asia*. Madras: New Era, 1982. Reprinted in Richard M. Eaton (ed.). *India's Islamic Traditions, 711– 1750*. New Delhi: Oxford University Press, 2003.

'Gupta History and Literature: A Bibliographic Essay'(with the assistance of Ann Whitfield). In Bardwell Smith (ed.). *Essays on Gupta Culture*. Delhi: Motilal Banarsidass, 1983.

'The World of Gundam Raul'. In Anne Feldhaus. *The Deeds of God in Rddhipur*. New York: Oxford University Press, 1984.

'Buddhist Sects in Contemporary India: Identity and Organization'. In Peter Gaeffke and David A. Utz (eds). *Identity and Division in Cults and Sects in South Asia*. Proceedings of the South Asia Seminar, University of Pennsylvania, I: 1980–1. Philadelphia: South Asia Regional Studies, 1984.

Translation of Vijay Tendulkar's *Ghashiram Kotwal*. Calcutta:

Seagull Books, 1984. (New York production by Pan Asian Repertory Theater, 1985.) Second edition 1999, reprinted 2002.

Consultant on Maharashtrian figure on the 'Peoples of South Asia' map. *National Geographic Magazine*. December 1984.

'The Buddhist Literature of Modern Maharashtra'. In Hugh van Skyhawk (ed.). *Minorities: On Themselves. South Asia Digest of Regional Writing*. vol. 11, 1985. Heidelberg: South Asia Institute, University of Heidelberg, 1986.

'The Political Thought of Dr B.R. Ambedkar'. In Thomas Pantham and Kenneth L. Deutsch (eds). *Contemporary Indian Political Thought*. Delhi: Sage Publications, 1986.

'Dr B.R. Ambedkar' and (with Anne Feldhaus) 'Marathi Religions'. In Mircea Eliade (ed.). *Encyclopedia of Religion*. New York: Macmillan, 1986. Newly edited version, in press.

'Eknath's Barude: The *Sant* as Link Between Cultures'. In Karine Schomer and W.H. McLeod (eds). *The Sants: Studies in a Devotional Tradition of India*. Berkeley: Religious Studies Series; Delhi: Motilal Banarsidass, 1987.

'Four Radical Saints of Maharashtra'. In Milton Israel and N. K. Wagle (eds). *Religion and Society in Maharashtra*. Toronto: Centre for South Asian Studies, University of Toronto, 1987.

Introduction to *Palkhi*, by D.B. Mokashi, translated by Philip Engblom. Albany: State University of New York Press, 1987. Reprinted by Orient Longman, Hyderabad, 1990.

'Untouchability'. In Ainslee Embree *et al.* (eds). *Encyclopedia of Asian History*. N.Y.: Charles Scribners Sons, 1988. Shorter entries: 'Dr B.R. Ambedkar', 'Poona Sarvajanik Sabha', 'Republican Party'.

Selections from the writings of Dr B.R. Ambedkar and comment for the revised edition of Stephen Hay (ed.). *Sources of Indian Tradition*. vol. II. *Modern India and Pakistan*. New York: Columbia University Press, 1988.

The Experience of Hinduism: Essays on Religion in Maharashtra. Eleanor Zelliot and Maxine Berntsen (eds). Albany: State University of New York Press, 1988. Reprint, Delhi: Sri Satguru Publications, 1992.

'Congress and the Untouchables'. In Stanley Wolpert and Richard Sisson (eds). *Congress and Indian Nationalism*. Berkeley: University of California Press, 1988.

'Dalit: New Perspectives on India's Untouchables'. In Philip Oldenburg (ed.). *India Briefing: 1991*. Boulder: Westview Press, 1991.

From Untouchable to Dalit: Essays on the Ambedkar Movement. New Delhi: Manohar, 1992. Second edition with new introduction, 1996. Reprinted 1998. Third edition 2001.

'Buddhist Women of the Contemporary Maharashtrian Conversion Movement'. In José Cabezón (ed.). *Buddhism, Sexuality and Gender.* Albany: State University of New York Press, 1992.

An Anthology of Dalit Literature (Poetry). Mulk Raj Anand and Eleanor Zelliot (eds). New Delhi: Gyan Publishing House, 1992.

'Mahar' and 'Chitpavan Brahman'. In Paul Hockings (ed.). *Encyclopedia of World Cultures.* vol. III (South Asia). Boston: G.K. Hall, 1992.

'Dr Ambedkar through Western Eyes'. In K.N. Kadam (ed.). *Dr B.R. Ambedkar: The Emancipator of the Oppressed.* Bombay: Popular Prakashan, 1993.

'New Voices of the Buddhists of India'. In A.K. Narain and D.C. Ahir (eds). *Dr Ambedkar, Buddhism and Social Change.* Delhi: B.R. Publishing Corporation, 1994.

'Daya Pawar's "The Buddha"'. Translated by Eleanor Zelliot. In *Oxford Anthology of Modern Indian Poetry.* New Delhi: Oxford University Press, 1994.

'Should We Study Caste in Order to Abolish it?'. In Sandeep Pendse (ed.). *Dalit Movement Today.* Bombay: Vikas Adhyayan Kendra, 1994.

'The Folklore of Pride: Three Components of Contemporary Dalit Belief'. In Gunther D. Sontheimer (ed.). *Folk Culture, Folk Religion and Oral Traditions as a Component in Maharashtrian Culture.* New Delhi: Manohar, 1995.

'Cokhamela: Piety and Protest'. In David Lorenzen (ed.). *Bhakti Religion in North India: Community, Identity and Political Action.* Albany: State University of New York Press, 1995.

'The Householder Saints of Maharashtra'. In Alan W. Entwistle, Carol Salomon *et al.* (eds). *Studies in Early Modern Indo-Aryan Languages, Literature and Culture.* New Delhi: Manohar, 1999.

'The Dalit Movement'. In John Webster (ed.). *Dalit International Newsletter.* vol. 1, no. 1, February 1996.

'Stri Dalit Sahitya: The New Voice of Women Poets'. In Anne Feldhaus (ed.). *Images of Women in Maharashtrian Literature and Religion.* Albany: State University of New York Press, 1996.

'The Poetry of Dalit Women'. In Saral K. Chatterji and Hunter P. Mabry (eds). *Culture, Religion and Society: Essays in Honour of*

Richard W. Taylor. Published for the Christian Institute for the Study of Religion and Society, Bangalore by ISPCK, Delhi, 1996.

'A Bibliographic Essay on Women in Maharashtra'. In Anne Feldhaus (ed.). *Images of Women in Maharashtrian Society*. Albany: State University of New York Press, 1998.

'Dalit Literature: Twenty-five years of Protest? of Progress?' (with Veena Deo). *Journal of South Asian Literature*. vol. 29, no. 2, 1994.

'The Religious Imagination of Maharashtrian Women Bhaktas'. In Shrikant Paranjpe, Raja Dixit, and C.R. Das (eds). *Western India: History, Society and Culture*. (Dr Arvind Deshpande Felicitation Volume). Kolhapur: Itihas Shikshak Mahamandal, 1997.

'Ovi' and 'Tamasha'. In Margaret A. Mills, Peter J. Claus, and Sarah Diamond (eds). *South Asian Folklore: An Encyclopedia*. New York/London: Routledge, 2003.

'Fifty Years of Dalit Politics'. In Yogendra Malik and Ashok Kapur (eds). *India: Fifty Years of Independence: Assessment and Prospects*. New Delhi: APH Publishing Corporation, 1998.

'Bhimrao Ramji Ambedkar'. In Henry Scholberg (ed.). *The Biographical Dictionary of Greater India*. New Delhi: Promilla and Co., 1998.

'Religious Leadership among Maharashtrian Buddhist Women'. In Ellison Banks Findly (ed.). *Women's Buddhism; Buddhism's Women*. Sumerville, MA: Wisdom Publications, 2000.

'Ordination'(with Ingrid Klass) and 'Buddhism: Modern Movements'. In Serenity Young (ed.). *Encyclopedia of Women and World Religion*, New York: Macmillan Reference, 1998.

'Roots of Dalit Consciousness'. In Harsh Sethi and Tejbir Singh (eds). *Seminar*. no. 471, November 1998.

'Women in the Homes of the Saints'. In Irina Glushkova and Rajendra Vora (eds). *Home, Family and Kinship in Maharashtra*. New Delhi: Oxford University Press, 1999.

'Dr Ambedkar Speaks to Government' and 'The American Experience of Dr B.R. Ambedkar'. In Verinder Grover (ed.). *Bhimrao Ramji Ambedkar: A Biography of His Vision and Ideas*. New Delhi: Deep and Deep, 1998.

'New Books on Dalits'. *Dalit International Newsletter*. vol. 4, no. 2, June 1999; vol. 6, no. 2, June 2001; vol. 8, no. 2, June 2003; and vol. 10, no. 2, June 2005.

'The Untouchable Women Saint-poets of Maharashtra'. In Mariola Offredi (ed.). *The Banyan Tree: Essays on Early Literature in New Indo-Aryan Languages*. New Delhi: Manohar, 2000.

'Sant Sahitya and Dalit Movements'. In Meera Kosambi (ed.). *Intersections: Socio-cultural Trends in Maharashtra*. Hyderabad: Orient Longman, 2000.

'Women Saints in Medieval Maharashtra'. In Mandakranta Bose (ed.). *Faces of the Feminine in Ancient, Medieval, and Modern India*. New York: Oxford University Press, 2000.

'Dr Ambedkar and the Empowerment of Women'. In Anupama Rao (ed.). *Gender and Caste*. New Delhi: Kali for Women, 2004.

'B.R. Ambedkar and the Search for a Meaningful Buddhism'. In Surendra Jondhale and Johannes Beltz (eds). *Reconstructing the World: B.R. Ambedkar and Buddhism in India*. New Delhi: Oxford University Press, 2004.

'The Meaning of Ambedkar'. In Ghanshyam Shah (ed.). *Dalit Identity and Politics*. Delhi/Thousand Oaks: Sage, 2001.

'Experiments in Dalit Education (Pre-Independence)'. In S. Bhattacharya (ed.). *Education and the Disprivileged*. Hyderabad: Orient Longman, 2002.

'Dalit Tradition and Dalit Consciousness'. In Niraja Gopal Jayal and Sudha Pai (eds). *Democratic Government in India: Challenges of Poverty, Development and Identity*. New Delhi: Sage, 2001.

'Dalit Samaj' for *Shahar Pune: Ekā Sāmskritik Samchitācā Māgovā....*, Aroon Tikekar (ed.). vol. 1. Pune: Nilubhāū Limaye Foundation, 2000. In English: 'The History of Dalits in Pune'. *The Journal of the Asiatic Society of Bombay*. N.S. vol. 74, 1999.

'Untouchables, Purity and Pollution' for the Eighth International Conference on Maharashtra Studies, held in Sydney, Australia in 1999, to be edited by Jim Masselos.

'Introduction', 'Glossary', and 'Biographical Notes'. In Vasant Moon. *Growing up Untouchable in India: A Dalit Autobiography*, translated from the Marathi by Gail Omvedt. Lanham, Maryland: Rowman and Littlefield, 2001. New Delhi: Sage, 2002.

'Kipling's *Kim* in the Classroom'. In *Asianetwork Exchange*. vol. 8, no.1, Fall 2000.

'Self Critical Honesty: The Writing of Urmilla Pawar'. *Manushi*. no. 122 (January–February 2001). Introduction to *Chauti Bhint* ('The Fourth Wall') by Urmilla Pawar.

'Ahilyabai Holkar'. *Manushi*. no. 124.

'Dr Ambedkar and the Constitution'. *Journal of the Asiatic Society of Bombay*. vols 77, 78, 2002–3.

Translation (with Vimal Thorat) of 'Whirlwind' by Datta Bhagat, in G.P. Deshpande (ed.). *An Anthology of Modern Indian Drama*. New Delhi: Sahitya Akademi, 2000.

'Bombay/Mumbai and the Ambedkar Movement: Past and Present'. In Sujata Patel *et al.* (eds). *Thinking Social Science in India: Essays in Honour of Alice Thorner*. New Delhi: Sage, 2002.

'The Search for Cokhamela'. *The Dalit*. March–April 2002.

'Immortalizing Babasaheb' (an interview with Meena Kandasamy), *The Dalit*. May–June 2002.

Foreword and Comments for Detlef Kantowsky, *Buddhists in India Today*, translated from the German by Hans-Georg Tuerstig. New Delhi: Manohar, 2003.

Sant Cokhamela: Vividh Darshan, edited with V. L. Manjul. Pune: Sugawa Prakashan, 2002, including Marathi translations of three articles by Zelliot: 'Cokhamelayaca shodh', 'Cokhamela ani Eknath', and 'Soyrabai ani Nirmala'.

'Ashok Kelkar and Dalit Literature'. *The Bulletin of Deccan College Postgraduate and Research Institute*. vols 62 and 63 (2002 and 2003). Professor Ashok R. Kelkar Felicitation Volume (published in 2004).

'A Maharashtrian Buddhist Family: The Kambles of Pune'. In P. K. Roy (ed.). *Family Diversity in India: Patterns, Practices and Ethos*. New Delhi: Gyan Publishing House, 2003.

'Relating to the Voices of India's Untouchables'. *AsiaNetwork Exchange*. vol. 11, no. 3, Spring 2004.

'A Note on Bhakti Poetry'. In Molly Daniels-Ramanujan (ed.). *The Oxford India Ramanujan*. New Delhi: Oxford University Press, 2004.

'Caste in Contemporary India'. In Robin Rinehart (ed.). *Contemporary Hinduism: Ritual, Culture and Practice*. Oxford: ABC-CLIO, 2004.

'Untouchability'. In *New Dictionary of the History of Ideas*. New York: Charles Scribner's Sons, 2004.

'Bhimrao Ramji Ambedkar'. In *Oxford Dictionary of National Biography*. Oxford: Oxford University Press, 2004.

'Untouchables (Dalits)'. In *Encyclopedia of the Developing World*. Chicago: Fitzroy Dearborn Publishers, 2004.

Untouchable Saints: An Indian Phenomenon, edited with Rohini Mokashi-Punekar. New Delhi: Manohar, 2005.

Dr Babasaheb Ambedkar and the Untouchable Movement. New Delhi: Blumoon Books, 2004.

'Ambedkar Abroad'. Sixth Dr Ambedkar Memorial Annual Lecture. Jawaharlal Nehru University, New Delhi, 2004.

'The Importance of Ambedkar's World View to India's Social Progress'. Fourth Manchester Ambedkar Memorial Lecture, Manchester, UK, 10 October 2005.

'Dr Ambedkar's Path to Buddhism: A Marg to Navayana?' In M. Naito, I. Shima, and H. Kotani (eds). *Marga: Ways of Liberation, Empowerment and Social Change in Maharashtra*. New Delhi: Manohar, 2007.

'The Early Voices of Untouchables: The Bhakti Saints'. In Mikael Aktor and Robert Deliège (eds). *Untouchables—Scheduled Castes—Dalits: Identity and Power in Early and Modern Expressions of Untouchability in India* (E-book). Copenhagen: Museum Tusculanum Press, forthcoming.

'Dalit', in John H. Moore (ed.). *Encyclopedia of Race and Racism*. New York: Macmillan Reference USA, 2007.

'Understanding Dr B.R. Ambedkar'. *Religion Compass*. Online Resource from Blackwell Publishing, 2008.

'Dalit Literature', in Braj Kachru and S.N. Sridhar (eds). *Language in South Asia*. Cambridge: Cambridge University Press, 2008.

CONTRIBUTORS

MEENA ALEXANDER is Distinguished Professor of English at Hunter College and the Graduate Center, The City University of New York (CUNY).

MANU BHAGAVAN is Assistant Professor in the Department of History at Hunter College-CUNY.

LAURA R. BRUECK is Visiting Assistant Professor in Comparative Literature at Hamilton College.

DILIP CHITRE is a poet who was until recently Professor and Head, Sant Jnanadev Adhyasan, University of Pune.

VEENA DEO is Professor of English at Hamline University, St Paul, Minnesota.

ANNE FELDHAUS is Foundation Professor of Religious Studies at Arizona State University.

MANI KAMERKAR (1925–2004) taught and also served as Principal at colleges affiliated with Shreemati Nathibai Damodar Thackersey (SNDT) Women's University in Mumbai.

ABIGAIL MCGOWAN is Assistant Professor in the Department of History at the University of Vermont.

SHAILAJA PAIK is a PhD student and a Ford fellow at the University of Warwick.

VIJAY PRASHAD is George and Martha Kellner Professor of South Asian History and Professor of International Studies at Trinity College in Hartford.

ANUPAMA RAO is Assistant Professor of History at Barnard College, Columbia University.

RAMNARAYAN S. RAWAT is a Mellon Postdoctoral Teaching Fellow in South Asian History at the University of Pennsylvania.

BALI SAHOTA is Assistant Professor of Indian Literary and Intellectual History in the Department of Asian Languages and Literatures at the University of Minnesota.

YASMIN SAIKIA is Associate Professor in the Department of History at the University of North Carolina at Chapel Hill.

SUKHADEO THORAT is the Chairman of the University Grants Commission, New Delhi, and Professor of Economics at the Centre for the Study of Regional Development, Jawaharlal Nehru University.

RAJENDRA VORA (1946–2008) was Lokmanya Tilak Professor of Politics and Public Administration at the University of Pune.